What Are Intellectuals Good For?

What Are Intellectuals Good For?

Essays & Reviews by

GEORGE SCIALABBA

2009 : PRESSED WAFER : BOSTON, MASS.

typeslowly designed

Cover: *Pyramid of Capitalist System*

Printed in Canada by Friesens on Rolland Enviro, a 100% PCW paper

Thanks to my editors: Deb Chasman, Elsa Dixler, Keith Gessen,
M. Mark, Askold Melnyczuk, Brian Morton, Kit Rachlis, Adam Shatz,
and Ben Sonnenberg; and to William Corbett, publisher of Pressed Wafer.

First printing in 2009

ISBN 978-0-9785156-6-9

Pressed Wafer / 9 Columbus Square / Boston, Mass. 02116

For Chomsky, Rorty, Lasch—

three answers.

TABLE OF CONTENTS

III. Fantasia

A Worried Mind

BY SCOTT McLEMEE

> The intellectuals: in God's menagerie, are they necessary? For what? Are they mediators or producers? If the latter, what do they produce? The word?
> Leszek Kolakowski, *Modernity on Endless Trial* (1990)

I.

We sometimes speak of a dog "worrying" a bone, chewing it with a certain obvious persistence of attention. George Scialabba worries books and ideas this way. His prose is graceful, but it manifests a quality of mind that seems, well, dogged. There is an urgency, a hunger to it, though also, at moments, a gentle humor. More than once while reading this book, I wondered whether the author had planted a self-effacing jest in the title and subtitle, which may, after all, be read as question and reply. What are intellectuals good for? Essays and reviews.

Kolakowsi's reflections on "God's menagerie" provide a clue to why we are recurrently curious about the place of the intellectual. We find ourselves, the philosopher notes, in a world that has somehow given rise to a symbolic universe, which is directly connected to experience while also being relatively autonomous and self-contained. He is thinking of language, which creates an order unto itself, as do money and power.

The financier and the politician work in the upper reaches of this symbolic universe. And so, in a way, does the intellectual. But while claims to expertise in the cultivation and control of money and power tend to be easily verifiable, things are rarely so straightforward with regard to those who handle words and ideas. In eras or cultures that have well-defined bodies of official doctrine —whether a theological tradition or a secular ideology such as dialectical materialism—the ability to manipulate important symbols will be invested with prestige and authority. There will be limits, though, to how much interrogation of basic terms is possible, even by those who have studied them most closely. The priest and the party theoretician are able to frame questions but also know the limits of questioning. Those known variously as *philosophes*, "men of letters," or "intellectuals" tend to disregard such limits. This can be disruptive. For one thing, their attention is almost inevitably drawn to the other quarters of the symbolic universe—so that they ask questions about how the money and power in a given society are being used. That might be one way of describing the role of the intellectual: someone whose capacity for analysis allows him or her to keep an eye on what the other symbol-manipulators are doing.

But the power of questioning eventually turns back upon those who wield it. What criteria do we use to make judgments about the world? How do we choose those criteria? And why trust intellectuals to make such determinations, anyway? The history of the past several decades has been an often appalling record of smart people making sophisticated arguments for murderous doctrines. Sometimes those arguments were couched in terms of utopian possibility; at other times, of the crassest realpolitik.

And so the strange fate of the intellectual is to be subjected to an almost obligatory form of self-questioning—the very sources and media of their power (words, symbols, ideas) turning back on them, reflexively. Perhaps bankers and politicians, too, have moments of doubt; let us hope so. Still, money and power are not obliged to be introspective or to challenge the conditions of their own existence. Critical intellect is.

2.

In the title essay, Scialabba offers a roll call of exemplary figures practicing a certain kind of writing. The list includes Randolph Bourne, Bertrand Russell, George Orwell, and Maurice Merleau Ponty, among others. "Their primary training and frame of reference," he writes, "were the humanities, usually literature or philosophy, and they habitually, even if only implicitly, employed values and ideals derived from the humanities to criticize contemporary politics. . . . Their 'specialty' lay not in unearthing generally unavailable facts, but in penetrating especially deeply into the shared culture, in grasping and articulating its contemporary moral/political relevance with special originality and force."

I am intrigued by that slash-mark in the phrase "contemporary moral/ political relevance." Is it the equivalent of an equal sign? Not quite; but it suggests that the relationship is both close and problematic. If we want to characterize the bone that Scialabba worries so tenaciously, this ambiguous bit of punctuation is perhaps a good clue.

His reflections on this matter follow from his effort to resolve the tensions within a certain political stance. It is a variety of democratic leftism, with a very pronounced egalitarian streak, in which there is no anchoring of those aspirations (so far as I can tell) in any a priori certainty about the necessity of progress. Reconciling the skeptical pragmatism of Richard Rorty and the geopolitical worldview of Noam Chomsky is not a simple project. Rarely do you find them treated as two sides of one ideological coin. But that seems like a reasonably accurate description of Scialabba's sense of the possible. If he were to write a manifesto, it would probably call for more economic equality, the dismantling of the American military industrial complex, and the end of metaphysics.

To hold such an ideal without any very robust confidence that History is the record of mankind's long march towards its fulfillment—well, that can make for gloominess. Nor is this the only shadow darkening his worldview. Another is a strong hunch that José Ortega y Gasset was correct in *The Revolt of the Masses* (1930):

> The most radical division it is possible to make of humanity is that which splits it into two classes of creatures: those who make great demands

on themselves, piling up difficulties and duties; and those who demand nothing special of themselves, but for whom to live is to be every moment what they already are, without imposing on themselves any effort toward perfection; mere buoys that float on the waves.

Something in this formulation must have struck a chord with Scialabba, who cites it more than once. "Is this a valid distinction?" he asks. "Yes, I believe it is. . . ." But the idea is troubling. It worries him (and vice versa).

Lumping humanity into two categories, the noble and the rest, may seem to lend itself to anti-democratic sentiments or even to a violently reactionary form of politics. But Scialabba affirms the distinction without snobbery. Perhaps he suspects that the division runs right down the middle of most of us. Even so, it can undermine the will to egalitarianism. Economic leveling means giving more to those who have less. Cultural leveling seldom has that implication. How, then, to resolve the tension? This volume reflects a series of efforts—provisional, personal, and not entirely successful—to work out an answer.

3.

So much for the Scialabban *problématique*. At this point, it might be appropriate to say a word about the man himself. George is a generalist and a public intellectual who works at Harvard University—but not in quite the way that sounds. He took his undergraduate degree at Harvard (1969) and has read his way through a canon or two, but he is a part-time office worker and freelance opinionator, not an academic.

The son of working-class Italian American parents, he grew up believing that he might have a religious vocation. Instead, he was drawn into Opus Dei —a conservative Catholic lay movement that sought to propagate a new kind of spirituality, combining the traditional virtues and devotions with a professional or business career.

But he read modern intellectual history at college and, like so many others, succumbed to Satan's lure. The present book is unmistakably the work of a man whose outlook is secular and modern, without nostalgia for the faith of his ancestors; but it also bears the traces of a struggle. It exemplifies Oscar Wilde's insight that criticism, in the right hands, can be a form of autobiography.

4.

The critic and essayist Harold Rosenberg defined an intellectual as someone who knows how to make questions out of answers. That is what you find Scialabba doing throughout these pages; and Rosenberg's nifty phrase also recalls another passage from Kolakowski:

> A view of the world does not emerge from an accumulation of facts; it also requires words to interpret, judge, and order the facts. Thus, by attempting to uncover, that is, to produce the meaning of facts, the intellectuals—as philosophers, poets, writers of fiction, and political thinkers—turn out to be ideologists. That is to say that they uphold an idea of the world as it ought to be, and from it they derive their picture of the world as it is. . . .[F]rom a world desired or imagined, they derive the rules for how the facts of the existing world must be interpreted—or what the facts are in their essence.

Among the phenomena to be examined, interpreted, and judged is the very fact that some people find themselves taking on such a role. Is this necessary? Is it just?

The priest of an established tradition may not need to frame such questions. If words exist within a sacred order, it is the order that matters, not any ambiguities about what the words may mean. "But the intellectuals are masters and rulers of the word," writes Kolakowski, "and not its servants—at least in their own estimation. For that reason, they are destroyers of tradition even if they attempt to preserve it with the best intentions, because to defend tradition on one's own already means to question it." So our author discovered while defending the Catholic tradition to his college classmates, until the effort drove him, unexpectedly, to embrace secular modernity.

But that, too, is a tradition of sorts: a "tradition of the new," in another phrase of Rosenberg's. We may not be sure of determining the true, the good, and the beautiful; but there is always some feverish crowd of novelties, intellectual or aesthetic, jostling for our attention. While much of his work takes the form of book reviews, Scialabba's attention is seldom purely topical. The pieces are, rather, engagements with aspects of modernity's tradition that try (Kolakowski again) "to preserve it with the best intentions . . . to defend tradition on [his] own."

He does not take refuge in the relative safety of some imagined postmodern condition.

"What are intellectuals good for?" It is a general question, but it has urgent moral overtones. There is more to it than the mind's abstract obligation to account for the uncertain status of its own reflexivity. That, of course; but the writings that follow are personal essays as well. You will find in them evidence of a hard moral discipline—a ceaseless and merciless self-questioning that has outlived whatever religious calling once fostered it. George Scialabba transfigures worry into something artful. And the grace of that effort earns the intellectual his place in "God's menagerie," if anything can.

Scott McLemee writes the weekly "Intellectual Affairs" column for *InsideHigherEd*, and blogs at Crooked Timber and Quick Study.

I. Definitions

What Are Intellectuals Good For?

Like the Spirit in Hegel's *Phenomenology*, intellectuals are inexhaustibly curious about the nature and conditions of their own activity. It is not an innocent curiosity. One way or another, in most discussions of the sociology of knowledge, intellectual legitimacy is at stake. To take either the alienation or the integration of intellectuals as a problem, to raise questions about objectivity or relativism, to emphasize or minimize the social and economic background of theoretical positions and aesthetic tendencies—all these choices presuppose, or at any rate seem to correlate with, political commitments.

So that what one makes of Russell Jacoby's story in *The Last Intellectuals*[1] about the decline and imminent disappearance of the "public intellectual" will likely reflect one's own notion of what intellectuals are good for. If one thinks them chiefly good for hallowing the national purpose, for generating new policy ideas, for revolutionizing academic disciplines, or for guiding the struggles of the oppressed, then Jacoby's lament will not seem to have much point. In fact, it is not always easy to discover his point, or point of view: a difficulty frequently posed by serious criticism of mass culture (which, as much as anything else, is what

[1]Basic Books, 1987.

3

The Last Intellectuals is up to). Jacoby's descriptions and analyses are shrewd, lively, plausible; but the meaning of the developments he chronicles remains uncertain.

Everyone knows that the gods dwelt among men a few decades ago and that Olympus was then called *Partisan Review*. Their thunderbolts took the form of essays, and their laughter rang through certain apartment buildings in Greenwich Village on Saturday nights. Actually, Jacoby offers a much wider range of examples of public intellectuals than the New York Jews and honorary Jews of the 1930s and '40s. He cites Lewis Mumford, Edmund Wilson, C. Wright Mills, Russell Kirk, Murray Bookchin, Jane Jacobs, and Paul Sweezy (though not, surprisingly, Randolph Bourne). All wrote in the vernacular, with vigor and clarity, for the general, educated reader. Their topics were large, their interests wide; however small their actual, engaged audience, their writings opened out, and so helped sustain at least the idea and the hope of a public culture.

That hope is now guttering out. The last generation has been "supplanted by high-tech intellectuals, consultants, and professors—anonymous souls who may be competent, and more than competent, but who do not enrich public life." Older intellectuals—Daniel Bell, John Kenneth Galbraith, Norman Podhoretz, Gore Vidal—have maintained a voice and presence, but few younger intellectuals write primarily for general-interest magazines rather than professional journals, for lay readers rather than academic colleagues. Few pursue, perhaps even envision, a life outside the university, unconstrained by its disciplines. Even the New Left, for all its promise of vitality, originality, engagement, now seems safely integrated into the university and the professions, largely insulated from public influence.

To attest decline is not to indulge in nostalgia. There have been gains as well as losses, Jacoby acknowledges: feminist scholarship, a robust Marxist presence in the social sciences, doubtless some liberating pedagogical effects on the next generation. Above all, things could not have been otherwise. "The restructuring of the cities, the passing of bohemia, the expansion of the university"—not to mention television-induced mass illiteracy—these secular processes, not any generational failing, have doomed the public intellectual to extinction. None but the superhumanly talented, energetic, ascetic, self-sufficient, or lucky writer can hope to make a living nowadays without an academic or journalistic base. Cheap, comfortable urban space, where the temporarily marginal can congregate, no longer exists. Little magazines can rarely afford to pay contributors more than nominally. The spectacular postwar growth of higher education sucked virtually an entire generation of intellectuals into college teaching; a contracting job market now reinforces their academic socialization, which emphasizes specialization and deference and subtly discourages ideological explicitness. And for this generation, at least, it is too late to change habits and habitat: "as intellectuals became academics, they had no need to write in a public prose; they did not, and finally they could not."

Jacoby's account is rich and his explanation compelling. But a question remains: is the sort of public political intellectual who is about to disappear the sort we now need? The defining characteristic of the great twentieth-century *politiques et moralistes*—exemplified in, say, Bourne's "Twilight of Idols," Dwight Macdonalds' "The Root is Man," Orwell's "Looking Back on the Spanish War," Camus' "Neither Victims Nor Executioners" and Sartre's "For Whom Does One Write?"—has been humanism. The word can mean nearly anything, of course; I mean that their primary training and frame of reference were the humanities, usually literature or philosophy, and that they habitually, even if often implicitly, employed values and ideals derived from the humanities to criticize contemporary politics. They were generalists: they drew, from a generally shared body of culture, principles of general applicability and applied them to facts generally available. Their "specialty" lay not in unearthing generally unavailable facts but in penetrating especially deeply into the shared culture, in grasping and articulating its contemporary moral/political relevance with special originality and force. They were arbiters, not investigators. "By impulse, if not definition," wrote Irving Howe in an afterword to "This Age of Conformity" (1954), still perhaps the best essay on the vocation of the public intellectual, "the intellectual is a man who writes about subjects outside his field. He has no field."

We look to public intellectuals of this sort for the clarification of important abstractions, for the demonstration of dialectical skills, for rhetorical solace or stimulus, for personal witness, for refinements and enlargements of moral imagination. And some of them—besides the writers already mentioned, Russell, Silone, Chiaromonte, Merleau-Ponty, Enzensberger, Grass, Kolakowski, Konrad, Goodman, Howe, Vidal come to mind, among others—have accomplished these things supremely well. Their writings are invaluable for the formation of a supple, humane political sensibility.

But the political culture has changed in a way that undermines not merely the viability, but also the authority, of the generalist. To put it crudely and provocatively: sensibility now matters less than facts; cultivated judgment is now (thanks in part to the example of earlier public intellectuals) commoner and far easier to acquire than adequate information. The following suggestive quote from Franz Borkenau's 1938 study of the Spanish Civil War, *The Spanish Cockpit*, may begin to bring this change into view:

> In this tremendous contrast with previous revolutions one fact is reflected. Before these latter years, counterrevolution usually depended on the support of reactionary powers, which were technically and intellectually inferior to the forces of revolution. This has changed with the advent of fascism. Now, every revolution is likely to meet the attack of the most modern, most efficient, most ruthless machinery yet in existence. It means that the age of revolutions free to evolve according to their own laws is over.

Borkenau clearly had in mind the military and police apparatus of the totalitarian state. But his observation also applies to the manufacture of consent within liberal societies. Before the era of opinion management and public relations, information sources allied to ruling classes (for example, lobbyists, government spokesmen, reactionary newspapers) were "technically and intellectually inferior." Intellectuals could evaluate such sources largely by their style, their timbre. Lying by business and government was comparatively unsystematic and inept; one needed chiefly a good ear, perhaps also in some cases a modest degree of enterprise. Today, by contrast, corporate and governmental propaganda services employ resources that dwarf those available to critics; it is they who command "the most modern, most efficient, most ruthless machinery [that is, of persuasion] yet in existence." One statistic will have to suffice: according to Thomas Ferguson and Joel Rogers in *Right Turn: The Decline of the Democrats and the Future of American Politics*, by the end of the 1970s corporations were spending more than $1 billion annually on political advertising and grassroots lobbying alone, apart from the large sums devoted to Congressional lobbying and the funding of conservative academics and research institutes. By way of comparison, in 1982 the combined net income of all national and international labor unions and associations, including the AFL-CIO, was only $324 million.

In charge of this modern, efficient machinery of persuasion is a new variety, or mutation: the anti-public intellectual, whose function is not criticism, not defense of the public against private or state power, but the opposite. "Experts in legitimation" was Gramsci's prescient phrase. One of the earliest American practitioners, the eminent political scientist Harold Lasswell, explained in the 1930s that the spread of democratic education "did not release the masses from ignorance and superstition but altered the nature of both and compelled the development of a whole new technique of control, mainly through propaganda." This new means of social control—"propaganda" is Lasswell's repeated usage— is "the one means of mass mobilization which is cheaper than violence, bribery, or other possible control techniques." Irving Kristol, the chief contemporary American strategist and impresario of this development, put the matter more suavely: "It has always been assumed that as the United States became a more highly organized national society, as its economy became more managerial, its power more imperial, and its population more sophisticated, the intellectuals would move inexorably closer to the seats of authority—would, perhaps, even be incorporated *en masse* into a kind of 'power élite.'"

One consequence of this new technique of social control is the near-absence of public accountability for vital economic and political decisions. As a result of the intellectuals' incorporation *en masse* into the "power elite," it now requires far more training, leisure, and resources to penetrate the screen of corporate or governmental propaganda about, say, environmental regulation, product safety, or foreign policy, than are available to the ordinary citizen. When amateurs were in charge of deceiving the public about American foreign policy, they did it badly; Henry Kissinger, Richard Perle, and Elliott Abrams are another matter.

In theory, a free press will defend the public interest. In practice, large media institutions are major corporations, affected like all others by government economic policy. Not even the most powerful are immune to pressure from advertisers, which are usually other corporations. Directly and indirectly, governments can place individual newspapers or networks at a considerable competitive disadvantage in reprisal for consistently hostile coverage. Social and financial ties between newspaper or network owners and government officials or corporate executives are common. All in all, the resistance of the press to "mass mobilization" and the engineering of consent by intellectuals in the service of elites is much weakened.

The situation calls for public political intellectuals of a new sort. One of the old sort—one of the most admirable—was Maurice Merleau-Ponty. To watch Merleau-Ponty in his writings think his way through the moral perplexities of the post-Second World War period, always excruciatingly sensitive to the temptations of oversimplification, remains inspiring. But he himself was dissatisfied and discouraged in this role. He went about as far in his political criticism as an old-style intellectual could, and he probably sensed it. In one of his last political essays, "On Not Voting" (1955), he wrote a passage that may be read in retrospect as a handing on of the torch to a new kind of public intellectual:

> We have yet to learn how to realize majority rule, how and with what institutions to protect it against manipulation. And this is not easy, for each man's sense of his life depends to an extraordinary degree upon ideologies. In a crisis, especially, the abstract itself comes to seem concrete, and each man is so influenced by social symbols that it is difficult to find in him his own certainties . . .
>
> The problem of majority rule, then, is wholly before us. We have not even caught a glimpse of what a society which had solved it would be like. But the first thing is to get what is said and done communicated. For we already know that a worthwhile society will not be less but more free than our own. *More instruction, more—and more precise—information, more concrete criticism, publicity given to the actual functioning of society and politics, all problems put in the most offensive terms—as offensive as suffering and as all true reasoning—here are the preliminary conditions for "transparent" social relations.* (Emphasis added.)

Two years before, in 1953, I.F. Stone had inaugurated his *Newsletter*, which succeeded brilliantly during the following two decades in giving "publicity . . . to the actual functioning of society and politics." A few years later, Ralph Nader launched his heroic crusade to bring "more—and more precise—information" about pretty much everything into the public domain. Recently two other "new" public intellectuals have, by producing endless "concrete criticism," done more than anyone else to protect the majority—or at least those readers they've been allowed to reach—against the "manipulation" by "ideologies" that Merleau-Ponty warned of. Both of them—Noam Chomsky and Alexander Cockburn—have recently released major anthologies: *The Chomsky Reader*[2] and Cockburn's *Corruptions of Empire*[3].

Curiously, the first question asked by James Peck in the interview that opens *The Chomsky Reader*, which has to do with "how seldom you [Chomsky] mention literature," seems to spring from a sense of some such contrast with older public intellectuals as I've suggested. Chomsky's answer requires, and eventually receives, qualification: "I've always been resistant to allowing literature to influence my beliefs and attitudes with regard to society and history"; still, the contrast with, say, Macdonald or Orwell is striking. In "The New York Intellectuals," Irving Howe vividly described that group's style:

> It is a kind of writing highly self-conscious in mode, with an unashamed vibration of bravura and display. Nervous, strewn with knotty or flashy phrases, impatient with transitions and other concessions to dullness, willfully calling attention to itself as a form or at least an outcry, fond of rapid twists, taking pleasure in dispute, dialectic, dazzle—such, at its best or most noticeable, was the essay cultivated by the New York writers . . .

This is precisely what Noam Chomsky's writing is not like. Lucid, penetrating, austere, unaffected: the absence of self-consciousness constitutes Chomsky's style. Which does not prove any moral superiority to the New York intellectuals, but does imply, correctly, that Chomsky's criticism is more "concrete."

The object of that criticism is the American state religion, whose central tenet, Chomsky claims, is this: "The United States is unique among the nations of past or present history in that its policies are governed by abstract moral principles, such as the Wilsonian ideals of self-determination, human rights, economic welfare, and so on, not by the material interests of groups that actually have domestic power, as is the case in other societies." Mainstream debate over American intervention in Indochina and Central America[4] has generally turned on narrow questions of feasibility: can the policy succeed at an acceptable cost?

---

[2] Edited by Jim Peck, Pantheon, 1987.
[3] Verso, 1987.
[4] And now (2008) Iraq.

Our right to intervene is rarely challenged, on the near-universal assumption that the United States is a reactive, not an aggressive, agent in world affairs, whose policies do not derive from selfish or merely particular national or class interests. Furthermore, such enormities as the United States commits or supports, especially in the Third World, fall under the category not of crimes but of "tragedies" and are attributable to "naïveté" or "misplaced idealism" or "policy-maker error." Acceptance of the essential virtuousness of American intentions is the price of admission to respectable discussion of these matters.

Chomsky has refused respectability. He has argued instead that the fundamental purpose of American foreign policy has all along been to maintain a favorable investment climate, a global economy open to penetration and, if possible, control by American business, which has often entailed sponsoring right-wing dictators or elites; that Cold War ideology (on both sides) has served primarily as a technique of social control and economic management, by securing popular support for foreign intervention, defense spending, and surveillance or repression of dissidents; and that the American intelligentsia, though less harshly and clumsily regulated than its Soviet counterpart, has been no less effectively subordinated to the goals of the state.

I have summarized Chomsky's argument in a paragraph. He has elaborated it through thousands of pages. Most of these pages are topical, of course, devoted to refuting official falsehoods of the moment or to demonstrating ideological bias in mainstream media and scholarship. His technique, typically, is to compare official statements or newspaper editorials with facts drawn from foreign and domestic news accounts, books, reports of international organizations, government documents, and other sources of a sometimes staggering range. After a televised performance full of misstatements, George Bush Senior is supposed to have remarked that political wisdom consists in saying whatever is convenient before an audience of eighty million and later, if necessary, issuing a correction for the benefit of the twenty thousand or so who really care. Obviously, the "realization of majority rule" depends on the latter. Judging from the ferocity and ingenuity with which he pursues misstatements convenient and conventional, Chomsky really cares.

Reading "Equality: Language Development, Human Intelligence, and Social Organization," a largely inaccessible 1976 essay reprinted in *The Chomsky*

Reader, the thought even crosses one's mind that perhaps he cares too much. "Equality" is an exquisitely reasoned piece of moral theory, disentangling more confusions in twenty pages—about the relation of freedom to equality, for instance, or of endowment to desert—than many professional philosophers manage to think their way through in a lifetime. Goldsmith's famous line about Burke prompts a peculiar reflection: perhaps Chomsky has given up to mankind what was meant for the pleasure and enrichment of the philosophical few.

In another sense, Chomsky undoubtedly does care too much. Yeats: "Too long a sacrifice/Can make a stone of the heart." Unlike younger, less eminent radicals, Chomsky has never suffered career-threatening reprisals. But to begin in his late thirties, having recently achieved recognition as the world's foremost linguistic theorist, to devote a large fraction of his time to political speaking and writing, often before tiny groups and in obscure publications, must have been a considerable sacrifice, which has not aroused universal gratitude. A well-known study by the sociologist Charles Kadushin found that in 1970 Chomsky was one of the ten most influential American intellectuals. The others (including a tie for tenth place, making eleven in all) were Daniel Bell, John Kenneth Galbraith, Irving Howe, Dwight Macdonald, Mary McCarthy, Norman Mailer, Robert Silvers, Susan Sontag, Lionel Trilling, and Edmund Wilson. It is hardly conceivable that any of these figures could not publish a major article on nearly any subject virtually anywhere he or she chose. Yet Chomsky, though by far the most prolific of the group, has not for the last fifteen years been published (apart from three brief symposium comments) in any of the following: the *New York Times Magazine*, the *New York Times Book Review*, the *Washington Post*, the *Atlantic*, *Harper's*, the *New Republic*, the *New York Review of Books*, *Dissent*, *Commentary*, *Partisan Review*, *Foreign Affairs*, or *Foreign Policy*. Nor has he once appeared on *Nightline*, the *MacNeil/Lehrer Newshour*, National Public Radio's *All Things Considered*, or NPR's *Morning Edition*. Except as a target of occasional ignorant sneers, he is largely a nonperson in most of our leading cultural/political organs.

This extraordinary collective pusillanimity—partly a result, I suspect, of Chomsky's forthright criticism of Israeli policies—has taken its toll. Chomsky's heart has not turned to stone, but his prose style has sometimes turned raw. The majestic, impersonal sarcasm of his earlier writings is now, on occasion, merely bitter and exasperated. Slight touches of exaggeration have crept in, such as he would never have permitted himself in the late 1960s, when he had a large and appreciative readership (as well as, perhaps, more experienced and self-confident editors). It does not happen often, but often enough to make even admirers wince.

Still, if his recent writing has occasionally lacked finesse, it has not decreased in power. He remains capable, and often, of producing passages like this one from *Turning the Tide: U.S. Intervention in Central America and the Struggle for Peace*:

> The US government and commentators here like to speak of the "symmetry" between El Salvador and Nicaragua; in both countries, it is alleged, indigenous guerrillas with foreign support are rebelling against the government. The comparison would have some merit if the guerrillas in El Salvador lacked any domestic base, having been organized in Nicaragua by the KGB for the purpose of sowing terror in El Salvador and overthrowing its government; were launching murderous attacks against civilians in El Salvador from Nicaraguan and Cuban sanctuaries, killing, torturing, and mutilating their victims; were led by thugs who had ruled El Salvador by violence for fifty years with Soviet support and had finally been driven out by an uprising of virtually the entire population; and were armed, trained, and controlled by Soviet military forces in a major Nicaraguan military base while the USSR maintained large naval units offshore, carried out overflights of El Salvador to supply the guerrillas and for military operations, used Cubans and Bulgarians to fly arms to guerrillas and to carry out major sabotage and terror operations which are attributed to the Soviet proxy army operating from its foreign bases, etc. All of this is, of course, utter nonsense. The fact that the "symmetry" can be discussed without eliciting ridicule is another tribute to the efficacy of "brainwashing under freedom."
>
> In fact, there is a "symmetry," but not one discussed in the press. In both cases, terrorist forces are carrying out large-scale torture and massacre and in both cases these terrorist forces (the army of El Salvador, the *contras*) are organized and controlled by the lord and master of the region.

Or this one from *The Culture of Terrorism*:

> Consider the crucial matter of freedom of expression. As we have seen, freedom of expression, while important, has limited consequences in Honduras or even Costa Rica, while in El Salvador and Guatemala, formal freedoms can easily be granted, with the understanding that, as in the

past, attempts to use such freedom will lead to mutilation, torture, disappearance, or execution. In Nicaragua, however, the situation is radically different, for reasons already discussed. Radio and television in much of the country are dominated, even in wartime, by foreign broadcasting. In the early 1980s, *La Prensa*, which has little relation except in name to the journal that opposed Somoza, was the only significant opposition journal in the region; indeed in the hemisphere, if by "opposition journal" we mean one that takes a stand in opposition to the basic structure of the socioeconomic order and is open to critics of it, and if by "significant" we mean that resources are available to reach beyond narrow segments of the population. If true internal freedom were permitted in Nicaragua, as surely it should be, then the resources of the terrorist superpower, of the international business community, and of domestic economic privilege would ensure that the media were dominated by right-wing elements linked to U.S. interests, merely by the workings of the "free market of ideas" under existing conditions. Again, Nicaragua must bear a burden from which other states, which conform to the requirements of U.S. power and privilege, are entirely exempt. None of this implies that the burden should not be borne; only that we should not succumb to the system of delusion carefully erected in our own business-run partial democracy.

No one else in the United States can write like this. By the standards of logical rigor and moral imagination these passages evoke, we are all midgets.

Chomsky's friend and favorite journalist, Alexander Cockburn, is, for better and worse, a more complicated case. While Chomsky sometimes seems like a *machine à penser*, Cockburn is a rake among radicals and a radical among rakes. He has not forsworn "bravura and display," and so is more fun to read than Chomsky, or almost anyone else, though he sometimes seems—perhaps because, unlike Chomsky, he lives by his pen—to take too seriously his obligation to be entertaining.

Although he is a considerable stylist, he is not a traditional public intellectual. Unlike Howe's "*Luftmensch* of the mind," Cockburn is committed to "concrete criticism." Besides the national press, he evidently also reads NACLA's *Report on the Americas*, MERIP's *Middle East Reports, Central America Update, Latin America Regional Reports, Israeli Foreign Affairs, Covert Action Information Bulletin, Multinational Monitor, Dollar & Sense, Left Business Observer*, the Pacific News Service, and the publications of the Council on Hemispheric Affairs, the

Washington Office on Latin America, the Israeli League for Civil and Human Rights, Oxfam, Americas Watch, and Amnesty International. And he uses them. His wit is a plus, but it's never been the point of his press criticism or, especially, of his superb political reporting with James Ridgeway in the *Village Voice* (his best work, and unfortunately underrepresented in *Corruptions of Empire*). The point is to explain the ideological function of apparently innocent words like "moderate" or "complexity" or "stability" in editorials and news stories; to explain why Duarte and Aquino are ciphers and why they are nevertheless so highly touted; to explain who Frank Carlucci really is, what Paul Volcker is really up to, what "reindustrialization" or a nuclear "freeze" or "tax reform" really amount to; to ask why the press has not covered the murderous air war in El Salvador; and to explain why it was sure to focus almost exclusively on Nicaraguan, rather than Salvadoran, Guatemalan, or Honduran compliance with the Arias peace plan. His jests and epithets decorate a structure of facts and distinctions. He can be as light as Liebling but also, and more important, as solid as Stone.[5]

Predictably and regrettably, it's for his wit that Cockburn is most popular and controversial. This was also his countryman Shaw's misfortune. In a letter of 1904, while still a terribly earnest young man, Bertrand Russell pronounced Shaw "on the whole . . . more bounder than genius." Russell gave some solemn reasons, but I think he was mainly irritated by Shaw's exuberance, which could not endure to leave anything clever unsaid. Most of us cannot, of course; but if potentially clever things occur to a writer at a preternaturally rapid rate, he is bound to have some difficulty in distinguishing the genuinely clever from the merely provocative. Shaw was notoriously afflicted with this perilous gift. By now it is clear that Cockburn is, too. From sheer excess of verbal energy, he must turn a criticism into an epithet, and so occasionally verges on bounderdom.

---

[5]David Denby has written that Cockburn "can't compare as a press critic to A.J. Liebling" (*New Republic*, 1/31/83). This is a foolish judgment. Liebling at his best (e.g., "The Great Gouamba") was very funny but incapable of the wild hilarity of, say, "The Tedium Twins," Cockburn's sendup of MacNeil/Lehrer, or "The Adventures of Mr. P.," his review of Gay Talese's *Thy Neighbor's Wife*, or "Adolf Hitler by A.W.," a mock *Interview* interview. As for Liebling's politics: they were enlightened enough, but too implicit, too merely genial, to be thoroughly admirable. When he died, the *New York Times* editorially intoned: "His death stills a pen that could inspire as well as wound. The press will be duller for the loss of his barbs." To Cockburn's credit, it is highly unlikely that the *Times* would confer a similar benediction on him.

Some unhappy instances: Denise Levertov's statement in the *Nation* on the 1982 Israeli invasion of Lebanon was not "noisome." Americas Watch was not "craven" in refusing to judge Contra human rights abuses more serious than Sandinista abuses before it could fully document that judgment. George Black and Michael Massing were not "spring-heeled self-seekers" merely because they referred to Sandinista errors and crimes and proposed a form of U.S.-Nicaraguan accommodation pretty close to the Sandinistas' eventual position. It is doubtful that Paul Berman "and [Martin] Peretz are of course at one on the Mideast." And it is not funny, nor serious, to assert that "Podhoretz and Orwell deserve each other, as far as I'm concerned." Still, these and similar examples add up to a minor failing. Sharp malice is, after all, less damaging to a political culture than dull malice. On the whole, Cockburn's occasional nastiness is significant chiefly for revealing how deplorably thin-skinned many of his colleagues are.

Of somewhat more substance are complaints about "even-handedness." Cockburn is regularly accused of having a double standard of political morality (often, to be sure, by those who have maintained a lifelong single standard of credulity toward official propaganda and support for the policies of some favored state.) In a letter to the *Nation*, Ronald Radosh put this accusation with maximum force and minimum nuance: "One can only conclude that Cockburn supports the tortures carried out by the left-wing dictators whose policies he favors." Is anything of the sort true?

No one has actually claimed, or could, that Cockburn defends such practices; rather, that he has failed to criticize them sufficiently (by some unspecified criterion). Is this distinction important? Only to the intellectually scrupulous, who will appreciate that the moral value of affirming a truth hardly anyone doubts—that is, a truism—is pretty close to zero. In a 1980 column Cockburn dealt with this issue, albeit offhandedly, in an item on the then-current editorial cliché about the "extremism of left and right" in El Salvador:

> This is the balanced view, which reached its apogee with the Indonesian coup of General Suharto in 1965, when nearly one million supporters of the Indonesian Communist Party were killed in the ensuing six months. As the U.S. government, World Bank, and IMF poured in money, editorialists, columnists and reporters once again proclaimed their distress

at the violence of left and right extremists—though always with the suggestion that it is the left which causes these unwholesome spasms of
violence to come to pass. If only the left would cease to exist, the right
would not have to torture them, etc., etc. Of course I should add that the
left has tortured the right, but no one would suggest that the U.S. government or its equerries in the press have taken a correspondingly sedate
and kindly view in such cases.

That last sentence seems to me an obvious and adequate answer to most of
his critics' self-righteous fulmination about "even-handedness."

Not to all of it, however. Cockburn himself has on occasion blurred the
distinction between supporting a régime and defending its right to be free of
external subversion. It is crucial for principled opponents of American military intervention to maintain this distinction. (Chomsky, for one, has done so
punctiliously.) It is not because contemporary Cuba and Nicaragua are, in some
respects, admirable societies that they deserve to be defended against American
aggression, but because they have legally sovereign, technically legitimate governments, and because international law, fragile though it is, nevertheless helps
prevent even more widespread and lethal superpower intervention. Besides,
Cuba and Nicaragua, like most other societies, are in some respects not at all
admirable. How one strikes a moral balance between the admirable and not-so-
admirable is strictly irrelevant, unless one claims that humanitarian intervention is warranted, which requires a showing of genocide or at least extensive mass
murder (as in the case of our ally Guatemala, for example). It is gallant of Cockburn, in the face of the cowardly near-unanimous refusal of politicians and edi-
torialists to acknowledge any positive achievements by the Sandinistas and the
Cuban Communists, to stress those achievements. And more: it is analytically
useful for explaining the "threat of a good example" that so largely motivates
American hostility to Third World revolutions. But it is a mistake, moral and
even logical, to refer to the Sandinistas or any other régime as "our side." Governments are not moral entities.

In general, of course, it is the objects of Cockburn's criticism who need continual reminding of that last point. A press prone to state worship, especially
when the state in question has, during his formative years, turned one part of
the world into a moonscape and another part into a torture chamber, is bound to

drive a passionate press critic to occasional intemperateness or injudiciousness. There are plenty of hoarse voices and contorted features among contemporary political writers, but none is so well entitled as Cockburn to invoke Brecht's great lines from "To Posterity" in extenuation.

As an undergraduate, I was induced to take an introductory economics course by the promise that it would "teach you how to read the newspaper." It didn't. Cockburn has. For example: right around the time *Corruptions of Empire* was published, several items appeared in the press that would have made no particular impression on me, and would doubtless have seeped into my political unconscious, except for several years of reading Cockburn (and Chomsky). In news stories a few weeks apart, *New York Times* Central America correspondents referred to "the war that has killed more than 60,000 Salvadorans since 1979" (James LeMoyne, 11/4/87) and "the eight-year-old civil war, which claimed more than 60,000 lives" (Lindsey Gruson, 10/5/87). What actually killed most of those 60,000 Salvadorans, overwhelmingly noncombatants, were military and police death squads, originally organized, trained, and equipped by the CIA, as detailed by Allan Nairn in a 1984 story in the *Progressive*, to which Cockburn has several times referred. But because the murderers are allies of the United States, the official American position is that the war, or "extremists of left and right," not the Salvadoran government, is responsible; and the *Times* tailors its phrasing accordingly. A *Times* AP story (10/26/87) referred to a Salvadoran political murder as "unusual, because the incidence of political assassinations has fallen sharply in El Salvador since the early 1980s, before the election of José Napoleón Duarte as president in 1984." The implication is that Duarte's election led to a sharp decline in political violence, testimony to his effectiveness and good will. That is also the American government's view. In fact, Duarte's election had no effect on the death squads, which simply ran out of victims by the mid-1980s, having murdered or driven into exile a majority of the leaders and potential leaders of the popular organizations. Duarte did, however, preside over a vast escalation of aerial bombardment in the countryside, which was aimed largely at the guerrillas' civilian supporters and which claimed civilian lives at a higher rate than the death squads had in any period. A final example: in an editorial on "Torture in Israel" (11/23/87), the *New Republic* commented matter-of-factly that "no country has been more punished by terrorism than Israel." Leaving aside

El Salvador and Guatemala, whose civilian populations have suffered traumatic levels of state terrorism (to which both Israel and the United States have made substantial contributions), and disregarding the tens of thousands of Palestinian and Lebanese civilians killed, wounded or displaced by the Israeli Defense Forces in 1982 (plainly political violence, since the purpose of the invasion was to weaken the allegiance of West Bank Palestinians to the PLO, which many regard as their political representative), this statement ignores the enormous terrorist campaign waged by the United States against Cuba throughout the 1960s, including bombings, assassinations, economic sabotage, and the poisoning of crops and livestock; and, more recently, American-sponsored Contra terror in Nicaragua. According to a study reported in *Ha'aretz* in 1982 and cited by Cockburn, 282 Israeli civilians had been killed by Palestinian terrorists since 1967. That is quite horrible; but most of the examples I've mentioned exceed this level of "punishment" by a large margin. What can the *New Republic's* statement possibly mean?

This sort of thing is bad enough and frequent enough. If not for Cockburn, there would doubtless be even more of it, and worse. And that, I imagine, will be the common form of epitaph for the new public intellectuals. Not that they created monuments of unaging intellect, but that they hemmed in everyday barbarism a little. Consider the legacy of such as Stone, Nader, Chomsky, and Cockburn: endless engagements with current deceits causing or threatening immediate suffering to a great many actual people. Unlike earlier public intellectuals, they have not written for the ages, but for present efficacy. And the price, which they have accepted in all seriousness, will be exacted: their writings will not live.

But their example will. Introducing Orwell's *Homage to Catalonia* in the 1950s, Lionel Trilling concluded:

> Its particular truth refers to events now far in the past, as in these days we reckon our past. It does not matter the less for that—this particular truth implies a general truth which, as now we cannot fail to understand, must matter for a long time to come. And what matters most of all is our sense of the man who tells the truth.

The countless "particular truths" that Chomsky, Cockburn, et al., have unearthed and published from week to week over the last several decades also imply a "general truth" which, alas, "must matter for a long time to come": that intellectuals have indeed been incorporated *en masse* into the power elite, making the "'transparent' social relations" Merleau-Ponty looked forward to that much more difficult and distant. And they imply something else as well: a performance, like Orwell's, of rare moral beauty. It is this—the energy and specificity, the "offensiveness," of their truth-telling—that will matter longest and most of all.

The Sealed Envelope

I.

A propos of Vietnam, W. H. Auden remarked exasperatedly: "Why writers should be canvassed for their opinions on controversial political issues I cannot imagine. . . . Literary talent and political common sense are rarely found together.' One sees his point. And yet the habit is incorrigible: the habit, that is, of deference to the political opinions of artists and intellectuals. It is by no means universal, of course, and is even arguably declining. But the reflex remains widespread.

Auden's remark notwithstanding, the assumption on which this deference is based is not hard to understand. As Lionel Trilling phrased it, art supposedly "makes one more conscious, more aware, more sensitive, and the more conscious, aware, and sensitive one is, the more sympathetic and responsive one is to other people." Though Trilling himself went on to question this assumption, he admitted its plausibility.

Surely it's at least plausible. The beginning of political decency and rationality is to recognize others' similarity in important respects to oneself; that is, to identify imaginatively. Which is what one does when reading fiction. Literature is, in this sense, practice for civic life. "The great instrument of moral good is the imagination," as Shelley wrote in *A Defense of Poetry*.

Besides largeness of imagination, art makes another gift to public life: fineness of discrimination, "A man with taste,' observed Joseph Brodsky in his Nobel Prize speech:

> particularly with literary taste, is less susceptible to the refrains and the rhythmical incantations peculiar to any version of political demagogy. The point is not so much that virtue does not constitute a guarantee for producing a masterpiece, as that evil, especially political evil, is always a bad stylist. The more substantial an individual's aesthetic experience, the sounder his taste, the sharper his moral focus, the freer—though not necessarily the happier—he is . . .

Yet Auden's complaint cannot be dismissed. A 20th-century dishonor roll of writers, including great writers, who've uttered left-wing or right-wing foolishness and even murderous rubbish could be drawn up with no difficulty. How is this possible?

The simplest answer is probably the most useful: don't trust the teller, trust the tale. Art never purveys murderous rubbish, though artists sometimes do. A few masterpieces have been disfigured by—a few even, some would argue, partly animated by—politically pernicious sentiments, but they are so rare that they may reasonably be considered freaks, Opinions are secondary in literature; the primary effect, always benign, is upon the reader's imagination and taste.

All true as far as it goes. That's far enough, at any rate, for my purpose here, which is neither to address Lionel Trilling's objection that teaching modern literature to young narcissists usually produces not brave and humane young citizens but only more cultivated narcissists; nor to arbitrate between the engaged and the skeptical, between, say, Sartre ("although literature is one thing and morality quite another, at the heart of the aesthetic imperative we discern the moral imperative") and Thomas Mann (form is "in its innermost core, indifferent to good and evil"). Instead I want only to reflect a little on the changing situation of intellectuals.

There is, after all, also a long honor roll of 20th-century writers who've articulated important and difficult truths. I'm thinking of Bourne, Russell, Orwell, Macdonald, Silone, Chiaromonte, Camus, Merleau-Ponty, among others.

Some were artists, others critics, but all were literary men. Their primary training and frame of reference were the humanities, usually literature or philosophy, and they habitually, even if often implicitly, employed values and ideals derived from the humanities to criticize contemporary politics. They were generalists: they drew, from a generally shared body of culture, principles of general applicability and applied them to facts generally available. Their "specialty" lay not in unearthing generally unavailable facts, but in penetrating especially deeply into the shared culture, in grasping and articulating its contemporary moral/political relevance with special originality and force.

But many large developments have combined to reduce the influence of such generalists. The public relations industry has far outstripped the intellectuals' restricted access to the public. Formerly, propaganda campaigns like the one sponsored by the British to bring about American intervention in World War I were effective but rare. Propaganda routinized became p.r., which was soon a major ingredient in local newspapers and radio broadcasts. Serious journals, even the larger ones, could not compete with such mass outlets.

Nor could intellectuals and other independents begin to match corporate and government support for academic departments and research institutes. Ideologically congenial experts were funded and publicized, while dissidents, predictably, were not. As a result, the prestige of natural and social science was regularly enlisted behind business objectives or government policy.

Finally, authoritative interpretation of the humanities could only command moral and political influence among a populace who revered that tradition, or indeed knew of its existence. The decline of print literacy and the advent of the "electronic millennium" (Sven Birkerts' invaluable phrase) has eroded not merely the extent but the basis of generalist intellectuals' influence.

No less important than these external developments is a change in the role or definition of intellectuals. In a classic essay on the intellectual vocation ("This Age of Conformity"), Irving Howe observed that "the intellectual is a man who writes about subjects outside his field. He has no field." in another, perhaps even more famous essay ("The New York Intellectuals"), Howe referred to "the idea of the intellectual as anti—specialist, or ... dilettante-connoisseur." These descriptions were especially true of the New York/*Partisan Review* intellectuals, but apply to all 20th-century "public" intellectuals, to all *politiques et moralistes*. Their breadth of reference was the source of their authority: they wrote on political and cultural matters as men and women upon whom nothing—at least nothing relevant—had been lost.

But this combination of range and authority may no longer be feasible. The cultural conversation has grown and now includes too many voices and perspectives, too much information. To be, or at any rate to seem, an expert on everything—which is implied by Howe's definition—is now not a challenge but an invitation to vertigo. To retain an active mastery of the humanities, to keep in touch with new art and new interpretations, is difficult enough. But political and social criticism has grown far more empirical, more specialized, than in the high season of the New York intellectuals. As we know from many a memoir, everyone in the City College cafeteria in the 1930s had a position on everything. Throughout the next couple of decades, everyone at *Partisan Review* meetings and Greenwich Village parties still had a position on everything. Today only Gore Vidal and Hilton Kramer seem to have positions on everything, positions usually generated simply by applying familiar rhetorical strategies to a new topic, without any complicating adjustment to new facts or perspectives. One sympathizes: the grand old anti-capitalist and anti-communist intuitions still have important work to do. And they unify the sensibility, supplying the abundant moral energy that makes both Vidal and Kramer (in spite of everything) admirable. But a unified sensibility and the critical self-confidence it bestows are, for most of us, no longer to be had.

Russell Jacoby's *The Last Intellectuals* persuasively identified the financial and institutional constraints on the freelance life. The intrinsic, evolutionary pressures mentioned above may be just as much to the point. The very ideal of cosmopolitanism, of the intellectual as "anti-specialist," uniting political and aesthetic interests and able to speak with some authority about both, may be obsolescent. Though almost always decried, this is an ambiguous prospect. The culture of professionalism and expertise, the bureaucratization of opinion and taste, are not merely mechanisms of social control or a failure of nerve. They are also in part a response to genuine intellectual progress. There's more to know now than in the '30s, and more people have joined the conversation. Perhaps the disappearance of the public intellectual and the eclipse of the classical ideals of wisdom as catholicity of understanding and of citizenship as the capacity to discuss all public affairs are evidences of cultural maturity. Intellectual wholeness is an almost irresistibly attractive ideal; but nowadays too determined a pursuit of it must end in fragmentation and superficiality.

Actually, that's not just true of nowadays. More than a century ago Matthew Arnold lamented:

> It requires in these times much more intellect to marshal so much greater a stock of ideas and observations. . . . Those who should be guides for the rest, see too many sides to every question. They hear so much said, and find that so much can be said, about everything, that they feel no assurance about anything.

Alas, the stock of ideas and observations relevant to political and cultural criticism has continued to increase. It might seem obvious, for example, that Reaganomics was bad for ordinary Americans —this, if nothing else, a contemporary left-wing intellectual ought to be able to affirm with confidence. Unfortunately, some undeniably honest and intelligent people affirm the contrary. One who is determined to see "all sides of every question" must then learn how to distinguish among ways of measuring median family income, job creation and job loss, unemployment, and several other economic indicators, along with the basics of monetary theory. For a literary intellectual, this is quite a chore.

Formerly a stance, a posture, a gesture, an eloquent affirmation or ironic negation was what was required of the literary-political intellectual. But as the print culture declines, eloquence is devalued. Allusions lose their resonance, rhetorical devices their effect; the habit of close, eager attention to, and the capacity to be intensely affected by, words on a page gradually dwindles.

The problem of scale is equally fundamental, The typically abstract and comprehensive political pronouncements of generalist humanist intellectuals can now no longer hope to be morally or rhetorically adequate. The phenomena in question—the state, the global or domestic political economy, the environment—are too big, and the arguments about them too many and too technical. To draw from a generally shared body of culture principles of general applicability and apply them to facts generally available is no longer possible. The relevant facts are not generally available anymore, but must be dug for; and which principles are applicable is fiercely contested.

There is another obstacle: the very legacy of Bourne, Orwell, Silone, Camus, Macdonald, et al. The success of these intellectuals in elegantly and forcefully articulating general truths of modern political morality leaves their succession problematic. Just as the great achievements of realist and modernist fiction has bequeathed contemporary novelists a crisis of narrative form, so in a sense have the achievements of the public intellectuals of the early and mid-20th century exhausted the possibilities of the political essay. (At least in the West: Konrad, Michnik, and others seem unfazed.) Of course the truths of political morality need frequent restatement. But much of what commands attention and respect about these writers cannot be recaptured: the authoritative tone and sense of responsibility produced by their immersion in European literature; the impression of high specific gravity produced by the historical circumstances and by the fact that all literate Europe and America was their audience; finally, their sheer virtuosity. Attempts to find some contemporary equivalent of the form and voice of the public intellectuals of the '30s and '40s are futile, for all the above reasons and also because, in the history of art, once is enough. Their best essays have something of the specificity and uniqueness of art, which means that their true successors (Alexander Cockburn and Michael Kinsley, for example?) will doubtless look, superficially, very different,

Early in *Armies of the Night*, Norman Mailer reminds himself that "one's own literary work was the only answer to the war in Vietnam." Later in the book, having disregarded his own advice, he finds himself sharing a jail cell with Noam Chomsky. That most influential of intellectual opponents of the war would eventually tell an interviewer: "I've always been resistant to allowing literature to influence my beliefs and attitudes with regard to society and history." Mailer's account of their mutual respect and mutual incomprehension is amusing. Inasmuch as it can stand for a division of labor and a division of sensibility among contemporary intellectuals, it is also, in retrospect, poignant.

II.

In my favorite communist manifesto, The Soul of Man Under Socialism, Oscar Wilde writes: "To the thinker, the most tragic fact in the whole of the French Revolution is not that Marie Antoinette was killed for being a queen, but that the starved peasant of the Vendee voluntarily went out to die for the hideous cause of feudalism." Before and since then, the masses have fairly consistently disappointed their well-wishers, including me. Savage enthusiasm for the First World War among the supposedly gentle and kindly English people astonished and permanently embittered Russell, Shaw, and Lawrence. Wittgenstein renounced his wealth and his career in order to teach children in rural Austria, only to conclude that peasants and children alike were as vile as Cambridge dons. The failure of the European proletariat to become a revolutionary subject hurt Gramsci, Lukacs, and Adorno into magnificent Marxist poetry. The American electorate's embrace of Ronald Reagan and George Bush— unaffected by almost daily news reports of procurement waste and fraud, failure to enforce environmental, occupational-safety, and consumer-protection regulations, the Executive Branch's continual usurpation of Congressional prerogative, the appointment of young and inexperienced but ideologically congenial judges, and plenty of straightforward sleaze—has all but broken my own heart.

Of course the people aren't always wrong. They made the Velvet Revolution. Danish and Scandinavian trade union members appear to be astonishingly enlightened. A large minority of American voters did, after all, vote against Reagan, and a majority (eventually) against Bush. Nevertheless, the problem for the utopian and the radical democrat (both of which I still consider myself, though on fewer days of the week than formerly) is what to make of the typically great gulf between the people's vision, or lack of vision, and our own.

There are at least two rationales for despair. One is the reproduction of culture, the ways political attitudes and beliefs are transmitted in each generation. The study of this process is a signal achievement of recent social science, from feminists on child-rearing (and innumerable other practices) to Stuart Ewen, Jackson Lears, and others on the historical roots of consumerism to Frances Fitzgerald on American history textbooks to Mark Crispin Miller and Todd Gitlin on television advertising to Noam Chomsky and Edward Herman on the "manufacture of consent" through the news media, along with very much other fruitful work. The upshot of all these investigations is, from one point of view, entirely predictable: he who pays the piper calls the tune. Donors, sponsors, stockholders, and trustees—in nearly all cases, businessmen or government officials—set the framework of critique, usually not by outright suppression or censorship, but indirectly, by declining to support work that calls into question, even implicitly, their prerogatives, interests, or values. There is nothing in the least conspiratorial or hypocritical about this, once it's granted that people ought to be able to do whatever they like with "their" money. Now at bottom it is a critical, skeptical attitude, a lack of automatic deference for official or corporate pronouncements—anything that reduces lethargy, passivity, credulity—which threatens the reproduction of social and political orthodoxy. A generalization therefore emerges: work which receives significant institutional or commercial support is likely to be mediocre, conformist, or esoteric. This is as true of popular culture as of academic social science.

The left's discouraging achievement consists in laying bare how subtly this control is exercised and how far it reaches. Considering the disparity of resources between right and left—and I don't mean between Republicans and Democrats—I can't see that a case for, say, the democratic control of production and investment will get a hearing in my lifetime. It would take tens of billions of dollars to mount an effective ideological challenge to contemporary industrial authority relations (a mouthful, that last phrase, but "capitalism" is no less difficult to specify nowadays than "socialism"), since this would include having formulated and if possible tested an alternative, Have-nots haven't got that kind of money.

The other case is less rigorous, but in a way even more troubling. It is the argument for elitism: that most people will always be incapable of the energy, imaginative range, sensual and familial detachment, and inner poise required for citizenship in a republic. There is no disgrace in this; most of us are not gifted musicians or mathematicians and feel no shame about it. It is not, obviously, a precise analogy: fellow citizens influence and sometimes govern us; musicians do not. But in another respect the analogy may be valid and actually encouraging. Mathematical and musical ability can be fostered, up to a point, especially if the effort begins in childhood. And generations of what might be called equal early-environmental opportunity may level differences in aptitude. Might a similarly benign civic pedagogy produce a similarly vast rise in the general level of republican virtue?

Once again, conservatives without imagination will wearily or indignantly object that civic pedagogy on a mass scale—any effort to produce rather than merely permit social virtue—must end in totalitarianism. Conservatives (and liberals and radicals) without imagination are, I suppose, always numerous and influential enough to be worth arguing with. Some other time, though; what haunts me most keenly at present are not Isaiah Berlin's and Leszek Kolakowski's pontifications nor the grandiloquence of the *nouveaux philosophes*, but rather these sadly, quietly authoritative observations of Ortega y Gasset:

> The most radical division that it is possible to make of humanity is that which splits it into two classes of creatures: those who make great demands on themselves, piling up difficulties and duties; and those who demand nothing special of themselves, but for whom to live is to be every moment what they already are; without imposing on themselves any effort toward perfection; mere buoys that float on the waves. . . . As one advances in life, one realizes more and more that the majority of men—and women—are incapable of any other effort than that strictly imposed on them as a reaction to external compulsion. The few individuals we have come across who are capable of a spontaneous and joyous effort stand out isolated. . . . These are the select men, the noble ones, the only ones who are active and not merely reactive, for whom life is a perpetual striving.

Any number of objections will doubtless spring to a generous mind, but one that can hardly do so is that the distinction Ortega proposes is not "the most radical division that it is possible to make of humanity." If humanity will always be a mass of dough leavened sporadically by a yeast of heroes, then why talk of "radical democracy"? Capitalist democracy requires only consumers, fermented occasionally by entrepreneurs. The resulting loaf is not very nutritious, but a lot more so than Stalinist or pre-modern brands. And if Ortega is even roughly right, what other kind of democracy is possible?

I've found two paths leading, if not altogether out of despair, at least toward endurance and a provisional hope. One is renunciation—always an attractive option for the beleaguered leftist. What has recently made this, for me, a live option is the example of Richard Rorty—whom I consider an (perhaps the) exemplary contemporary intellectual. Rorty has associated himself, far more often and more explicitly than most of his philosophical peers, with a humane, egalitarian politics. And so my reflexive resistance is suspended when he urges, delicately and persuasively, that the sweet dreams of perpetual progress notwithstanding, we may have to concede to Nietzsche that democratic societies have no higher aim than what he called "the last men"—the people who have "their little pleasures for the day and their little pleasures for the night." But maybe we should just make that concession, and also concede that democratic societies do not embody anything, and cannot be reassured by anything, larger than themselves (e.g., by "rationality"). Such societies should not aim at the creation of a new breed of human being, or at anything less banal than evening out people's chances of getting a little pleasure out of their lives. This means that citizens of those societies who have a taste for sublimity will have to pursue it in their own time, and within the limits set by On Liberty. But such opportunities might be quite enough.

The other path, or tactic, is a frankly tenuous, even willful, faith in the utopian visionary tradition. As with all the other problems I've touched on in this essay, I've dealt scarcely at all in evidence, almost exclusively in quotidian impressions. And this not solely for brevity's sake. The perennial philosophical questions, the immemorial answers, may gradually fade away, as Rorty and I hope and expect, or may at any rate mutate into now unimaginable forms. A good reason to think so is that now, as always, one argues about them by opposing a single idiosyncratic (though, one hopes, somehow persuasive) vision to another. Ortega himself splendidly disdains evidence: "As one advances in life, one realizes more and more . . ." To his distressingly plausible pessimism I can only oppose the (to me) hearteningly plausible utopias of Wilde and William Morris. In News from Nowhere, there is virtue and (infrequent) transgression, happiness and (infrequent) grief, but no mechanical miracles; it is undeniably heaven, but undeniably no more than human; and there is no distinction between an inert "majority of men" and a few heroes "for whom life is a perpetual striving." Life for all is an exquisite balance of striving and rest. The Soul of Man Under Socialism is less graphic and less convincing, but Wilde's rhetoric is nearly irresistible; and he almost seems to have anticipated Ortega when he redefines socialism as "Individualism": "It is the differentiation to which all organisms grow . . . the perfection that is inherent in every mode of life, and towards which every mode of life quickens." Where Ortega saw fixity, Wilde saw evolution. I agree—I want to agree—with Wilde.

For quite a while, it appears, the question may be moot. Even the most fervent faith in the heroic capacities of ordinary people may need to be passed on "in a sealed envelope," as Rilke says of love between selfish lovers. Class stratification, sometimes violently enforced, and ethnic or religious civil wars are the immediate human prospect, for which no intensive pedagogy will be required to enlist most ordinary people.

In a sealed envelope, then, along with many of the values adumbrated by the writers I most admire, whose works are a small flotilla bearing that envelope towards other generations, less and more enlightened than ours, who will make their own unforeseeable use of its contents.

II. Intellectuals

The Promise of an American Life

The death of Randolph Bourne in 1918, at the age of 32, was as great a loss as American intellectual life has ever sustained. "In no one," wrote Alfred Kazin about Bourne's generation, "did 'the promise of American life' shine so radiantly." His career lasted seven years, during which he wrote more than 150 essays and reviews for the leading literary and political journals of his time. His book on the experimental public schools of Gary, Indiana, was an important event in the history of the progressive education movement. His essays on Dreiser largely rescued that novelist from critical neglect. His attack on Puritanism and the genteel tradition helped found cultural radicalism in America. Above all, his lonely, bitter opposition to American participation in World War I was a brief but unforgettable demonstration of the dignity of the intellectual vocation. He was "the intellectual hero of World War I in this country," said Dwight Macdonald, who was the intellectual hero of World War II in this country.

Bourne was born in suburban New Jersey in 1886. The family doctor bungled the birth, and Bourne's face was badly deformed. At the age of four he suffered a severe case of spinal tuberculosis, which left him a hunchback and less than five feet tall throughout his life. His father, a business failure and an alcoholic, was banished by the stern maternal uncle who supported the family. When Randolph graduated high school he was accepted by Princeton, but his uncle refused any further financial support. He tried to find a job in New York City, but his looks told against him. "Not once in two full years of applying," writes his latest biographer, Bruce Clayton, "did he ever get past the receptionist or initial interview." He gave up on the city and scrounged work in his home-town; he gave music lessons, punched out piano rolls in a local workshop, did factory work and odd jobs.

Somehow he kept his spirits up, and after six years, at the age of 23, entered Columbia with a full tuition scholarship. It was like entering Paradise. The teachers were stimulating and accessible; his classmates were friendly; Bourne blossomed into a brilliant student and conversationalist. As a freshman he began contributing to the Columbia literary magazine. As a sophomore he began contributing to the *Atlantic Monthly*. His first essays for the *Atlantic* ("The Two Generations" and "The Handicapped") were immensely popular; halfway through college, he was a nationally known writer.

His early pieces for the *Atlantic* were a little callow, full of vague and occasionally vapid uplift, which presumably appealed to the attenuated Transcendentalism of that magazine's readership. "Youth" began: "How shall I describe Youth, the time of contradictions and anomalies? The fiercest radicalisms, the most dogged conservatisms, irrepressible gayety, bitter melancholy—all these moods are equally part of that great showery springtime of life." These essays probably owed their popularity to a kind of tame iconoclasm: for all that they twitted the older generation and lamented American provincialism and conformism, their upbeat, healthy-minded tone was also reassuring. The young Bourne preached "the experimental life," "vitality," "variousness," and openness to "American promise." Liberal, prosperous, prewar middle-class America read these sermons indulgently, rather proud of its youthful chastiser and confident that it could afford a certain quantity of self-improvement.

As graduation approached he hoped for a teaching post at Columbia. But he had lampooned several professors and supported a strike of scrubwomen against the university. The English Department would as soon appoint him a professor, a friend told him, as "the Catholic Church would appoint Voltaire a bishop." He won a traveling fellowship and spent a year in Europe, meeting writers and radicals, observing architecture and town planning. While he was there, the flower of America's liberal intelligentsia came together to found

The New Republic. Bourne was made a contributing editor.

After returning from Europe and joining *The New Republic* in the autumn of 1914, Bourne's radicalism became more forceful but also more worldly and sardonic. He had been reading Nietzsche, Dostoevsky, and the Fabian socialists, had watched Europe slide into war hysteria, and had begun to take stock of the American left (this last a sobering experience in any epoch). His wary editors asked him to concentrate on education and city planning, and his series on progressive education at Gary, Indiana (soon afterward expanded into a book) was enormously influential. But his reports and reviews pushed on to larger themes, toward a criticism of American life as a whole.

Bourne's cultural criticism was partly an attempt to apply the pragmatic, instrumentalist philosophy of James and Dewey. Today it may be hard to believe that pragmatism once seemed fresh, liberating, subversive; but it did. Philosophical pragmatism was the last, best blossom of Victorian agnosticism, the modest, tentative Yea that followed the Everlasting Nay. It amounted to a cosmic wager on the adequacy of secular styles of thought and democratic forms of social life, a wager inspired and underwritten by the success of science. In the experimental, antidogmatic, and—not least important—communal character of scientific practice, pragmatists beheld the image of a possible future. Dewey had shown, Bourne wrote, that "scientific method is simply a sublimely well-ordered copy of our own best and most fruitful habits of thought." From this apparently innocuous formulation, Bourne drew a radical (though not fully worked out) conclusion: maximizing the national welfare was a technical problem, to be tackled with a resolute disregard of intellectual superstitions, traditional privileges, or special interests. Ingenuity, flexibility, good will, good nature—Americans' "best and most fruitful habits"—would, if imported into public life, gradually overcome America's class, ethnic, and generational conflicts.

Bourne would outgrow this cheerful meliorism, but it was a generous and plausible illusion. Faith in "the promise of American life" (the title of one of the most influential books of the era, by the first editor-in-chief of *The New Republic*) was not obviously misplaced in the years before World War I. Bourne took that promise more seriously than most. "Transnational America," his finest *Atlantic* essay, asked "whether perhaps the time has come to assert a higher ideal than the 'melting pot.'" The assimilationist ideal was misguided, Bourne argued, because "there is no distinctively American culture. It is apparently our lot rather to be a federation of cultures." This was an exceptional historical opportunity: "America is a unique sociological fabric, and it bespeaks poverty of imagination not to be thrilled at the incalculable potentialities of so novel a union of men." But "poverty of imagination" was precisely the characteristic failing of America's middle class. And so Bourne warned, in a prescient though fragmentary critique of mass culture, that dynamic capitalism and aggressive "Americanization" would produce not cosmopolitanism but deracination.

To read "Transnational America" and other essays and reviews from Bourne's last three years is to ache with regret that his astonishing trajectory was cut so short. "The Price of Radicalism," a 1000-word book review, is a better manifesto for the New Left than the Port Huron Statement. "What Is Exploitation?", a 1500-word account of Bourne's correspondence with an unabashedly reactionary factory owner, is an exquisite specimen of stylish nondoctrinaire, unpatronizing socialist propaganda (not a thickly populated genre). And he was maturing rapidly. As late as 1917 there were still occasional touches of high-sounding vagueness, of undergraduate wistfulness, in his writing. But America's entry into World War I concentrated his mind wonderfully and provoked the series of furiously eloquent essays for which he is best known today.

"The war—or American promise," he pleaded; "one must choose." As censorship and irrationalism increased throughout the country, Bourne insisted, nearly alone, that cultural pluralism could not survive national mobilization. War enhances state power and undermines local, decentralized initiative; it makes passivity, apathy, conformism, and cynicism the normal relation between the citizen and the state; paradoxically, modern bureaucratized war makes public-spiritedness superfluous. In Bourne's memorable phrase: "War is the health of the State."

These arguments did not impress his fellow intellectuals, who lined up in support of American intervention. *The New Republic*'s editors and contributors, especially John Dewey, urged "realism" and a more indulgent view of the uses of force. They were confident that "intelligence" (that is, they, the intelligentsia) could turn the forces let loose by the war to creative social purposes at home and abroad, could turn mechanized lunacy into a "democratic war." But to do this it was necessary to ally themselves with—in fact, to subordinate themselves to—

state power. They did so enthusiastically, and thereafter (like many liberal supporters of the U.S. invasion of Iraq) devoted a good deal of polemical energy to jeering at radicals and pacifists, whose scruples, the "realists" claimed, could lead only to isolation and impotence.

All this outraged Bourne, who replied with a combination of penetrating analysis and coruscating sarcasm. In his colleagues' eagerness to subserve official policy he saw the corruption of pragmatism and, more generally, the proneness of intellectuals to a mystique of "action" and "commitment." They had supported intervention, he charged, from a "dread of intellectual suspense"—a readiness to minimize their own principled objections to the war for fear of ending up in a posture of futile opposition or of offering an appearance of sentimental idealism. They convinced themselves that power would allow itself to be guided by expertise—their expertise. Bourne exposed this illusion ruthlessly:

> But what then is there really to choose between the realist who accepts evil in order to manipulate it to a great end, but who somehow unaccountably finds events turn sour on him, and the Utopian pacifist who cannot stomach the evil and will have none of it? Both are helpless, both are coerced. The Utopian, however, knows that he is ineffective and that he is coerced, while the realist, evading disillusionment, moves in a twilight zone of half-hearted criticism, and hopes for the best, where he does not become a tacit fatalist. The latter would be the manlier position, but then where would be his realistic philosophy of intelligence and choice? . . . War determines its own end—victory; and government crushes out automatically all forces that deflect, or threaten to deflect, energy from the path of organization to that end. All governments will act in this way, the most democratic as well as the most autocratic. It is only "liberal" naiveté that is shocked at arbitrary coercion and suppression. Willing war means willing all the evils that are organically bound up with it. A good many people still seem to believe in a peculiar kind of democratic and antiseptic war. The pacifists opposed the war because they knew this was an illusion, and because of the myriad hurts they knew war would do to the promise of democracy at home. For once the babes and sucklings seem to have been wiser than the children of light.

Bourne's best antiwar writing forms part of a remarkable series of essays by American literary and philosophical radicals: Thoreau's "Civil Disobedience,"

Bourne's "War and the Intellectuals," "A War Diary," and "Twilight of the Idols"; Dwight Macdonald's "The Responsibility of Peoples"; and Noam Chomsky's "The Responsibility of the Intellectuals" and "Objectivity and Liberal Scholarship." There are differences, of course, most notably along a stylistic axis from the epigrammatic bravura of Thoreau to the documentary doggedness of Chomsky. But the similarities are striking: they were all outbursts of passionate moralism occasioned by an imperialist war (in Macdonald's case, a morally dubious military strategy); they were aimed at the national chauvinism of the populace, the complacent pragmatism of the educated, and the routine mendacity of the state; and their authors were ignored, or derided as naïve and unserious, by the "realists" of their epoch. Perhaps more important, their authors were all amateurs; they asserted a kind of Protestant principle of private judgment against the quasitheological mystifications of the government and the policy intelligentsia. Taken together, they constitute something like a prophetic tradition within American radicalism, and the content of their prophecy is: "War is the health of the State."

As a prophet, Bourne met the usual fate. *The New Republic* politely declined to publish his antiwar essays, though it continued to accept book reviews from him. Bourne's antiwar writings appeared in *Seven Arts*, a new journal that featured several other young writers—Van Wyck Brooks, Paul Rosenfeld, Louis Untermeyer—and many established ones—Frost, Dreiser O'Neill, Mencken, Sandburg, Max Eastman, Amy Lowell, Sherwood Anderson. *Seven Arts* was a brilliant success; but its wealthy sponsor, aghast at Bourne's radicalism, withdrew her support, so it folded. Bourne began publishing more frequently in *The Dial*, but editorial control passed to a friend of John Dewey, and Bourne was frozen out. By the end of the war he was one of the most famous and least publishable writers in America.

Once again, he kept his spirits up. He began a novel and a philosophical study of the modern state. As the war wound down, he was poised to resume his place as one of the country's leading literary and social critics. And he found the "golden person" he had always—with an intensity heightened by his deformity—yearned for: the talented, beautiful, aristocratic Esther Cornell. They became engaged a few weeks before Bourne's fatal influenza attack.

Bruce Clayton's *Forgotten Prophet*[1] has not much of interest to say about Bourne's ideas, but it does manage to get inside his emotional life. There is something a little adolescent about the personality that emerges from Bourne's letters, which Clayton quotes extensively: the ardor, the high-mindedness, the wry self-mockery. Only a little, though; on the whole, Bourne's character was as admirable as his intelligence. He suffered a good deal from having to go about with one of the best minds of his time in a child's body. But he succeeded in growing up, and in making himself loved as well as admired.

Clayton concludes by speculating that Bourne would have become a socialist Reinhold Niebuhr: skeptical, unaffiliated, anti-utopian, mindful of human limitations and the tragic dimension. Maybe so; he could not have remained indefinitely in the rarified, supercharged atmosphere of the great antiwar essays. But he would doubtless have soared again, on occasion; and those later flights are much missed. As Sartre wrote after Camus's death: "Rarely have the qualities of his work and the conditions of the historical moment so clearly required that a writer live."

Today, Bourne occupies an obscure place in the tiny pantheon of the American left. But he captured the imagination of his contemporaries, including John Dos Passos, who wrote in *U.S.A.*:

If any man has a ghost
Bourne has a ghost
a tiny twisted unscared ghost in a black cloak
hopping along the grimy old brick and brownstone streets
still left in downtown New York,
crying out in a shrill soundless giggle:
"War is the health of the State."

[1] Louisiana State University Press, 1985.

An Exemplary Amateur

In Saul Bellow's novel *Humboldt's Gift*, the narrator/protagonist returns to New York and meets an old friend, Orlando Huggins, who is clearly Dwight Macdonald:

> It came back to me that more than twenty years ago I had found myself at a beach party in Montauk, on Long Island, where Huggins, naked at one end of the log, discussed the Army McCarthy hearings with a lady sitting naked and astride opposite him. Huggins was speaking with a cigarette holder in his teeth, and his penis, which lay before him on the water-smooth wood, expressed all the fluctuations of his interest. And while he was puffing and giving his views in a neighing stammer, his genital went back and forth like the slide of a trombone. You could never feel unfriendly toward a man of whom you kept such a memory.

It seems to have been difficult for anyone in American intellectual life to feel unfriendly toward Dwight Macdonald. In the course of his long career as a political and cultural critic, he took issue with virtually everyone on the scene at one time or another, including (most emphatically and often, whenever he had occasion to reconsider his own previous opinions) himself. Macdonald was a gadfly: a debunker of kitsch and propaganda, of radical, conservative, and mainstream sentimentality, vulgarity, and duplicity. Yet this inveterate argufier inspired nearly universal affection. What beguiled his readers was less his arguments—though these were never negligible—than the distinctiveness of the voice in which they were delivered: "persnickety, contentious, vain, unafraid, passionate, garrulous, sometimes irritating, always honest," wrote one reviewer, who might have added "and often extremely droll." That admirable voice was stilled in December of 1982, but Da Capo press has lately[1] begun to reissue his books, starting with *On Movies*, a collection of film criticism, and *Against the American Grain: Essays on the Effects of Mass Culture.*

Macdonald's career traced an arc from literature to politics and part way back. He attended Phillip Exeter Academy and then Yale, and like a few other gifted adolescents amid the intellectual torpor of upper-class schools in the 1920s, he enlisted for life in the avant-garde. At Exeter he idolized Oscar Wilde, published a short-lived student magazine "of extreme preciosity," as he later described it, and joined an exclusive club (there were two other members) called the Hedonists, whose motto was "Cynicism, Estheticism, Criticism, Pessimism." At Yale he hectored the president, faculty, and student body about dress codes, compulsory chapel, and professorial dullness. Yet all of this flippancy was serious. His friends at Yale later became his colleagues at *Partisan Review*. And when an English teacher at Exeter put him in touch with James Agee, who arrived a few months after Macdonald left, they began an ardent lifelong correspondence about literature and film.

After graduating Yale in 1928, he joined a management-training program at Macy's. "My plan was to make a lot of money very rapidly and retire to write literary criticism." He didn't last long. A Yale classmate got him a job on the staff of Henry Luce's new magazine, *Fortune*. There Macdonald learned the craft of journalism—the research and expository skills he picked up at *Fortune* were the foundation of his later, "higher" journalism—and acquired an intimate, enduring dislike of American business civilization. American business civilization, in the person of *Fortune*'s editors, did not exactly take a shine to Macdonald either, and after his series of articles excoriating the US Steel Corporation was bowdlerized, he quit.

[1]1984.

In the late 1930s Macdonald's political education began in earnest. He read the Marxist classics plus an enormous quantity of economics and sociology, hung out with several Trotskyist groups, and became an editor of the newly revived *Partisan Review* (which had temporarily suspended publication because of the editors' disillusionment with Stalinism and socialist realism). In the intellectual hothouse that New York was in those years, he evolved "with amazing speed." as he later commented wryly, from New Deal liberal to neophyte radical to Communist sympathizer to anti-Stalinist Trotskyist revolutionary to unaffiliated, unprogrammatic anarchist-pacifist. When World War II broke out, the other editors of *Partisan Review* supported American participation and tempered their radical opposition to capitalism and bourgeois society. But the logic of the lesser evil did not appeal to Macdonald. In 1943 he left the magazine, and the next year, with his wife, Nancy, he started his own magazine, *Politics*.

Politics was a phenomenon. It was published from the Macdonalds' living room (Dwight was the entire editorial staff), and for the five years of its existence it was arguably the best political journal ever published in the United States. Macdonald's own varied and prolific commentary (collected in *Memoirs of a Revolutionist*, to be reissued by Da Capo in 1985) was the magazine's staple, but some of the most remarkable radicals of the time were also contributors: Albert Camus, Simone Weil, Nicola Chiaromonte, Victor Serge, Paul Goodman, George Woodcock, George Orwell. All of them, like Macdonald, were morally fastidious, ideologically heterodox, and fed up with brutality and propaganda, both official and oppositional. They made a program and an ideology of honesty; it was an impractical program and they accomplished nothing, but their writing illuminated these dark times better than anyone else's.

Among many extraordinary articles in *Politics*—including Camus's "Neither Victims Nor Executioners," Weil's "The Iliad or the Poem of Force," and Bruno Bettelheim's "Behavior in Extreme Situations"—two by Macdonald stand out. "The Responsibility of Peoples" asked why, if all Germans were held responsible for Nazi atrocities, all Americans should not be held responsible for Allied atrocities. The latter included the saturation bombing of German and Japanese cities (which took perhaps a million civilian lives), widespread starvation in liberated Europe, bloody repression of the Greek resistance, refusal to allow more than a few European Jews to immigrate to the United States, and the reckless initiation of atomic warfare. In part the essay was an anarchist argument against the "organic" corruption of the State, which underlay notions of "collective responsibility" for war crimes. But equally it was a challenge to national chauvinism, a rebuttal of the tacit assumption that the other side's atrocities somehow extenuate one's own. And since his audience consisted largely of leftists, Macdonald felt obliged to address their own chauvinisms: much of his most scathing wartime criticism, in "The Responsibility of Peoples" and elsewhere, was directed at Soviet crimes and their American apologists. It required almost a heroic disinterestedness to say, or even perceive, such things in an atmosphere of inflamed patriotism and partisanship. That disinterestedness, his apparent lack of any temptation to equivocation or self-deception, was and is the basis of Macdonald's reputation.

"The Root is Man" was more speculative. It was not only the war that had disillusioned Macdonald and his comrades, it was the whole sorry history of the organized left. How had the splendid ideals of the nineteenth-century socialists been perverted into Stalinist barbarism and Trotskyist scholasticism? Were there ethical values—socialist values—by which Marxism itself might be judged? "The Root is Man" claimed to find in Marxism a contradiction between two legacies of the Enlightenment: individualism and humanism on the one hand, historical and scientific materialism on the other. Marx had shown that in every society, moral values and property relations are connected. From this suggestive but ambiguous proposition, most of his followers concluded that morality was irrelevant to "real" politics, i.e., the class struggle, which progressed inexorably according to dialectical laws deducible from *Capital*. "Pragmatic" liberals drew analogous lessons from John Dewey's philosophy, and both Marxists and liberals tended in practice, as Macdonald demonstrated at length, to cynicism, opportunism, and state worship.

So Macdonald proceeded to reconsider the Enlightenment, modestly proposing to rethink "Determinism v. Free Will, Materialism v. Idealism, the concept of Progress, the basis for making value judgments, the precise usefulness of science to human ends, and the nature of man himself." He ended, predictably, perplexed. But he did succeed in arguing one crucial point against the Marxists/pragmatists, or "Progressives," as he called them: "What can possibly be the content of this future *real* morality [i.e., the one vaguely invoked in the *Communist*

Manifesto] if it is not the persisting core of past morality stripped of all class-exploitative perversions?" It was in that "persisting core" of classical and modern humanism, rather than in an undefined (and, as he came to feel, largely mythical) Progress, that radical hope lay. As others were quick to point out, the explication and defense of "past morality" was what conservatives claimed to be up to. Was Macdonald a socialist, a conservative, both, or merely confused? Confused he was, yet "The Root is Man" may be worth the entire corpus of twentieth-century moral and political philosophy. But for Macdonald it was, politically, the end of the road.

Turgenev remarked about politics that "the honorable man will end by not knowing where to live." By 1950 Macdonald was politically homeless. "There is very little that we can honestly say in praise of the institutions and culture of Western capitalism," he wrote in 1949, "beyond the statement that, now that we have seen thirty years of Communist development, the comparison is greatly in favor of Capitalism." And the next year, in an even bleaker mood: "The scale of things is too big, the levers of power too far removed from people like us (perhaps from people like Stalin and Truman), the mood of the general population, after generations of Pavlovian conditioning by industrialism, world wars, and state bureaucracies, too demoralized and apathetic to respond to our appeals. Even if we could make them with the old fervor and rationality. Which we can't. For fervor we now have routine moralizing; for reason, the old stock of antiquated abstractions. . . . The pacifist and the socialist writings of today are to those of two generations as hay is to grass. Which is why I am no longer a pacifist, a socialist, or any kind of ist."

Turgenev went into exile; Macdonald went to work for the *New Yorker*, writing what he called "social-cultural reportage and analysis." There were several reasons for this internal migration: ideological burnout; financial burnout— *Politics* had lost a lot of money, and he had children to support; and a conviction —or at least a hope—that "the correction of taste" (T.S. Eliot's definition of the purpose of criticism) might be a form of political action. Mobilizing the masses was not on the docket anymore, but perhaps one could begin to counteract, or anyway to document, that "Pavlovian conditioning."

Macdonald's essays, profiles, and reviews for the *New Yorker*, collected, along with occasional pieces from *Partisan Review* and other journals, in *Against the American Grain* and *Discriminations*, ranged over the American scene, surveying how-to books, bestselling novels, the careers of Mark Twain and Ernest Hemingway, the state of literary journalism, the culture of poverty depicted in Michael Harrington's *The Other America* (which Macdonald's lengthy review rescued from obscurity), and much else. He punctured Marshall McLuhan, Tom Wolfe, Norman Cousins, and Mortimer J. Adler. He grumbled about the damage to language wrought by Webster's Third International Dictionary, the Revised Standard Version of the Bible, and the theory of structural linguistics. He composed a perceptive, slightly querulous meditation on "The Triumph of Fact" before that theme became commonplace.

The point of all this witty, erudite grousing was to keep American culture honest. That tenuously persisting core of "past morality," of ethical and aesthetic values, seemed encrusted by commercialism and bureaucracy and in need of large doses of critical solvent. Macdonald's most influential effort of cultural hygiene was "Masscult and Midcult" (1960), an anatomy and theory of popular culture. Actually, Macdonald called his subject "mass culture," which highlights a fundamental distinction in his essay between "communities" and "masses." Communities (city-states, craft guilds, artistic schools, political factions) have traditions, and their members have individual functions. But masses are "in historical time what a crowd is in space: . . . not related to *each other* but only to some impersonal, abstract, crystallizing factor. In the case of crowds, this can be a football game, a bargain sale, a lynching; in the case of the masses, it can be a political party, a television program, a system of industrial production." Art is individuality, so members of a community can produce genuine culture, either High or Folk. But masses are composed of "inchoate and uncreative" atoms capable only of an anonymous and homogenized nonculture, "Masscult."

So far, familiar: Macdonald (and plenty of others) had been making this argument for decades. But there was something new, he claimed, about post-World War II American culture: it was so abundant, various, and flexible as to induce acute anxiety. "The pattern of our cultural lives is 'open' to the point of being porous. For a lucky few, this openness of choice is stimulating. But for most, it is confusing and leads at best to that middlebrow compromise called Midcult." Midcult may be defined as the tribute mediocrity pays to excellence. It was a hybrid, combining the essential qualities of Masscult—"the formula, the built-in reaction, the lack of any standard except popularity"—with ersatz mimicry of High Culture, employing modern idiom and technique in the service of the banal. Midcult's intentions were good, but its effect was insidious: unlike Masscult, Midcult competed with serious new art for prestige and financial support.

Most of "Masscult and Midcult" was devoted to a review of typical Midcult phenomena: the Book-of-the-Month Club, Norman Rockwell's *Saturday Evening Post* covers, Rodgers and Hammerstein musicals, Hemingway's *The Old Man and the Sea*, Thornton Wilder's *Our Town*, and so on. Macdonald's detailed criticism was scintillating and salutary, and his historical diagnosis was persuasive. But his prescription was bizarre: to re-create a cultural (though *not* a social, political, or economic) elite. "Let the masses have their Masscult, let the few who care about good writing, painting, music, architecture, philosophy, etc., have their High Culture, and don't fuzz up the distinction with Midcult." Macdonald admitted that this solution was both unattractive and impractical. Still, it seemed to him the only alternative to an even more farfetched (though much more desirable) solution: the creation of real, i.e., decentralized, communities within which lively popular cultures might flourish. Macdonald was a cultural elitist, but only by default. His democratic hopes were in abeyance, and he thought of High Culture, with its subversive playfulness and its fidelity to noncommercial, non-bureaucratic standards, worth defending against the encroachments of Midcult.

For all Macdonald's etiological shrewdness, the criticism of popular culture has come a long way since "Masscult and Midcult." And even in 1960 there was no excuse for lumping Elvis Presley with Zane Grey and Cecil B. De Mille. There was something *ancien régime* about Macdonald's radicalism, which produced too many somber and untenable formulations like this: "Folk art was the people's own institution, their private kitchen-garden walled off from the great formal park of their masters. But Masscult breaks down the wall, integrating the masses into a debased form of High Culture and thus becoming an instrument of domination." In fact, kitchen garden and formal park are too cozy a setting for the best popular art. It's true that industrial civilization has given rise to new and unexpected forms of cultural debasement. But it's also given rise to new cultural possibilities, to which Macdonald was largely impervious. An increase in scale does not always entail reductiveness: one effect of the best of mass culture is to trace or forge the connections among the unprecendentedly diverse experiences of its unprecendentedly broad audience. When artists find this common ground, the experience, however fleeting, of so enormous a community is visionary and exalting. When they fail, they can retreat into an irony that thrives in the vast range and dense detail of American consumer culture.

Most of mass culture may be junk, but some of its vast wares will be goofy or frenzied or self-indulgent in original, unpredictable ways—and more to the point, in ways that are made possible only by the relationship of artist and mass audience. The inevitable commercialism of that relationship offended Macdonald, and rightly. But sometimes indignation is a critical liability. A critic of popular culture needs a large measure of negative capability, i.e., a sense of when to disregard one's own standards, or in Keats's definition, the ability to refrain occasionally from "any irritable reaching after fact and reason." Like all doctrines, Macdonald's aristocratic moralism was both enabling and disabling.

Fortunately, he was no doctrinaire. His movie reviews, mostly written for *Esquire* between 1960 and 1966 (and collected in *On Movies*), are much less programmatic than the essays in *Against the American Grain*. They're wry and informative, and though less tense with polemical energy, they're still bracing. In 1966 Macdonald switched the subject of his monthly column at *Esquire* to politics, in time to fulminate splendidly against the Vietnam war. Among his later essays were a startlingly detailed program for "Updating the Constitution" (included in *Discriminations*) and a homage to Buster Keaton (in the *New York Review*, October 1980; as far as I can tell, his last major piece). When he died in 1982 he was making dilatory efforts at writing his memoirs.

Did Macdonald matter? Some people (including Macdonald) have disparaged him affectionately (some, like Hilton Kramer, not so affectionately) as a "dandy," charming and talented but fickle and, finally, lightweight. I think he mattered, in a general way and in a great many particular ways. For one: "The Responsibility of Peoples" directly inspired the finest political essay of the last several decades, Noam Chomsky's "The Responsibility of Intellectuals." That alone is more than most of his contemporaries accomplished. For another, there was Macdonald's effect on the *New Yorker*. During the Vietnam war, the magazine's "Notes and Comment" section featured a good deal of surprisingly pungent criticism of American policy. An outsider can only guess, but I'd guess that Macdonald was partly, even if indirectly, responsible. And that gracefully phrased, quietly indignant commentary has become a tradition. From week to week, "Notes and Comment" is some of the best editorializing in America: well-informed, discriminating, magnanimous. Like Macdonald.

He mattered in a larger way, too, at least to those of us trying to be citizen-critics. He was an exemplary amateur. Like Chomsky and Randolph Bourne—his only peers among twentieth-century American political writers—Macdonald was aroused by a calamitous war to a passionate moralism. Like them, he was dismissed or derided by "pragmatic" liberals as naïve and unserious. And in each case, while the "realists" were steeped in intellectual disgrace, the naïve moralists redeemed, in a small way, the humane promise of the intellectual vocation.

Macdonald despaired of politics—but only of "professional," organized politics and its ideological sideshows. He remained a political dilettante, in the pristine sense of that honorable old word: someone who prizes nobility or skill. In 1968 Nicola Chiaromonte, a frequent contributor to *Politics*, responded to the French student uprising by admonishing the students to adopt "a non-rhetorical form of 'total rejection'": to approach politics with the integrity of artisans, to apply to social life "the standards of the craft itself, standards that in themselves are the simplest and strictest of moral principles and, by their very nature, cut out deception and prevarication, charlatanism, and the love of power and possession." That was also Macdonald's creed. He sought to apply to our politics and culture the strict critical standards of an honest intellectual craftsman—standards at one deeply conservative and deeply subversive.

Not his uncommon wit but his common decency was Macdonald's best legacy. Lionel Trilling observed of George Orwell: "If we ask what it is that he stands for, what he is the figure of, the answer is: the virtue of not being a genius, of fronting the world with nothing more than one's simple, direct, undeceived intelligence, and a respect for the powers one does have, and the work one undertakes to do." Like his friend Orwell, Macdonald was not a genius, but he was all the more useful for that. "We admire geniuses, we love them," Trilling went on, "but they discourage us." To see this freelance intellectual tilting year after year at the political and commercial barbarities of the age, armed with no system but only some peculiar moral and aesthetic intuitions, was—and still is —encouraging.

Citizen Karp

One of Jacques Derrida's more entertaining *jeux d'esprit* was his "signature" theory. There seems to be, he observed, a curiously frequent correspondence between an author's name and the title or subject of his/her work: e.g. *North American Songbirds* by Gay Lee Trilling or *Urology Illustrated* by C.M. Passwater. (Derrida's examples, needless to say, were infinitely subtler.) Perhaps we gravitate toward similarly signed things out of unconscious identification and ontological narcissism, or perhaps it's just another of Language's little jokes. At any rate, my favorite example is Walter Karp, who until his death four years ago was one of the republic's preeminent political scolds.

Karp was a member of not one but two endangered species: the independent scholar and the public intellectual. Without academic or journalistic affiliation, he wrote scores of essays and eight books, of which at least two (the only ones I've read) are tours de force. *The Politics of War* (1979) is a study of the causes and consequences of America's entry into the First World War, which drastically— according to Karp, designedly—transformed American politics from republican to statist. *Indispensable Enemies* (1973) reinterprets twentieth-century American history as the reign of a bipartisan oligarchy: viz., the leadership of the two major parties, who perennially collude to maintain the appearance and prevent the substance of political competition. Both books are resplendently amateur performances, utterly lacking in professional myopia, timidity, and prosaism (as well as, less endearingly, footnotes), full of embattled eloquence and high civic purpose. Karp was also a frequent contributor to *Harper's*, whose editor, Lewis Lapham, has collected and introduced these essays from Karp's last decade and a half.[1]

They range widely, from the contemporary relevance of Thucydides, the Bobby Kennedy legend, and the origins of the Cold War to soap operas, fallout shelters, and the history of Central Park. But they all have the same moral: the enemies of liberty never sleep. "My politics is simple," he once wrote, quoting Lincoln: "'Give all of the governed a voice in their government; and that alone is self-government.' It is amazing," Karp continued, "how radical that proposition turns out to be and how much of the political history of this country is an effort to prevent its realization."

Amazing, for example, how little American participation in World War I had to do with making the rest of the world safe for democracy and how much with quelling the democratic stirrings expressed in Populism and Progressivism. No less clearly than Randolph Bourne, Karp demonstrates, Woodrow Wilson and the war party saw that "war is the health of the state" (only John Dewey and the other *New Republic* liberals failed to see this) but thought its centralizing, authoritarian, and chauvinistic consequences all to the good.

Amazing, too, how stable a condominium the two parties have achieved at the state and local levels, and how eager both leaderships are to help put down independent initiatives of any sort, from within either party. According to standard political science doctrine, parties exist in order to win elections; but in case after case, party bosses have favored unpopular hacks, even from the opposing party, over popular insurgents. At the national level, too, collusion reigns. The Southern Bourbon hegemony that throttled the Congress until the mid-1970s cannot be explained in terms of ideology, regional interests, or the mechanics of the seniority system but only, Karp argues, by an alliance between the Bourbons and the Northern urban machines to maintain control of the national Democratic

---

[1] *Buried Alive: Essays on Our Endangered Republic* by Walter Karp. Edited by Lewis Lapham and Ellen Rosenbush. Franklin Square Press, 1992.

Party. And the amazing performance of the Congressional Democratic leadership from the mid-1970s to the mid-1980s—its persistent undermining of Carter, supine acquiescence in Reaganism, and support for the hapless Mondale—is best explained not by Carter's (hardly unique) ineptness or Reagan's allegedly invincible popularity but by the leadership's determination to reverse its defeat by reformers.

In Karp's account, the antidemocratic spirit, like the democratic spirit, is protean and inextinguishable. His discussion of Frances Fitzgerald's *America Revised* suggests that the shift in the curriculum from narrative history to "social studies" was something more insidious than a triumph of nonpartisan banality. Whatever the intentions of curricular innovators (many of them earnest Deweyite progressives), the very form of the new pedagogy, by de-emphasizing individual ambitions and achievements, by leaching out the drama and glamour of the past, starved children's moral and political imagination, thereby weakening a crucial source of resistance to illegitimate authority. The newly powerful educational bureaucracies may not have aimed at this result, but it did not displease them.

Another essay looks at the Cold War from a resolutely noninternationalist perspective. The deformation of American political life that followed World War II—the overgrowth of the executive branch, the cult of secrecy, the national security culture—was not, Karp contends, a byproduct of imperialism but the motive for it. "The imperial republic was born not of the strife between capitalism and communism; that is the grand misdirection. It was born of the ineluctable republican struggle between those who would 'limit,' in Tocqueville's words, and those who would 'extend the authority of the people.'" As Dean Acheson put it, less elegantly than Tocqueville: "You can't run this damned country any other way . . . [than] to say politics stops at the seaboard—and anyone who denies that postulate is a son-of-a-bitch and a crook and not a true patriot. Now if people will swallow that then you're off to the races."

The linchpin of *Buried Alive* is an essay titled "The Two Americas." They are, on the one hand, the republic, the "constitution of liberty and self-government," the spirit of freedom together with the memories and practices that embody that spirit; and on the other, the nation, a mystic unity that is separate from and greater than its members and that is best served not by the skepticism and self-assertation of an active citizenry but by incuriosity and automatic deference. This is a fundamental antagonism. One can't be loyal to both the republic and the nation. Republicans (not, needless to say, GOPers) love their country partly because it is theirs, but mostly because it is free, as Lincoln said, a sentiment that enrages "nationists" (Karp's useful coinage). Republicans are wary of talk about national "greatness" or the "national interest," especially in support of foreign adventures, always suspecting that such talk means pockets are being picked and liberties eroded. Nationists go abroad, ostensibly in search of monsters to destroy but actually in order to aggrandize the federal executive and whip the population into shape, to "forge a national soul . . . a new religion of vital patriotism—that is, of consecration to the State," as one of the pro-war party put it in 1916. Nationists profess to want prosperity, security, and efficiency, but are willing for this purpose to minimize accountability and participation, which is anathema to republicans. Karp does not name names, but as I understand him, William F. Buckley, Charles Krauthammer, and—notwithstanding his empty chatter about civic virtue—George Will are nationists, I.F. Stone and Ralph Nader republicans.

The difficulty of sorting out the deplorable from the admirable in American history, and of doing justice to both, has bedeviled radicals. The crude chauvinism of the right is a continual, all too frequently irresistible, provocation, eliciting compensatory inanities about inequality and repression being "as American as apple pie." Karp's categories, amply and subtly elaborated, show how to distinguish this country's republican core from nationist accretions, how to cherish America by giving it hell.

One piece of Karp's argument sticks in my craw, though. He insists too much on the autonomy of the political. Karp is fond of quoting Thucydides' maxim: "Of the gods we believe, and of men we know, that by a necessary law of their nature they rule wherever they can." In other words, ambition is a given, and arbitrary power is sought for its own sake. We should not look to social or economic forces to explain history but to "our nature as *political* beings." Even greed is pretty much beside the point. Party bosses, union bosses, corporate bosses want above all to rule; the prerequisites of power are a distant second.

Actually, one of the few things we've learned since Thucydides' time is that the phrase "human nature" does no explanatory work. Like everything else, having power is desired for the sake of its consequences—which may, of course, be too many or too obscure to yield a usable explanation in any individual situation. And philosophy aside, it's rash to dismiss all talk of social forces. The Constitution is certainly something more than a "bankers' plot," as a few doctrinaire leftists have made it out, but it was not an immaculate conception. "The hardest way to make a million dollars is to become a United States senator," Karp scoffs. "Any vicious, impudent, brazen, shrewd, gifted person can think of an infinite number of better ways to become rich than to become a crooked politician." Maybe so, but this is not the last word on money and politics. Individual action is indeed the text, but institutions are the context. In a capitalist society, market power constrains political action. Even an enlightened citizenry and incorruptible politicians are helpless in the face of a capital strike.

This is my cavil about Karp. No one's perfect, I suppose. *Buried Alive* does, however, contain one perfect essay. "Liberty Under Siege" may be the finest political essay I've ever read, equal to anything by Bourne, Orwell, Macdonald, even Chomsky. It is a chronicle and analysis of the Reagan Administration's campaign against democracy: executive order by executive order, O.M.B. guideline by O.M.B. guideline, Justice Department ruling by Justice Department ruling, Congressional capitulation by Congressional capitulation. It's a horrifying story, yet so august is the theme, so compelling the exposition, so fierce and luminous Karp's rhetoric, so genuine and generous his passion, that reading the essay is, in spite of everything, an exalting experience. *Felix culpa*, I felt, the wretched corruption that evoked such magnificent indignation.

Karp was fond of quoting two other phrases: Franklin's "a republic, if you can keep it," and Jefferson's "we are never permitted to despair of the commonwealth." If we keep it (which is by no means certain), Karp will deserve more thanks than most of us. And if we—I, at least—did not altogether despair during these last dozen dark years, it was in part through the grace of his example.

The Worst Policy

Steven Koch, director of the creative writing program at Columbia, has recently published *Double Lives: Spies and Writers in the Secret Soviet War of Ideas Against the West*.[1] It is full of fascinating details and provocative speculations about the long and sorry romance between Western intellectuals and Soviet Communism. Wells, Rolland, Gide, Malraux, Hemingway: all duped, duped utterly, along with countless others, by brilliant, unscrupulous cultural double agents like Willi Munzenberg and Otto Katz. The Bloomsbury/Cambridge milieu that produced Guy Burgess and Anthony Blunt; the corps of literary auxiliaries in the Spanish Civil War; the creation of an American espionage and propaganda network in Washington and Hollywood: all these are fully and vividly evoked. Perhaps Koch's most astounding contention is that the legendary Reichstag Fire trial was a fraud, a shadow play, and that long before the Pact, Hitler's and Stalin's secret police and propaganda services were cooperating extensively, "supplying each other with disinformation against each other's domestic enemies. Thus, Stalin used the Gestapo to discredit and destroy [Marshall] Tukhachevsky and

[1]Free Press, 1994.

the Red Army general staff, while Hitler used the Comintern and the Munzenberg operation to discredit and destroy Ernst Rohm and the SA."

Double Lives has taken its knocks from reviewers, and I'm in no position to comment favorably or unfavorably on its scholarship. But insofar as its purpose is to get leftish literary intellectuals thinking (and fuming) about our ideological ancestry, it is unquestionably successful. Trails of reflection lead in every direction. I'll simply meander along one of them, without stopping to indicate the others.

Koch has some unkind words about a figure I've long found intriguing: Claud Cockburn, who in the 1930s and 40s was, as Koch says, "the most visible and best-connected Stalinist journalist in England." He was, Koch continues, "the perfect incarnation of a certain glib tone of sneering condescension—the Cockburn tone was Bloomsbury vulgarized—fused with a wholeheartedly Stalinist soul and mind. Guy Burgess talked very much the way Cockburn wrote."(*Mutatis mutandis*, this is also true—although it is, I'd say, no more than one-tenth the whole truth—of Claud's no less brilliant son, Alexander Cockburn.) "In Claud Cockburn," Koch concludes, "Stalin was in full and public possession of his man."

This catalyzed my longstanding resolve to read Cockburn's deliciously witty memoirs. There I found an episode that illuminates—by no means simply or straightforwardly—one of Koch's chapter headings: "Lying for the Truth." During the Spanish Civil War, at the behest of the Soviet agent Otto Katz, Cockburn concocted an account of a great Republican military victory in order to influence the French government to let a crucial arms delivery to the Republicans pass over the border. It worked; the fabricated story made a sensation, and the arms got through. Years later, when Cockburn revealed the truth, he was denounced by Richard Crossman, the British Labour Party leader and editor of *The God That Failed*, who had himself done propaganda work for British intelligence in World War II, but who had, he insisted in his defense, "detested" it.

> A comfortable ethical position [Cockburn replied], if you can stop laughing. To me, at least, there seems something risible in the spectacle of a man firing off his propaganda-lies as, presumably, effectively as he knows how, but keeping his conscience clear by "detesting" his own activities. After all, if he does not think the cause for which he is fighting

worth lying for, he does not have to lie at all, any more than the man who sincerely feels that killing is murder is forced to shoot at those enemy soldiers. He can become a conscientious objector, or run away. *Paris vaut bien une messe*, and I do not recall that Henry of Navarre ever claimed that he had detested his own "cynical" behavior.

Through sheer literary bravado, Cockburn wins this round. But this is hardly the last word on "lying for the truth." In another volume of memoirs (his wife's), Cockburn tells another Spanish story. A left-wing American journalist has filed an accurate report about an imminent Republican defeat. Assailed by the Comintern agent Koltzov, one of Cockburn's closest friends, he replies in admirable American fashion that "facts are facts, and the reader has a right to them." Koltzov retorts scornfully:

> If you were a little more frank, you'd say that what you're really inter-ested in is your damned reputation as a journalist. You're afraid if you don't put out this stuff, and it comes through someone else, you'll be thought a bad reporter, can't see the facts under his nose. Probably in the pay of the Republicans. That's why you, as the French say, have lost an excellent opportunity to keep your mouth shut.

This round is a little harder to call. The American is actually no fool, and the allegedly clever and dashing Koltzov seems a smug brute. But for me, the main interest of this episode lies elsewhere, in the light it throws on still another passage in the Cockburn memoirs. Claud is complaining that the West's impla-cable mistrust of Soviet intentions was based on a failure of understanding:

> When the Russians talked of peace and non-aggression they meant it. They had to. Westerners hoaxed themselves into the idea that all this was a mere smoke-screen. The economic condition of Russia absolutely required not only peace but the maximum possible co-operation with the capitalist states in terms of trade and concessions to foreign capital operating in Russia itself.

This is largely true. When the Russians talked of peace and non-aggression in the 1920s and 30s, they *did* mean it; they *did* have to. But there is one disingenuous word in this passage: Westerners did not exactly "hoax" themselves into mistrusting the Soviets. They didn't have to. The Communists were, as Cockburn and Kolt-zov forthrightly acknowledge, unashamed, uninhibited, and extremely skillful liars, a tradition stretching back well before the Revolution. It was only rational to disregard their protestations. True, enlightened Western diplomacy would have coopted and corrupted rather than confronted the Soviets. But enlightened diplomacy is rare in any age. At the very least, it was profoundly unintelligent of Lenin, Trotsky, Koltzov, Cockburn, et al. not to know who they were dealing with—not, that is, to recognize how vulnerable their chronic mendacity ren-dered their appeal to Anglo-American public opinion. In this case (in virtually all cases, I would argue, given unlimited space and less limited energy and inge-nuity), dishonesty was the worst possible policy.

But even that is not the last word on "lying for the truth." What is truth, anyway? Actually, I agree with Lenin, Trotsky, Koltzov, and Cockburn that truth is whatever serves the revolution; or as Trotsky put it in *Their Morals and Ours*: "That is permissible . . . which *really* leads to the liberation of humanity." And I agree with Dewey, who in his reply to *Their Morals and Ours* rejected "as definitely as does Mr. Trotsky himself" all forms of "absolutistic ethics based on the alleged deliverance of conscience, or a moral sense, or some brand of eternal truths."

Only, I don't believe Lenin, Trotsky, et al. had a very well-worked-out idea of what might "*really* lead to the liberation of humanity." In particular, they seem not to have seriously entertained the thought that the liberation of humanity was most likely a long way off and could only be delayed still further by starv-ing, shooting, or imprisoning recalcitrant Russian peasants, workers, and poets. They were right in principle: the liberation of humanity is certainly worth lying and murdering for, if these can be shown (though I doubt they can) to be the best way of achieving it. But after all, the Bolshevik Revolution did not lead to the liberation of humanity; it led to . . . Stalin. And Stalin led to contemporary, post-Communist Russia, quite possibly the most corrupt, violent, altogether wretched country on earth, at any rate in the Northern Hemisphere.

So what is the last word? For now, let it be the first word—the first word, that is, of *Double Lives*. The book's epigraph is Matthew 5:37: "Let your speaking be, 'yea, yea,' or 'nay, nay'; for whatsoever is more than these cometh of evil." This was not, of course, even Christ's last word; he also said, "Be ye wise as serpents."

And as Koch acknowledges, many deep-dyed Stalinists were brave and selfless. But Christ's injunction to singleness of heart has resonated down the ages for a good reason. With the rarest of exceptions, double lives are futile and self-consuming. Bad policy.

Grand Disillusions

The disintegration of the Old Left in the first half of the twentieth century produced an engaging and, on the whole, admirable type: the "virtuous" intellectual. Disillusioned by firsthand involvement with wars and totalitarianisms, undeceived by the ideological enchantments of the left or right, these writers undertook to preserve an amateur, nonpartisan status and to bring Cold War controversies before the bar of common sense and uncommon candor. One might say—though the phrase is a trifle ambiguous—that they made a career of honesty. For this they were rewarded with widespread affection and loyalty, if not quite celebrity, during their lifetime and a sort of minor immortality afterward. I'm thinking of Orwell in England, Camus in France, Dwight Macdonald in the United States, and Nicola Chiaromonte in Italy.

Chiaromonte was born in southern Italy in 1905. He joined a libertarian socialist group, *Giustizia e Libertá*, in his twenties and fled Mussolini's regime in 1934. He later fought in the Spanish Civil War (he appears, as the philosophical Scali, in Malraux's *Man's Hope*). During World War II he came to the United States; he moved in *Partisan Review* circles and contributed to Dwight Macdonald's *Politics*, where the ingenuous socialist radicalism of the early twentieth century was metamorphizing into disenchanted humanism with ambiguous political implications. He returned to Europe after the war, wrote essays and theater criticism (occasionally for *Dissent* and other American journals), and co-edited *Il Tempo Presente* with Ignazio Silone. He died in 1972. *The Worm of Consciousness*, a collection of his best-known pieces—among them his graceful, searching meditations on "Modern Tyranny" and "The Mass Situation and Noble Values"—came out in 1976. *The Paradox of History*[1], the Christian Gauss Lectures at Princeton in 1966, was published in England in 1970 and appears now, for the first time, in the United States. Summing up as it does a full life of both action and erudition, it is an unusual and intensely interesting testament.

There is a passage in *The Paradox of History*, on the aftermath of World War I, that very well describes the "virtuous" intellectual and at the same time sounds the central theme of Chiaromonte's book:

> The individual who has lived through a great historical upheaval has not only been dispossessed of his beliefs. He has found himself face to face with a reality that goes far beyond him and everyone else. He has discovered that one cannot be satisfied with substitutes for truth, and that one cannot at will believe in anything or nothing at all. He has seen that in the relations between man and world something exists that cannot be changed. At the same time, he has sensed the reality of a Power which nobody can control. Finally, he has found himself personally in question, and he knows that, under any circumstances whatsoever, there is only one thing that matters: the relation between individual conscience and the world. This is something that cannot be counterfeited.

The "Power which nobody can control" is fate. Chiaromonte proposes to trace "the resurgence of the idea of fate in a world . . . dedicated to the idea of progress."

Autonomy, self-confidence, mastery of the environment—these notions are the essence of cultural modernity. Through a complex alchemy presided over by nearly all the modern masters, these ideas were transmuted into a kind of philosophical precious metal, a key to interpretation and action: history as Progress. The strands of this concept are various, but they include at least two chains of

[1]*The Paradox of History: Stendhal, Tolstoy, Pasternak, and Others*
by Nicola Chiaromonte. Univ. of Pennsylvania Press, 1985.

reasoning. First: the physical world is intelligible and, to some extent, controllable; contrary to religious cosmology, human beings are part of the physical world; therefore, human relations are also, at least in principle, intelligible and controllable. Second, each individual life involves a progression, mediated by education, from helplessness to self-control; so, too, humankind is bound to grow into control of its collective destiny. The story of this growth is History. Obviously the cornerstone of this optimism is Reason; or rather, faith in Reason. Understanding means mastery; as Bacon said at the outset, knowledge is power.

All that is familiar enough, as are the main historical objections to modern optimism: the theological-conservative doctrine of Original Sin, the Romantic idea of organic hierarchy, and the neo-Marxist critique of Enlightenment as instrumental reason. Chiaromonte's objection is different. It is an intuition derived from the shadowy but powerful Greek notions of Moira, Ananke, and Nemesis, jointly interpreted as Fate. What these notions have in common is a suggestion that the reach of rationality is limited, because physical nature is full of unforeseeable accidents and human nature of incomprehensible impulses. To describe those limits precisely is impossible; to defy them, even for noble purposes, entails tragedy. Chiaromonte's explanation of Fate is at times obscure and unsatisfying; but at its most lucid, it conveys some of the cosmology behind the tragic spirit.

As befits its imaginative and mythical origins, Chiaromonte's argument takes the form of a commentary on a body of fiction: the novels of Stendhal, Tolstoy, Roger Martin du Gard, Malraux, and Pasternak. "Only through fiction and the dimension of the imaginary," he writes, "can we learn something real about individual experience." What we learn is that "individual experience" perennially refutes historical optimism.

Chiaromonte contends that the works of Stendhal et al. make up a tradition: the antihistorical novel, in which the idea of History as rational and progressive, as the working out of an intelligible human destiny, is shown to be an illusion. As far as I know, no one has ever before linked these authors in quite this way; whatever the merits of Chiaromonte's argument as political philosophy, it is, as literary criticism, a brilliant conception.

In *The Charterhouse of Parma* the ardent, empty-headed young Fabrizio del Dongo sets out to join Napoleon's army. What ensues is farce: he is robbed by the first people he meets, thrown into jail as a spy, taken in by a worldly woman, an army provisioner, who outfits him in a dead hussar's uniform and sends him off to the great battle at Waterloo. Fabrizio wanders around the battlefield, alternately delighted and horrified, but always uncomprehending. And in fact the event as Stendhal describes it is largely incomprehensible—even, it seems, to Napoleon and his marshals, who gallop to and fro to little purpose and less effect. The scene is a masterly deflation of martial heroics, and especially of Napoleonic mythology. Hegel is supposed to have called Napoleon "the Idea on horseback." Stendhal's exquisite mockery is the antithesis of this apotheosis.

Tolstoy avowed that the antiheroic philosophy of *War and Peace* had its source in Stendhal's irony. *War and Peace* and Isaiah Berlin's essay on its epilogue, "The Hedgehog and the Fox," are the center of gravity in Chiaromonte's book. According to Chiaromonte (and Berlin), Tolstoy's antipathy to the "great man" theory of history stemmed from a deep skepticism that anyone—great or ordinary, individually or collectively—could control, or even comprehend, the direction of history. In the novel, those who pretend otherwise, whether French or Russian, are shown to be either deluded or self-serving. Wisdom comes only to those who, like Pierre and the dying Prince Andrey, are forced to recognize the insignificance, the radical contingency, of their grandest projects. After such an awakening, one can only abandon the unreal hope of making history. Real life is rooted, intractable, impervious to abstractions.

It is a commonplace to compare Homer and Tolstoy, for their epic scope and vivid descriptions of nature, ritual, and warfare. Chiaromonte points out a deeper resemblance. Simone Weil called the *Iliad* "a poem of force." She meant that, more than anything else in Western literature, the *Iliad* insists on the futility of attempting to use force "rationally," as a means. Chiaromonte suggests that *War and Peace* is a second "poem of force," because it depicts world-historical ambition as hubris, the willful disregard of human limitations.

Chiaromonte's chapters on Malraux, Pasternak, and Martin du Gard's magnificent, neglected *Summer 1914* extend his argument: "individual experience" undermines ideology. The Second International, the Russian Revolution, the Spanish Civil War, the Communist movement in China appear in these novels not as stages in the progress of Absolute Spirit or the Dialectic, but as so many installments of chaos. Disillusionment is the lot of every honest, undoctrinaire character. What they all learn is not so much that power corrupts as that large-scale historical designs necessarily transgress a certain limit—the limit of human predictability, the horizon of free will. Ideologies ignore the "irrational forces . . . hidden in society, in nature, and within the individual himself" (the Greek word for "divine," *theion*, originally meant "hidden"). They are guilty, according to Chiaromonte, of "cosmic impiety."

The mystery of free will is at the core of his critique of historical determinism; it is in terms of free will that he formulates the "paradox" of history. "If we could get to know all the consequences of our actions, history would be nothing but an idyllic and constant harmony of free wills, or the infallible unfolding of rational design. We would then always act rationally, that is, we would not act at all, since we would simply follow a preestablished and sterile pattern. But then we would not be free. We are free, however, and that means literally that we do not know what we are doing." He is taking aim at dialectical materialism; but if true, his thesis discredits every utopia, William Morris's no less than B.F. Skinner's.

One can quibble with Chiaromonte's "paradox" on logical grounds. His equation of freedom with uncertainty is a hoary fallacy: freedom is not indeterminacy but self-determination, for which knowledge is not an obstacle but a prerequisite. And anyone who harbors the slightest strain of residual positivism will find it flaring up when Chiaromonte prescribes humility before "the eternally impenetrable whole" and "all that is ineffable, arcane, and secret in the world" as a cure for "the sickness of our times."

But these objections miss much of the point and all the undeniable power of Chiaromonte's warning. What he meant, I believe, is not that an "idyllic and constant harmony" among human beings would be sterile or oppressive, but that it is unattainable; that perfectibility is the premise of utopianism, a premise empirically disproved by fascism, Stalinism, and mechanized global war. In *Summer 1914* the pragmatic Antoine Thibault exclaims, with love and exasperation, to his brother Jacques, a socialist dreamer: "You will not succeed in changing man!" Jacques trembles with defiance and doubt—for these characters, the question of progress is still open, which is why Chiaromonte calls *Summer 1914* "the last great novel of the classical nineteenth century." For Chiaromonte in 1966, after half a century of barbarism, the question is closed. Utopianism in the late twentieth century is at best contemptible naiveté, at worst a murderous pretext. The party of humanity has been reduced, for the time being, to chastened silence.

Do these dark counsels represent the beginning of wisdom or a failure of nerve? Perhaps both. The quality of Chiaromonte's thinking (not to mention his life) inspires immense respect, even trust. And anyone who could live through the horrors experienced by Chiaromonte's generation without an occasional loss of nerve must simply have lacked imagination. Mass murder is awful enough; mass murder rationalized by appeals to science and socialism—this must have seemed to "progressive" intellectuals like the death of all hope.

Hope is a sturdy weed, though. Two years after Chiaromonte traveled to the New World to deliver his gloomy meditation on the necessity for limits, the gay-est of revolutions broke out in the Old World, tossing off, among innumerable impudent slogans, "All Power to the Imagination" and "Love Without Limit, Play Without Restraint, Live Without Dead Time." To his credit, Chiaromonte met the French student revolt with the wisest, most generous response of any from his generation. He challenged the students to adopt a

> nonrhetorical form of "total rejection"; [to] detach [yourselves] without shouting or riots, indeed, in silence and secrecy; not alone but in groups, in "real societies" that will create, as far as possible, a life that in independent and wise, not utopian or phalansterian, in which each man learns to govern himself first of all and to behave rightly toward others, and works at his own job according to the standards of the craft itself, standards that in themselves are the simplest and strictest of moral principles and, by their very nature, cut out deception and prevarication, charlatanism and the love of power and possession.

This is a skeptical voice, but not a cynical one. It is, at any rate, a far cry from neoconservatism. The twentieth century hurt Chiaromonte into metaphysics but not into despair, and still less into callous chauvinism.

Camus is not mentioned in *The Paradox of History*, but I suspect Chiaromonte's book was written under the influence of *The Rebel*. There is the same rejection of ideology, concentration on art and literature, impossibly high-flown prose style, distaste for programmatic detail, and stress on limits and Mediterranean *mésure*. Both are unforgettably eloquent about what must not be done and irritatingly vague about what, if anything, should be done. They are, in their way, the *dernier cri* of twentieth-century literary radicalism, by which I mean the attempt to derive from art a criticism of politics and an explanation of the apparently inexplicable history of this century. Nowadays their legacy has been claimed by the Parisian "new philosophers"—a sad dénouement to an honorable enterprise.

Chiaromonte was no Cold Warrior—nor were the rest of the "virtuous" cohort. They were not any sort of warriors, except insofar as they proposed, in Camus's words, "to fight within History to preserve from History that part of man which is not its proper province." What this meant was not a retreat from politics into art but a desire to infuse politics with the values of art: intellectual detachment, emotional honesty, imaginative fullness. That was, and remains, a radical program.

The Liberal Intelligence

In 1975 Lionel Trilling died, at the height of his reputation and influence as America's foremost literary and cultural critic. Twenty years later, nearly all his books were out of print. Fortunately Trilling was survived by his remarkable wife Diana, who wrote an extraordinarily affecting memoir of their marriage, *The Beginning of the Journey*, and who encouraged Leon Wieseltier, literary editor of *The New Republic*, to assemble a new collection of her husband's essays. *The Moral Obligation to Be Intelligent*[1] is the result. It contains thirty of Trilling's finest essays, his two famous prefaces to *The Liberal Imagination* and *Beyond Culture*, and a well-judged introduction by Wieseltier. It is exactly what anyone urgently needs who has no Trilling on his or her bookshelves.

Trilling was one of the "New York intellectuals," the brilliant writers and critics connected with *Partisan Review* who played a large part in American culture from the 1930s through the 1960s. In some ways he was central to this group, perhaps the one most respected internally and most visible externally. But in other ways he was untypical of them, notably in passing his career as a professor

---

[1] *The Moral Obligation to Be Intelligent: Selected Essays* by Lionel Trilling. Edited and with an introduction by Leon Wieseltier. Farrar Straus & Giroux, 2000.

(of English, at Columbia) rather than as an institutionally unaffiliated man of letters like, say, Edmund Wilson or Philip Rahv. This made a difference to his writing, both in substance and in style. For one thing, his writing was less topical than that of most other New York intellectuals. Though nearly everything Trilling wrote had an ultimate political relevance, almost nothing he wrote had an immediate political reference. And then, though he was not a scholar, he was surrounded by scholars. This undoubtedly made him a little more circumspect, more respectful of expertise, and more inclined to deal in depth with individual works of literature and to reckon with their traditional interpretations than his almost defiantly non-professional fellow New Yorkers were.

It also made him more inward. Academics work and socialize at closer quarters than freelancers; and since an intellectual hatred is the worst, or at least the most uncomfortable, kind, academics place a high—sometimes excessive—value on courtesy. To reconcile this necessary academic civility with the boldness, even aggressiveness, prized by his more freewheeling *Partisan Review* colleagues required—what Trilling achieved—a style of incomparable tact and gracefulness. Some comments by Irving Howe on the "characteristic style" of the New York intellectuals may suggest how far Trilling was and wasn't a typical specimen. "The kind of essay they wrote was likely to be wide-ranging in reference, melding notions about literature and politics, sometimes announcing itself as a study of a writer or literary group but usually taut with a pressure to 'go beyond' its subject, toward some encompassing moral or social observation." So far, pure Trilling. But Howe went on: "It is a kind of writing highly self-conscious in mode, with an unashamed vibration of bravura. Nervous, strewn with knotty or flashy phrases, impatient with transitions and other concessions to dullness, calling attention to itself as a form or at least an outcry, fond of rapid twists, taking pleasure in dispute, dialectic, dazzle . . ." Trilling's style was not nervous, knotty, flashy, impatient, or ostentatious; it was grave, smooth, deliberate, and restrained. But it had force as well as grace. As Wieseltier observes: "Trilling was not noisy in the New York manner. For that reason, he wrote the most lasting prose of any of the New Yorkers."

Every piece in *The Moral Obligation to Be Intelligent* is rewarding, but someone making a first acquaintance with Trilling's work might best begin with these acknowledged classics: "Keats in His Letters," "Mansfield Park," "Huckleberry

Finn," "The Princess Casamassima," "George Orwell and the Politics of Truth." These essays, like the others, are full of illuminating juxtapositions, discriminations, and asides as well as subtle, shapely exposition. But the subjects of these essays evoke Trilling's keenest sympathies, and his affection kindles his usual intelligence to some unusually stirring formulations.

> [*The Princess Casamassima*] is a novel which has at its very center the assumption that Europe has reached the full of its ripeness and is passing over into rottenness, that the peculiarly beautiful light it gives forth is in part the reflection of a glorious past and in part the phosphorescence of a present decay, that it may meet its end by violence and that this is not wholly unjust, although never before has the old sinful continent made so proud and pathetic an assault upon our affections.

> [Keats] stands as the last image of health at the very moment when the sickness of Europe began to be apparent—he with his intense naturalism that took so passionate an account of the mystery of man's nature, reckoning as boldly with pleasure as with pain, giving so generous a credence to growth, development, and possibility; he with his pride that so modestly, so warmly and delightedly, responded to the idea of community.

> If we ask what it is [Orwell] stands for, what he is the figure of, the answer is: the virtue of not being a genius, of confronting the world with nothing more than one's simple, direct, undeceived intelligence, and a respect for the powers one does have and the work one undertakes to do. We admire geniuses, we love them, but they discourage us.... He is not a genius—what a relief! What an encouragement.

Trilling's enthusiasms were immensely attractive. But, some asked, were they specifically *literary* enthusiasms? In a generally admiring review of *The Opposing Self*, Denis Donoghue entered a few shrewd reservations. Speaking for the New Criticism, he wondered whether Trilling's "central interest is not in literature at all but in ideas; which are not, need it be said, the same thing"; whether "in the last instance [Trilling] is not really interested in the fact that the words of an individual poem are *these* words and not some others, in *this* order and not another"; whether "he is happiest when roaming about the large triangle whose sides are Sociology, Politics, and Literature (in that order)." Wieseltier's introduction touches on this question, a bit defensively, conceding that

Trilling was "a very un-literary literary critic," but countering immediately that "his conception of his critical duty was less professional and less playful—and bigger." Finally, Wieseltier concludes, "he was a historian of morality working with literary materials."

Wieseltier's "and bigger" strikes me as mere assertion. But I would also query Donoghue's "need it be said." It does, actually, and patiently explained, at least to the likes of me. The relation of form and content in literature may be a pseudo-question, as many claim, but like other such questions it recurs continually.

It's true, though, that Trilling was best known for his exploration of (to use his celebrated phrase) "the dark and bloody crossroads where literature and politics meet." In the decades when he began to write, the 1930s and 40s, liberalism was, as he noted, America's "sole intellectual tradition." Like any one-party state, the state of American political culture had become, in certain ways, lazy and intolerant. It had become intolerant of complexity, of limits, of doubt—in short, of mind. Trilling thought he detected a "chronic American belief that there exists an opposition between reality and mind, and that one must enlist oneself in the party of reality." Which usually meant the revolutionary or, as we now more soberly say, the progressive party.

Trilling was quite willing to enlist in the progressive party, but only on one condition. Progressives must acknowledge that "to act against social injustice is right and noble but that to choose to act so does not settle all moral problems but on the contrary generates new ones of an especially difficult sort." There is, for example, the problem of elitism vs. mediocrity. "Civilization has a price, and a high one . . . all civilizations are alike in that they renounce something for something else. . . . To achieve the ideal of widespread security, popular revolutionary theory condemns the ideal of adventurous experience. All the instincts of radical democracy are against the superbness and arbitrariness which often mark great spirits." There is, for another example, the problem of individual liberty, of limiting collective power once we have "learned something of what may lie behind abstract ideals, the envy, the impulse to revenge and to dominance." These are not insoluble problems. But there are no final or perfect solutions, only imperfect, temporary, revisable ones.

Trilling called this attitude "moral realism" and defined it as "the free play of the moral imagination." The phrase recalls Matthew Arnold, and is meant to.

Trilling began his career with a book on Arnold, and the resemblances between the two men—philosophical, political, and temperamental—go deep. They both wrote a marvellously flexible, musical, allusive prose. They both suffered fools— i.e., intellectual antagonists—if not gladly then at least kindly and courteously. They both considered literature primarily in its moral aspect, as a criticism of social and political life. And they both saw their special contribution as helping to keep their fellow progressives (liberals, radicals, reformers, social democrats, or what you will) up to the mark, helping them to fail a little less often in detachment, discrimination, receptiveness, patience, magnanimity. Literature could teach this, perhaps because it has no political designs on us, or because stories get around psychological defenses that often defeat arguments, or because rhythm, harmony, symmetry, and other aesthetic qualities induce a deeper attentiveness. Whatever the reason, literature *can* teach us the moral virtues, at least the second-order, intellectual ones, as Trilling showed repeatedly in his discussions of Hawthorne, Twain, Howells, James, Kipling, Eliot, Dos Passos, Dreiser, Hemingway, Orwell, and others.

Yes, yes, impatient progressives will (and did) reply, the second-order virtues are fine, but what about the first-order ones: solidarity, compassion, a hunger and thirst for justice? Aren't these still in short supply? Characteristically, Trilling put this objection to his position better than anyone else has. "However important it may be for moral realism to raise questions in our minds about our motives, is it not at best a matter of secondary importance? Is it not of the first importance that we be given a direct and immediate report on the reality that is daily being brought to dreadful birth? . . . To speak of moral realism is all very well. But it is an elaborate, even fancy, phrase and it is to be suspected of having the intention of sophisticating the simple reality that is easily to be conceived. Life presses us so hard, time is so short, the suffering of the world is so huge, simple, unendurable—anything that complicates our moral fervor in dealing with reality as we immediately see it and wish to dive headlong upon it must be regarded with some impatience."

Trilling's answer is that the first-order moral virtues are dangerous without the second-order ones. "The moral passions are even more willful and imperious and impatient than the self-seeking passions. All history is at one in telling us that their tendency is to be not only liberating but also restrictive." Certainly the history of the Russian Revolution, which was present to the minds of all Trilling's readers, should have taught that. So should the histories of the Puritan Revolution, the French Revolution, the Chinese Revolution, the Cuban Revolution, and the Iranian Revolution.

But Trilling was not, as leftists have charged, a "quietist," any more than Arnold was. His position, like Arnold's, was in essence, "Yes, but . . ." Yes to greater equality, inclusiveness, cooperation, tolerance, social experimentation, individual freedom . . . but only after listening to everything that can be said against one's cherished projects, assuming equal intelligence and good faith on the part of one's opponents, and tempering one's zeal with the recognition that every new policy has unintended consequences, sometimes very bad ones. But after all that . . . yes. "It is not enough to want [change]," Trilling wrote, "not even enough to work for it—we must want it and work for it with intelligence." Although neither the left nor the right appeared to notice, "we" included Trilling.

In fact, both the left and the right heard "Yes, but . . ." as simply "No," which must have discouraged Trilling horribly. Both sides have assumed he was a proto-neoconservative, the left blaming him for it and the right blaming him for not owning up to it. But Trilling was not a neoconservative. He was, like Arnold, a friend of equality, of progress, of reform, of democratic collective action—a wistful, anxious, intelligent friend. He was, that is, a good—actually, the very best kind of—liberal.

The Lady and the Luftmensch

Why do we still care about the New York intellectuals? Partly, perhaps, because they embodied, conceivably for the last time in American history, a venerable modern ideal, practiced also by the *philosophes* and praised by Goethe and Marx: *vielseitigkeit* or many-sidedness. Their versatility was astonishing; their apparent mastery in pronouncing on both culture and politics, and in relating one set of judgments to the other, now seems as attractive as it does unattainable. In the Age of Information, mastery even of a single field is an implausible aspiration, and casual authority over a whole range of them an anachronistic one.

Then, too, their pronouncements seemed to matter. To the live moral imagination, all times are dark times; but the late thirties and early forties have a special pathos. Rarely can so many catastrophes—global economic depression, world war, the Gulag, the Holocaust—have thronged a single decade. The need to make sense of these traumas was widely felt; and with so many people listening, even those tough-minded erstwhile historical materialists may be forgiven for forgetting about the structural irrelevance of radical ideas in a capitalist democracy—or, to put it less theoretically, for taking themselves so seriously.

Certainly we have been a long time saying goodbye. In the twenty-five years since Irving Howe wrote the first and best retrospective ("The New York Intellectuals," *Commentary*, October 1968), one after another of them, like the players

72

in Haydn's "Farewell" Symphony, has come forward with a valediction and then bowed off the stage or returned quietly—for the most part—to his or her seat: Mary McCarthy, Edmund Wilson, Howe himself, William Barrett, William Phillips (still fiddling away, but *rallentando*), Norman Podhoretz (also fiddling, *molto agitato*). Although by and large I can't get enough of the genre, I'm glad Phillip Rahv didn't weigh in—though a fine and underappreciated literary critic, he was apparently not good at personal relations and was particularly embittered late in life. My chief regret has always been the absence of memoirs by two of my favorite NYints, Dwight Macdonald and Lionel Trilling. A double pleasure, then, this publishing season: the first full biography of Macdonald[1] and Diana Trilling's memoir of her life with Lionel[2].

Michael Wrezsin is a diligent, conscientious, fair-minded scholar and so has produced a well-informed, even-handed, thoroughly useful and enjoyable biography. Diana Trilling is a New York intellectual (*emerita*) and so might have been expected to produce, depending on where one's ideological sympathies lie, either a brilliant, contentious, unreliable, and self-serving portrait of those fraught decades or a brilliant, contentious, and illuminating one. She has confounded expectations. *The Beginning of the Journey* occasionally takes sides, settles scores, dips into mere brilliance. But in its novelistic proportions and detail and its sustained inwardness, it is what few of those "*Luftmenschen* of the mind" (Howe) achieved or even attempted: a work of art.

Diana Trilling's style has often seemed to me a bit fussy. A fine, tortuous line separates the exquisite from the precious. Lionel Trilling navigated that boundary expertly, almost infallibly. Unlike some readers of *The Beginning of the Journey*, I have no trouble believing that Mrs. Trilling in good measure formed her husband's prose style (see, for one example among several that make this claim plausible, her superb essay on Virginia Woolf in *Claremont Essays*). But the pupil undeniably—she of course does not deny it—surpassed his teacher.

[1] *A Rebel in Defense of Tradition: the Life of Dwight Macdonald* by Michael Wrezsin.
    Basic Books, 1994.

[2] *The Beginning of the Journey: the Marriage of Lionel and Diana Trilling* by Diana Trilling.
    Harcourt Brace, 1993.

The enchanting combination of lightness and gravity that he regularly attained, she rarely attained.

In *The Beginning of the Journey* she attains something else: not quite a world but a milieu of lively, rounded, ridiculous, admirable characters, her family and Lionel's and their friends and colleagues during the first half of their marriage. (The memoir ends in 1950.) She herself is her own most memorable creation, or re-creation. "I was an excessively fearful child," she announces on page three, and offers a mind-boggling, side-splitting list of things she feared, above all burglars, for whom she lay awake listening night after night. Fear—especially "fear of public display," induced by parental strictures—is the hidden theme of this formidable woman's life. A gifted singer, she came down with a psychosomatic illness that foreclosed a musical career. As a beginning writer of anonymous short reviews for the *Nation*, she almost gave up in terror, aborting her career, when offered a byline. To this day, she is "unable to attend a concert or lecture or any public performance without at some moment having my throat tighten with the temptation to scream and thus divert, in a most unpleasant way, the attention of the audience from the onstage display to my own imprisoned self." They fucked her up, her Mum and Dad; they may not have meant to, but they did. Lionel's, too. She dramatizes it all marvelously, with impeccable moral delicacy and without a quaver of self-pity.

There are revelations—Lionel's rages and depressions, his blissful paternity, their lifelong financial difficulties, Diana's amazing misadventures in psychoanalysis. But most surprising and affecting of all is her voice: at once elegiac and pungent, magnanimous and unsparing, dignified and intensely, dauntingly intimate. Mrs. Trilling's intelligence was always plain on every page she wrote (though I will presently quarrel with her politics). But I never suspected she had so much soul.

There was, of course, never any doubt on that score about Dwight Macdonald, and there are fewer surprises in *A Rebel in Defense of Tradition*. He drank a lot, had a squeaky laugh, and drove recklessly; he was not the best of fathers; he occasionally—for example, when exercised by Rahv's or Phillip's subtleties —tossed off an anti-Semitic crack; and his late-life writer's block makes painful reading. But for the most part he was what he reads like, decency itself, universally liked even if not always (by truly serious people, that is) respected.

No major historical or interpretive novelties in Wrezsin, either, though a few nuggets. His versions of the 1949 Waldorf-Astoria Conference and Macdonald's stint at *Encounter* are full and entertaining. There are generous selections from Dwight's correspondence, most notably with Nicola Chiaromonte. And the New Yorkers' summer frolics on Cape Cod are high comedy. But for all Wrezsin's thoroughness and judiciousness, Stephen Whitfield's much shorter *A Critical American* (1984) is still the best introduction (apart from Macdonald) to Macdonald.

Whatever they may have disagreed about (practically everything), the New York intellectuals seem to have been virtually unanimous in regarding Macdonald with exasperated condescension. He was "Yogi Macdonald" (Rahv and Phillips), a "sentimental dilettante" (James Burnham), "bohemian . . . irresponsible" (Sidney Hook), "the thirteenth disciple" (Howe), a "kibitzer . . . thinks with his typewriter" (Paul Goodman), "has made a fetish of confusion and drift" (C. Wright Mills), a "truant" (William Barrett), a "dandy" (Hilton Kramer), a "boyish innocent . . . singularly lacking in self-consciousness" (Diana Trilling, 1957); "Nothing was easier than to be angry at Macdonald, whether in or out of print, but it was difficult to stay angry at him; he was too childlike, too seemingly innocent. Certainly he was innocent of the consequences of his ideas" (Diana Trilling, 1993). Even Trotsky chimed in: "Everyone has the right to be stupid on occasion, but Comrade Macdonald abuses the privilege."

Can so many and diverse eminences have been wrong? I think so. Turgenev once observed that in politics, "the honorable man will end by not knowing where to live." He might have added that such a man's less brave and imaginative contemporaries will mock his homelessness. The thirties and forties (even more than the fifties, sixties, seventies, and eighties) confronted political critics with dilemmas to which one, perhaps the only, honest response was confusion and despair. Macdonald initially opposed American participation in World War II, believing that capitalist governments could not effectively prosecute the war without themselves veering toward fascism. His more dramatic predictions, at least, were mistaken and occasioned much sarcasm. But they proceeded from a sound intuition—that war is the health of the state—which his polemical opponents gave no evidence of sharing. This inchoate, global skepticism allowed Macdonald to perceive the Allies' criminal misconduct: the mass bombings of civilians, the insistence on unconditional surrender, the refusal of asylum to the

Jews, and "the annihilation of all European underground movements against fascism and Nazism, which succeeded because it was one of the very few items on which the Allied powers wholeheartedly agreed . . . [and] for which only now are we beginning to pay the full price" (Hannah Arendt, "Introduction to *Politics Past*," 1968). It was Macdonald and his fellow contributors to *Politics* who documented and denounced all these things and so in a small way redeemed the honor of American intellectuals, not the *Partisan Review* "realists" (nor Diana Trilling, who in *The Beginning of the Journey* rebukes even the latter for their insufficient partisanship). The Cold War blueprint NSC 68, the existence of high-level State Department and Council on Foreign Relations planning groups that in effect designed the Pax Americana, and the evolution of huge, uncontrollable national security bureaucracies originating in this period also seem, in retrospect, to validate Macdonald's confused intuitions about the untrustworthiness of governments. At least one can say that a reader of *Politics* probably would not have been surprised by these developments, while a reader of the post-Macdonald *Partisan Review* very well might.

Macdonald's "negativism" also earned him a good deal of superior admonition. In "The Root Is Man" (1946) and elsewhere, he confessed his disenchantment with all the available forms of organized political action. (That essay prompted a young wiseguy named Irving Howe to send *Politics* a 6,000-word critique, which Macdonald published in full.) "What seems necessary," Macdonald wrote, after surveying in the preceding pages (and embracing in the previous decade) virtually every form of radical ideology, "is to encourage attitudes of disrespect, skepticism, ridicule towards the State and all authority." The only hope he could see, modest enough, "seems to be through symbolic individual actions, based on one person's insistence on his own values, and through the creation of small fraternal groups which will support such actions, keep alive a sense of our ultimate goals, and both act as a leavening in the dough of mass society and attract more and more of the alienated and frustrated members of that society."

It is difficult to understand why, except to the terminally tough-minded, any of this should have sounded frivolous, irresponsible, quietist, or defeatist. It's not as though there were practical alternatives, then or now. "Negativism" did not mean abandoning radical politics, just pruning it of empty pretensions and bad faith. It meant resisting the simplifying urgencies of war and cold war, admitting one's impotence and uncertainty, sitting tight, listening. It required moral poise, a kind of ideological negative capability. It required genuine—rather than professed, which is a very common article—intellectual humility. No wonder his fellow New York intellectuals thought him wacky. (Others, however, saw his floundering differently. Czesław Miłosz, for one, paid tribute to Macdonald as a successor to "Thoreau, Whitman, and Melville . . . a specific American type—the completely free man, capable of making decisions at all times and about all things strictly according to his personal moral judgments.")

And even at his most confused, discouraged, or doctrinaire, Macdonald *criticized*. He quotes Alexander Herzen on "two Russian liberals who made their peace with Czar Nicholas I: 'I shall be told that under the aegis of devotion to the Imperial power, the truth can be spoken more boldly. Why, then, did they not speak it?' So, too, with the critical supporters of the war—why, then, do they not criticize?" Actually, a similar question crossed my mind when I came upon Diana Trilling's remark in *The Beginning of the Journey* that after she and Lionel left a communist front organization in disillusionment, "we never again raised our voices on behalf of the worker's homeland." Well and good—Macdonald himself was as sharp and effective a critic of Stalinism as anyone in the history of the American left. But did the Trillings ever again raise their voices on behalf of their homeland's workers? Not that I can discover, whereas *Politics* was read fervently in army camps and union halls across the country, and frivolous, irresponsible Yogi Macdonald more or less single-handedly launched the War on Poverty with "Our Invisible Poor," his essay-review of Michael Harrington's *The Other America*. Altogether, Hook-Burnham-Rahv-Phillips-Kramer-Trilling disparaging Macdonald strikes me as no less implausible than, say, James Gould Cozzens ridiculing D.H. Lawrence or Mortimer J. Adler lecturing Wittgenstein.

Having praised *The Beginning of the Journey*, I must here parenthesize to defend Macdonald against a more particular reproach in it. Mrs. Trilling writes: "In 1968, with the outbreak of the campus disturbances at Columbia, [Macdonald] was at once on the scene, loaded for bear. He had no connection with Columbia; to him it mattered not at all if the institution lived or died—he had found himself a revolution . . . He and I quarreled during this period . . . he found my indignant refusal to help the SDS 'hilarious'—what more laughable than to want a university to endure?"

On the contrary, as an invited speaker at Columbia's counter-commencement, Macdonald told the strikers:

> While I find your strike and your sit-ins productive, I don't think these tactics can be used indefinitely without doing more damage than good to the university. It would be a pity if Columbia became another Latin American type of university in which education is impossible because student strikes and political disruptions have become chronic. Nor do I think that our universities should be degraded to service as entering wedges to pry open our society for the benefit of social revolution. I'm for such a revolution but I don't think it is a historical possibility in the foreseeable future in this country, and premature efforts to force it will merely damage or destroy such positive, progressive institutions as we have. Their only effect—if any—will be to stimulate a counterrevolution which will have far more chances of success.

These remarks probably contributed as much to Columbia's survival as anything Mrs. Trilling said or did in the spring of 1968.

From the 1950s on, Macdonald mainly occupied himself with what he called (borrowing T.S. Eliot's definition of the function of criticism) "the correction of taste." He became, as Stephen Whitfield put it, mid-century America's Mencken as well as its Bourne, slaying various middlebrow dragons such as the pseudo-populist third edition of Webster's Dictionary, the vulgarized Revised Standard Version of the Bible, and the ineffably pompous University of Chicago Great Books project.

But this was not really a flight from politics; it was a continuation of politics by other means. In the decades since Macdonald resigned as a revolutionist, systematic social theory, both liberal and radical, has lumbered around to an understanding of the strategic importance of mass culture and moral psychology; has begun to appreciate the ideological functions of cant, kitsch, crudity, and superficiality. Macdonald theorized a bit himself (his 1953 essay, "A Theory of Mass Culture," was fairly widely reprinted), but mostly he went in for practical criticism, with significant effects on American intellectual hygiene.

Eventually he took to calling himself a "conservative radical"—partly, one suspects, to pull everyone's leg, but also because the standards he sought to apply to our culture, the strict standards of honest intellectual craftsmanship, are at once deeply conservative and deeply subversive. "To think clearly is a necessary first step towards political regeneration," Orwell wrote in "Politics and the English Language," "so that the fight against bad English is not frivolous and is not the exclusive concern of professional writers." Macdonald's career is an almost unimprovable gloss on Orwell's essay.

A Critical Life

To be universally respected at the close of one's career can be a bitter fate. For nearly five decades Irving Howe has scolded and coaxed, reasoned with and preached to, American society, on the whole futilely, as he would be the first to admit. McCarthyism, the Cold War, the Vietnam War, the Reagan regression, the conformism of intellectuals, and the commercialization of culture have rolled along unaffected by the forceful, eloquent, scrupulously nuanced criticism perseveringly produced by Howe and his democratic-socialist comrades in their journal, *Dissent*, and elsewhere. Though radical in substance, that criticism has generally been moderate in tone; so American society, impervious to enlightenment but sensitive to ridicule, has gratefully accorded Howe a measure of moral prestige as an elder statesman for the "responsible" left. Even veteran radicals usually cherish respectability. But I don't doubt that Howe would gladly trade his for, say, the prospect of a modest national health-insurance program or a slight reduction in arms sales abroad.

Howe is by no means exclusively a political writer. Most of *Selected Writings*[1] is in fact literary criticism: Howe was a professor of English for thirty years and

---

[1] *Selected Writings: 1950–1990* by Irving Howe. Harcourt Brace, 1990.

has published books on Hardy, Faulkner, and Sherwood Anderson, besides several collections of essays and reviews. Nor are his literary interests and approach limited by ideology. Predictably, he has written with sympathy and insight about Zola, Dreiser, and Silone; less predictably, but equally well, about Wharton and Frost, Leskov and Pirandello, Whitman and Stevens, Edward Arlington Robinson and T.E. Lawrence. And his three major essays on modernism (two of them, "The Idea of the Modern" and "The City in Literature," are included in *Selected Writings*; the other, "Mass Society and Post-Modern Fiction," is not) are definitive.

But Howe's first love, or first vocation, was politics. The East Bronx in the 1920s and 1930s, where he grew up, was an ideological hothouse, from which the children of immigrant Jewish unionists generally emerged as one or another variety of socialist. At City College, this cohort of young radicals—Howe, Daniel Bell, Irving Kristol, and a couple of hundred others—sharpened their dialectical skills, debating one another about *Capital*, current events, and, above all, Trotskyist schism and Stalinist orthodoxy. (There's a piquant sketch of this milieu in Howe's 1982 memoir, *A Margin of Hope*.)

Howe was an active member of a small Trotskyist group, editing its journal and speaking at its forums, when he was drafted in 1942 and sent to Alaska. There he sat out World II in an undemanding clerical job and read, read, read. This enforced turn inward, and perhaps also the postwar collapse of revolutionary fervor throughout the American left, accelerated Howe's ideological evolution. After a brief spell of renewed party activity, he abandoned Trotskyism for a nonsectarian, unaffiliated radicalism—moved, so to speak, from agitation to dissent. In 1954, with $2,000 and a few like-minded radicals, he started *Dissent*.

Meanwhile, on the strength of his freelance literary criticism in *Partisan Review* and *Commentary*, he was offered a job teaching at newly founded Brandeis University. Eventually he returned to New York, teaching at his alma mater and at Hunter College. Like many other children of immigrants, Howe returned also to his ethnic roots, editing and writing about Yiddish literature even as it became virtually extinct in the 1960s and 1970s, and producing *World of Our Fathers*, a panoramic (and best-selling) portrait of Jewish immigrant life.

The world of the children has, however, attracted even more attention. In the last decade or so, a spate of histories, biographies, and memoirs has traced the career of the New York intellectuals, from their spectacular debut in the 1930s and 1940s via *Partisan Review*, through their ascent to cultural prominence, their reconciliation with American society in the 1950s, and their (sometimes) re-radicalization or (more often) conservative turn in the 1960s and 1970s. The research has been assiduous, the interpretations ingenious, the polemics fierce. And with reason: they were an unusually coherent and distinguished group, including Lionel Trilling, Dwight Macdonald, Sidney Hook, Meyer Schapiro, Philip Rahv, Hannah Arendt, Mary McCarthy, Harold Rosenberg, Delmore Schwartz, Bell, Kristol, Howe, and quite a few others equally or only slightly less eminent. For a brief Golden Age, they seem to have attained or at least approached an intellectual ideal: a union of independence and community, integrity and commitment, cosmopolitanism and authority. All this, in turn, made their political evolution especially significant, as though it marked the inevitable trajectory of intellectual radicalism in America.

There was not, of course, only one trajectory, or even two. But there was a general movement that had, if not a common destination, at least a common point of departure. The illusions painfully and publicly shed by one after another of the New York intellectuals were, first, that a socialist revolution was possible in the foreseeable future; and second, that a pseudo-socialist or Leninist revolution, which would leave a single party in control of the state and the economy, was desirable, if only as a step toward genuine socialism.

Renouncing these beliefs did the New York intellectuals credit. But where did it leave them politically? Most of them it left in an apolitical limbo, from which they sallied forth only for an occasional *Partisan Review* symposium or *cause celebre*, such as the controversy over Hannah Arendt's 1963 report on the trial of ex-Nazi Adolf Eichmann or the student strike at Columbia in 1968. Some let themselves be carried by the momentum of their rejection all the way into neoconservatism. Howe took the path of most resistance, determined to avoid the simplicities of orthodoxy and apostasy alike, to keep faith both with socialism's original vision and with the victims of those who have falsely claimed to be realizing that vision in the twentieth century.

It has been a struggle. In a much-quoted anecdote from Howe's autobiography, a friend observes that although Howe's politics are entirely admirable, they are, alas, "boring"; an abashed Howe agrees. I don't, on either count. Howe's politics have at times been less than admirable, but his political development has been a complicated, continuously interesting moral drama.

The essence of drama is conflict. Howe's career has been marked by a symmetrical pair of conflicts: with the older intellectuals who, after World War II, made an ignoble peace with American society, and with the young radicals who, in the late 1960s, made incoherent war on it. "This Age of Conformity" (1954) was occasioned by the intellectuals' response, or lack of response, to McCarthyism, and more particularly by the famous *Partisan Review* symposium, "Our Country and our Culture." The willingness of Sidney Hook, Irving Kristol, and other proto-neoconservatives to minimize McCarthy's threat to civil liberties; the pseudo-religious vagaries of many New Critics; even Lionel Trilling's Olympian nods of approval at mid-century American civilization—for Howe, these were symptoms of a subtle abdication of the critical spirit. "We have all," he wryly lamented, "even the handful who still try to retain a glower of criticism, become responsible and moderate."

"This Age of Conformity" was an effective polemic. Even the middlebrow journals, Howe noted ruefully a few years later, were soon "alive with chatter about conformity." But the essay transcends polemic. Concisely and cogently, Howe identified the historical processes that had produced inescapable pressures toward conformism—above all, the advent of mass society, "a society in which ideology plays an unprecedented part." Intellectuals were recruited en masse into administration, advertising, education, and entertainment. Appearances notwithstanding, the resulting gain in status was not a gain in real social power; it was, in fact, a loss, not of power (critical intellectuals had none to lose) but of autonomy:

> The institutional world needs intellectuals because they are intellectuals, but it does not want them *as* intellectuals. It beckons to them because of what they are but it will not allow them, at least within its sphere of articulation, to either remain or entirely cease being what they are. . . . A simplified but useful equation suggests itself: the relation of the institutional world to the intellectuals is like the relation of middlebrow culture to serious culture. The one battens on the other, absorbs and raids it with increasing frequency and skill, subsidizes and encourages it enough to make further raids possible—sometimes the parasite will support its victim.

Resistance to these pressures was undermined by the disappearance of bohemia, a casualty of prosperity and urban renewal. Three decades before Russell Jacoby's acclaimed *The Last Intellectuals*, Howe's essay described the integration of the literati into the universities and the transformation of the man of letters into the academic critic. The result was a "gradual bureaucratization of opinion and taste," the creep of massification into the realm of the spirit.

"This Age of Conformity" was a masterpiece, one of the pearls in *Partisan*'s crown. Combining a rhetorical verve equal to anything of Sartre's, a historical penetration akin to Trotsky's (with a far more restrained and effective deployment of sarcasm), and an unsentimental humanism reminiscent of Orwell, it was not just astute but exciting. Not boring at all.

Howe's reputation for tedious correctness is mostly derived, though, from his other major public controversy, with the New Left. As readers of Maurice Isserman's *If I Had a Hammer*, Todd Gitlin's *The Sixties*, or any other serious account of the period will know, relations were not always hostile. *Dissent* welcomed, even celebrated, the early New Left. Why things turned sour in the mid-60s has lately been the subject of almost as much research and debate as the political peregrinations of the New York intellectuals. The protagonists—Howe, Michael Harrington, Tom Hayden—all wrote memoirs during the 80s in which each one graciously assumed a large share of blame. But the issues remain.

What the older radicals—Howe, Harrington, and others from *Dissent* and the League for Industrial Democracy—wanted from the younger ones was a consistent, explicit, comprehensive anti-communism. The younger ones —Hayden and other leaders of SDS—demurred. Because they had learned anti-communism from J. Edgar Hoover and *Reader's Digest* rather than from Rosa Luxemburg and Victor Serge, they mistrusted it. Because Castro and Ho Chi Minh were targets of imperial violence, the younger radicals saw them as victims (which they were) but not as dictators (which they also were). It is notoriously difficult to keep two opposing truths in one's mind at the same time, let alone figure out how to act on them. The young radicals couldn't manage it, and the older ones were no help.

They were even, at times, a hindrance. It's true the young were terribly provoking—the leadership's swaggering arrogance eventually produced an open revolt among New Left women, which was the Lexington and Concord of contemporary American feminism. But although most of Howe's strictures throughout the 60s were justified in tone and content, he finally, fatally, stopped complaining *to* the young radicals and started complaining *about* them. The result, predictably, was a deterioration of relations and an escalation of angry rhetoric, and sometimes petty malice, on both sides. The episode was one of Howe's few lapses from political grace.

Another is his apparently invincible antipathy to Noam Chomsky, the leading left-wing critic of American foreign policy, with whom Howe has, as far as I can tell, few or no fundamental political differences. Chomsky's criticism's of some of Howe's more embattled formulations about the New Left and the Middle East, while largely correct in substance, have been excessively harsh in tone. Still, Howe edits a journal and Chomsky does not, a circumstance that imposes unequal obligations. That the best journal of the American left is, in effect, closed to the most important writer on the American left, however personally difficult; that Chomsky's awesome logical powers and appetite for facts and Howe's verbal, psychological, and moral subtlety and tact have, instead of supplementing each other, reacted on each other like gasoline and water—this is a large misfortune. And that the embargo, or at least inhospitality, extends to Gabriel Kolko, Michael Klare, Thomas Ferguson, Joel Rogers, and other talented radicals who might both improve *Dissent*'s foreign-policy coverage and themselves benefit from comradely criticism by its editors and other contributors—this is a small tragedy.

Howe's politics have never been more admirable than in his frequent restatements of the socialist ideal. From "Images of Socialism" (1954) to *Socialism and America* (1985), Howe has anxiously but unflinchingly demanded: "Can one still specify what the vision of socialism means or should mean?" After Stalinism and Maoism, it's obvious what socialism doesn't mean. Less obviously, perhaps, but just as surely, it doesn't mean merely the electoral triumph of a socialist party, as Mitterrand's painful experience shows. The only way to answer Howe's question is to gather up fragments from the tradition—cries of protest and invocations of solidarity, heroic lives and utopian fantasies, analytic strands and programmatic patches—and fuse them imaginatively. The resulting unity will be only temporary; the ideal will need to be reimagined in every generation. But this is how traditions live. In our time, Howe's efforts, as much as anyone else's, have kept the socialist tradition alive.

A volume of selected writings, especially one covering four decades, invites a summing up. After all his political positions are noted and literary judgments weighed, what kind of writer/critic/intellectual has Howe been? Anyone considering Howe's work must first of all be impressed—whether favorably or unfavorably, as superb ambition or absurd presumption—by its extraordinary range. Howe has lived by his own dictum: "By impulse, if not definition, the intellectual is a man who writes about subjects outside his field. He has no field." Howe has in fact characterized his work better than anyone else could, in yet another brilliant, definitive essay, "The New York Intellectuals":

> The kind of essay they wrote was likely to be wide-ranging in reference, melding notions about literature and politics, sometimes announcing itself as a study of a writer or literary group but usually taut with a pressure to "go beyond" it subject, toward some encompassing moral or social observation. It is a kind of writing highly self-conscious in mode, with an unashamed vibration of bravura. Nervous, strewn with knotty or flashy phrases, impatient with transitions and other concessions to dullness, calling attention to itself as a form or at least an outcry, fond of rapid twists, taking pleasure in dispute, dialectic, dazzle . . .

The New York style, like every other, had the defects of its virtues. "Impatience with dullness" could decline into smugness and condescension; an exquisite sense of the problematic could turn into a fetish of complexity. "No easy certainties," Howe once write about the responsibility of intellectuals, "and no easy acceptance of uncertainty." The later failing is rarer and in a way more honorable. But it is still a failing, one to which Howe himself is prone. His frequent thrusts at the "crude simplicities of left and right" occasionally sound reflexive—as though it's the energy rather than the crudity of his opponent's formulation that really annoys him. A less sophisticated leftist—Howard Zinn, say—may not be as sensitive to the analytic and strategic difficulties that exercise Howe. But Zinn has done immensely useful work over the years in rousing the citizenry. *Dissent* aims to produce a refined and complicated political awareness among its readers. It's a noble aim. But someone or something else must first have produced an elemental political awareness.

The New York intellectuals are passing from the scene, along with the conditions that produced their distinctive style: the immigrant background, fascism, Stalinism, global depression, the innovations of the great modernists. So much is inevitable and even desirable. No style can remain fresh and original for long. But as Howe, Jacoby, and many others by now have lamented, the very ideal of cosmopolitanism, of the intellectual as "anti-specialist," uniting political and aesthetic interests and able to speak with some authority about both, is obsolescent.

It's a troubling prospect, and an ambiguous one. The cult of professionalism and expertise, the "bureaucratization of opinion and taste," are not merely mechanisms of social control or a cultural failure of nerve; they are also in part a response to genuine intellectual progress. Perhaps the demise of the "public intellectual," of the "dilettante-connoisseur," is a symptom of inevitable crisis, a sign that intellectual wholeness is no longer attainable and that the classical ideals of wisdom as catholicity of understanding, and of citizenship as the capacity to discuss all public affairs, must be abandoned. Perhaps we'll have to learn to live with that. If so, then those who come after, when reckoning the costs of progress, will want to consider a few exemplary specimens from the world they have lost. Among twentieth-century American intellectuals, they could do worse than to choose Irving Howe.

Inside the Cave

One of the strangest and saddest specimens of social criticism in American history was a short-lived publication called *Osawatomie*, the journal of the Weather Underground. "Where We Stand," announced in stupefying prose the group's aim—"we are building a communist organization to be part of the forces which build a revolutionary communist party to lead the working class to seize power and build socialism"—and its discovery that "Marxism-Leninism is the science of revolution, the revolutionary ideology of the working class, our guide to the struggle." The Weather collective exhorted the rest of the American left to follow the group's example, to "begin with the resources and lessons from the triumph of proletarian revolution in many countries and with the great victories of national liberation."

What makes this episode lamentable rather than merely ludicrous is that the Weather Underground was the organizational—if not spiritual or political—successor to Students for a Democratic Society. SDS had also begun by announcing where it stood, but the Port Huron Statement remains as vivid and relevant as *Osawatomie* is dull, dated, and doctrinaire. Much of the reason for this difference is surely the determination of the Statement's authors to "speak American" (Tom Hayden), to "find a way to talk about socialism in an American accent" (Robert Ross). It begins:

We are people of this generation, bred in at least modest comfort, housed now in universities, looking uncomfortably to the world we inherit.

When we were kids the United States was the wealthiest and strongest country in the world; the only one with the atom bomb, the least scarred by modern war, an initiator of the United Nations that we thought would distribute Western influence throughout the world. Freedom and equality for each individual, government of, by, and for the people—these American values we found good, principles by which we could live as men. Many of us began maturing in complacency.

As we grew, however, our comfort was penetrated by events too troubling to dismiss.

Immediately the source of the Statement's perennial appeal is clear. These were fellow citizens speaking, not cadre. And they were *speaking*: of generous illusions, widely shared, followed by painful disillusion; they were not intoning ideological cabalisms or shouting obscure slogans.

The Port Huron Statement is an example of what Michael Walzer, in *Interpretation and Social Criticism*[1] and *The Company of Critics: Social Criticism and Political Commitment in the Twentieth Century*,[2] calls "internal criticism": it "challenges the leaders, the conventions, the . . . practices of a particular society . . . in the name of values recognized and shared in that same society." An effective critic, Walzer argues, is likely to be a member of the community he or she criticizes, formed within and by it, intimate with its traits and traditions, serious about its morality—more serious, in some important respect, than the community's leadership or even membership. The community's dereliction in that respect will arouse indignation, sometimes rage, but not radical hostility, much less rejection. Disappointed but not disaffected, the critic will stand a little apart, yet not altogether outside. "Critical distance," Walzer writes, "is measured in inches."

Even when criticism is fundamental, directed at the social structure rather than at some specific policy, the critic must be able to connect it with common values and aspirations, to interpret the history and mores of the community in a

[1]Harvard University Press, 1987.
[2]Basic Books, 1988.

way that calls the legitimacy of the structure into question. To appeal directly to universal principles that have little apparent purchase or resonance in the moral history of a particular society can only evoke incomprehension and defensiveness.

But will such insider criticism have sufficient bite? Can every—can *any* —society's standards be relied on to generate radical criticism of itself? Won't critics frequently need to invent or import principles not available, even implicitly, in the moral culture of their own society? Most of Walzer's writing throughout the last decade—in the books under review, in *Spheres of Justice* (1983), and in two essays for the journal *Political Theory*, "Philosophy and Democracy" (1981) and "Liberalism and the Art of Separation" (1984)—has been addressed to one or another version of these crucial questions.

The Company of Critics discusses eleven representative (more or less) twentieth-century social critics. Walzer claims that each of them, to the extent he or she did useful work, was an internal, connected critic, and to the extent any faltered or consistently struck a false note, was disconnected, excessively detached. It is a skillful demonstration—in some cases (Bourne, Silone, Orwell, Breytenbach), relatively straightforward; in others (Camus, de Beauvoir, Marcuse, Foucault), more problematic; in at least one (Gramsci) a *tour de force*—as well as a richly textured narrative. Walzer's ability to individuate each of these figures even while fitting the grid of his analytic categories over their work is remarkable. Some of his local judgments are debatable: Julien Benda seems to me a less valuable critic, and Marcuse a more valuable one, than Walzer allows. But the general argument is persuasive. Walzer has successfully located a pattern, a "standard form" of social criticism, in his subjects' careers: "the identification of public pronouncements and respectable opinion as hypocritical, the attack upon actual behavior and institutional arrangements, the search for core values (to which hypocrisy is always a clue), the demand for everyday life in accordance with the core."

This description may seem unexceptionable but unilluminating until contrasted with a different and in fact more conventional view of the critic, as outsider. The radically detached critic, according to Walzer,

> breaks loose from his local and familial world . . . escapes with much attendant drama, detaches himself from all emotional ties, steps back so

as to see the world with absolute clarity, studies what he sees . . . discovers universal values as if for the first time, finds these values embodied in the movement of the oppressed (class, nation, gender . . .), decides to support the movement and to criticize its enemies, who are very often people such as he once was [and] attaches himself . . . sometimes negotiating, sometimes not, about the terms of the attachment.

This is a stereotype, but one plausibly derived from the theory and practice of two of the most influential groups of social critics in the twentieth century: the Bolsheviks and the mid-century French intellectuals, notably Sartre, associated with *Les Temps Modernes*. Part of Walzer's purpose is to deflate the prestige of this ideal—and in consequence, of its practitioners. It is, necessarily, a corollary purpose, incidental to vindicating his own preferred model, and some readers may wish Walzer had more fully acknowledged the attractions (or temptations) of outsider criticism. Still, most will, I suspect, find his deft citation of Gramsci's euphemism about the Bolshevik intelligentsia—"Having thus performed its intellectual apprenticeship, it returns to its own country and compels the people to an enforced awakening, skipping several historical stages in the process"—as well as his reference to Sartre's all-too-human refusal to criticize Third World "liberation" movements, more than sufficient to illustrate the dangers of radical detachment.

Walzer has rather more to say about the alleged dangers of insufficient detachment. He defends Martin Buber's renunciation of the cause of Arab-Jewish binationalism after 1948, Silone's abandonment of Marxism for a sympathetic exploration of "the heresies and utopias of peasant consciousness," Orwell's insistence (still unacceptable to the cosmopolitan English left) that "popular culture . . . is not wholly estranged from the hegemonic culture of English capitalism," and Camus's futile but honorable advocacy of federal status for Algeria. Again, by and large, persuasively. And part of his defense addresses the misgivings mentioned earlier, about the adequacy of internal standards. Surely the social critic needs, if not abstract, universal principles, at any rate enough moral imagination to recognize the existence of other societies' common values, and then enough moral courage to insist that one's own society accord them due respect. Doesn't the intimacy Walzer endorses militate against such recognition and such insistence? Walzer himself, in "Philosophy and Democracy," formulates this objection well:

> Engagement always involves a loss—not total but serious enough—of distance, critical perspective, objectivity, and so on. The sophist, critic, publicist, or intellectual must address the concerns of his fellow citizens, try to answer their questions, weave his argument into the fabric of their history. He must, indeed, make himself a *fellow* citizen . . . and then he will be unable to avoid entirely the moral and even the emotional entanglement of citizenship. He may hold fast to the philosophical truths of natural law, distributive justice, or human rights, but his political arguments are most likely to look like some makeshift version of those truths, adapted to the needs of a particular people: from the standpoint of the original position, provincial; from the standpoint of the ideal speech situation, ideological.

The best defense against chauvinism, Walzer replies, is not a search for universal principles, for "philosophical truths," but a deeper appropriation of particularity. For societies as for individuals, the secure possession of a specific identity is what enables the recognition of otherness. A subject fully aware of his/its constitutive history will, faced with others, imaginatively *reiterate*, will ascribe a similar (but not identical) history and sense of self to them. Reiteration is the form of morality underlying Buber's persistent critique of Jewish messianism, Orwell's apparently eccentric combination of patriotism and internationalism, and Camus's complicated but uncompromised position on the Algerian War. Here and elsewhere in *The Company of Critics*, Walzer is chiefly (not, of course, exclusively) concerned with the integrity of his subjects' practice rather than with the correctness of their politics: a distinction that requires considerable scrupulousness on the part of both author and reader to maintain, even provisionally. Perhaps inevitably, those who reject Walzer's political judgments will be unappeasably suspicious of his moral psychology. That would be unfortunate; "reiteration," far from being an ad hoc, apologetical construction, is an original and suggestive formula, available to criticism of any degree of rigor.

There is, in any case, no alternative to some such conception. For there are no abstract, formal principles of distributive justice capable of immediate and universal application within and between societies. As Walzer has long argued, most fully in *Spheres of Justice* and with extraordinary economy in *Interpretation and Social Criticism*, moral argument is always, beyond a certain point, interpretive, a matter of elaborating (and occasionally revising) the meaning of some social good or practice. Formal definitions, however ingenious, invariably require historical completion. The minimal code of near-universally recognized rights that underwrites international law is too thin to support a dense moral culture. Only a shared history—which usually means a national history—of moral discourse, political conflict, literary achievement can generate values of sufficient thickness and depth. And what may appear to be genuine philosophical invention, e.g., the principle of equal justice under law, is in general better understood, Walzer convincingly suggests, as inclusion, as the extension, through social criticism and political conflict, of old principles to new groups.

"It is impossible . . . to step outside our skins—the traditions, linguistic and other, within which we do our thinking and self-criticism—and to escape from the [limits] of one's time and place, the 'merely conventional' and contingent aspects of one's life." I chanced on this passage from the writings of Richard Rorty, which nicely summarizes Walzer's moral epistemology, during the composition of this review. There is no intersection, as far as I know, between the work of these two men. So it is noteworthy that, in order to answer what is probably the most common objection to his moral theory, Walzer enlists a metaphor of which Rorty has also made memorable use: culture—in this case, moral culture—as conversation.

According to his critics, "the idea of a shared moral tradition cannot do the work Walzer wants; if society is divided on some issue, the tradition runs out where the dispute begins." In which case, "politics must . . . replace justice," and "justice all but disappears for us. We are left with the politics of selfishness" (Ronald Dworkin). Here is the familiar insistence that only secure philosophical foundations can prevent intellectual and moral chaos. In *Interpretation and Social Criticism* Walzer acknowledges that indeterminacy "prompts, not without reason, a certain philosophical apprehension. And from this there follows the whole elaborate apparatus of detachment and objectivity, whose purpose is not to facilitate criticism but to guarantee its correctness." In response, he tells the Talmudic story of Rabbi Joshua, who rebuked God for attempting to intervene in a rabbinical dispute with an authoritative interpretation of the Law, which He had irrevocably committed to fallible humanity.

> [Moral] argument implies common possession, but common possession does not imply agreement. There is a tradition, a body of moral knowledge; and there is this group of sages, arguing. There isn't anything else. No discovery or invention can end the argument; no "proof" takes precedence over the (temporary) majority of sages. That is the meaning of, "It is not in heaven."

There is no guarantor, no guarantee.

Still, the renunciation of the absolute—like the achievement of maturity—exacts an aesthetic and emotional price in exchange for intellectual and practical gain. Connected criticism has a sober coloring. Concerned not to cut himself off from his fellow-citizens, the internal critic will be tempted to moderate, if not his indignation, then at least the expression of it: his rhetoric. And sometimes—usually—he will be right to do so, to set political effectiveness above literary effect.

But indignation is not always manageable. And however conscientiously the critic tries to reiterate, to reconstruct the moral history of those in other communities, it will always be difficult for him to give their suffering due weight. We are properly skeptical of the habitually enraged critic; but we are also disappointed on occasion—and they may be the most important occasions—by the invariably judicious one. Perhaps this is why, though I largely share Walzer's political positions, I have seldom been profoundly moved by his own social criticism—enlightened, yes, but rarely inspired. The young Kafka wrote: "If the book we are reading does not wake us, as with a fist hammering on our skull, why then do we read it?" Walzer is, alas, far too polite ever to have hammered on anyone's skull. Other connected critics have done so, it is true, including some of those Walzer discusses. But if the connection is not to be endangered, the tact required is extraordinary, and the critic's inhibitions will therefore be considerable.

Kafka went on: "What we must have are books that come upon us like ill-fortune and distress us deeply . . . A book must be an ice-axe to break the sea frozen inside us." I have often exclaimed with pleasure while reading Walzer's graceful prose, but never with distress. Inside every citizen of a state responsible for so much misery in the rest of the world there is, one must assume, a frozen sea. In normal times, for ordinary purposes, the temperate, scrupulously nuanced, moderately forceful criticism of the typical connected critic—of Walzer himself—is appropriate. But sometime maximum intensity—an axe, a charge of verbal explosives, a burst of white heat—is required, whether for immediate effect or in helpless, furious witness. A sense of the simultaneous urgency and futility of much social criticism—i.e., the tragic sense—is a necessary part of the critical temperament. To resist this sense is the critic's everyday responsibility. To give in to it, to risk excess, loss of dignity, disconnection, may also, on occasion, be his duty.

In the book's introduction, Walzer speculates, troublingly: "It may be that my list of critics, arranged in rough chronological order, tells a story: of the rise and fall, the making and unmaking, of critical connection. The revolt of the masses opened certain possibilities, seized upon in exemplary fashion, it might be said, by writers like Ignazio Silone and George Orwell. But a long series of defeats has closed off these possibilities. The critic is alone again . . . deprived of any close relation to an audience, driven to recover authority by establishing his distance. Silone and Orwell now look like figures from a faraway past—modern figures seen from a postmodern age. Maybe." He disavows this interpretation of his narrative and promises reassurance, but little or none is forthcoming.

Though engaging, *The Company of Critics* is also a little bit exasperating. Walzer's fidelity to democratic socialist values is attractive, and his strictures against Marcuse and Foucault for their infidelities are just. But he doesn't seem to appreciate as fully as they did the extent to which contemporary culture threatens to make those values, along with the forms of political community in which they might flourish, obsolete. The shared values and social meanings to which internal criticism appeals are durable, no doubt, once internalized. But they must be internalized anew by each generation. Currently, their transmission to many, perhaps most, of the young is radically weakened and degraded. To point out only the most superficial of causes: political socialization depends in part on the vivid impressions associated with communal symbols, rituals, festivals, narratives. But after several formative years of Saturday-morning television, few children retain the capacity for responding deeply to most of the relatively plain images and stories that make up the national political tradition (such as it is). That is a speculative claim, but anyone to whom it seems hyperbolic should consult Tom Engelhardt's chilling essay "The Shortcake Strategy" (in *Watching Television*, edited by Todd Gitlin).

True, Marcuse got overexcited about this sort of thing. There is no excuse for calling it, or even a society full of such phenomena, "totalitarian." But Walzer gets underexcited. The "long series of defeats" he refers to means, presumably, political defeats: fascism and Stalinism; the failure of labor-based parties to gain state power; the inability of workers and consumers to form effective, permanent, democratic organizations. But the creation of contemporary American culture has also entailed a long series of defeats, with effects no less insidious. Neither set of defeats, political or cultural, is as yet irreversible; energetic, connected criticism remains the responsibility of intellectuals. Still, at certain haunted moments, The *Company of Critics* looks—to paraphrase its author—like a modern book seen from a postmodern age.

Farewell, Hitch

If a Hall of Fame were established for contemporary book reviewers—well, why not; there's one for ad executives, real estate salesmen, and probably croupiers—Christopher Hitchens would very likely be its second inductee. (James Wood, of course, would be the first.) About an amazing range of literary and political figures—Proust, Joyce, Borges, Byron, Bellow, Orhan Pamuk, Tom Paine, Trotsky, Churchill, Conor Cruise O'Brien, Israel Shahak, and a hundred or two others—he has supplied the basic information, limned the relevant controversies, hazarded an original perception or two, and bestowed half a dozen fine phrases, causing between fifteen and forty-five minutes of reading time to pass entirely unnoticed. His too frequent political columns have occasionally seemed tossed off, it's true; but his books about Cyprus, the Palestinians, the British monarchy, and the Elgin marbles are seriously argued. He lives in Washington and is said to be very fond of fancy parties, yet he has famously insulted and called for the incarceration of a sitting President and an ubiquitously befriended diplomat and Nobel laureate. And he gets to appear on all those fatuously self-important TV talk shows without wearing a tie. How can you not admire someone like that?

Actually, it's possible, I've discovered. All the someone in question has to do is begin thinking differently from me about a few important matters. In no time,

I begin to find that his qualities have subtly metamorphosed. His abundance of colorful anecdotes now looks like incessant and ingenious self-promotion. His marvelous copiousness and fluency sound like mere mellifluous facility and mechanical prolixity. A prose style I thought deliciously suave and sinuous I now find preening and over-elaborate. His fearless cheekiness has become truculent bravado; his name-dropping has gone from endearing foible to excruciating tic; his extraordinary dialectical agility seems like resourceful and unscrupulous sophistry; his entertaining literary asides like garrulousness and vulgar display; his bracing contrariness, tiresome perversity. Strange, this alteration of perspective; and even stranger, it sometimes occurs to me that if the someone changed his opinions again and agreed with me, all his qualities would once more reverse polarity and appear in their original splendor. A very instructive experience, epistemologically speaking.

Then again, it's not *just* Hitchens's changing his mind that's got my goat. His and my hero Dwight Macdonald did that often enough. But one may do it gracefully or gracelessly. Even when all the provocations Hitchens has endured are acknowledged (especially the not-infrequent hint that booze has befogged his brain), they don't excuse his zeal not merely to correct his former comrades but to bait, ridicule, and occasionally slander them, caricaturing their arguments and questioning their good faith. Not having recognized a truth formerly ought to make you more patient, not less, with people who do not recognize it now; and less certain, not more, that whoever you currently disagree with is contemptibly benighted. Besides, if you must discharge such large quantities of remonstrance and sarcasm, shouldn't you consider saving a bit more of them for your disagreements—he must still have some, though they're less and less frequently voiced, these days—with those who control the three branches of government and own the media and other means of production?

Hitchens might want to insist, contrarily, that although he has changed his allies, he has not changed his opinions. Unlike, say, David Horowitz, he still believes that the Cold War was an inter-imperial rivalry, the Vietnam War was immoral, the overthrow of Allende was infamous, and American support for Mobutu, Suharto, the Greek colonels, the Guatemalan and Salvadoran generals, the Shah of Iran, and the Israeli dispossession of Palestinians was and is indefensible. He still believes in progressive taxation, the New Deal, vigilant environmental, occupational-safety, and consumer-protection regulation, unions (or some form of worker self-organization), and in general, firm and constant opposition to the very frequent efforts of the rich and their agents to grind the faces of the poor. It's just that he now cordially despises most of the people who actively proclaim or advocate these things. Why?

It began with the Balkan wars. Hitchens supported NATO intervention, in particular the bombing of Serbia in March 1999. Some of his opponents on the left argued that NATO gave up too easily on (or indeed sabotaged) diplomacy, was wrong not to seek UN authorization to use force, and may have precipitated a humanitarian catastrophe (the flight and deportation of hundreds of thousands of Kosovar Albanians after the bombing began) that might not otherwise have occurred. Hitchens replied furiously—though not, by and large, to these arguments; rather, to other ones, either non-existent or easier to refute: e.g., imagined opposition "in principle in any case to any intervention," or insistence that in view of its imperialist past the United States could never in any circumstances be a force for good. His most reflective comments did seem to take his opponents' point: "Skeptical though one ought to be about things like the reliance of NATO on air power and the domination of the UN by the nuclear states, the 'double standard' may still be made to operate against itself." But such moments were few.

Since 9/11, reflectiveness and skepticism have gone on holiday from his political writing. Also logic and good manners. "Embattled" is too mild a description of his state of mind; it's been inflamed. Those who returned different answers than he did to the questions "Why did 9/11 happen?" and "What should we do about it?" were not to be taken seriously. They were Osama's useful idiots, "soft on crime and soft on fascism," their thinking "utterly rotten to its very core."

What provoked that last spasm of pleonasm was a suggestion that "Bin Laden could not get volunteers to stuff envelopes if Israel had withdrawn from Jerusalem . . . and the US stopped the sanctions and bombing of Iraq." Hitchens went ballistic. The hapless fool who wrote this, he thundered, either "knows what was in the minds of the murderers," in which case "it is his solemn responsibility to inform us of the source of his information, and also to share it with the authorities," or else he doesn't know, in which case it is "rash" and "indecent" even to speculate.

Hitchens proceeded to speculate. Al-Qaida, like their allies the Taliban, aim first "to bring their own societies under the reign of the most pitiless and inflexible declension of shari'a law," and then, since they regard all unbelievers as "fit only for slaughter and contempt," they will seek to "spread the contagion and visit hell upon the unrighteous." Talk of "Muslim grievances" is rubbish; al-Qaida's only grievance is that they have not yet enslaved the whole world. *Jihad* means, simply, the obligatory conquest or destruction of everything outside Islam.

Hitchens has asserted this insistently: for him, to talk about "grievances expressed by the people of the Middle East" in connection with 9/11 is obscene. Bin-Laden and al-Qaida are "medieval fanatics"; they "wish us ill"; no more need be said. To presume to "lend an ear to the suppressed and distorted cry for help that comes, not from the victims, but from the perpetrators" just amounts to "rationalizing" terror. Denouncing one's opponents as soft on terror has been the first or last resort of many scoundrels in the political debates of the last few decades in America. (Actually, it's such a dubious tactic that even the scoundrels don't usually get further than broad hints.) One is surprised to see Hitchens doing it. But even more important: Is he right about al-Qaida? Does he know "what was in the minds of the murderers"?

In *Imperial Hubris* and its predecessor *Through Our Enemies' Eyes*, veteran CIA analyst Michael Scheuer, former head of the Agency's al-Qaida task force, writes:

> Bin Laden and most militant Islamists [are] motivated by . . . their hatred for a few, specific US policies and actions they believe are damaging—and threatening to destroy—the things they love. Theirs is a war against a specific target and for specific, limited purposes. While they will use whatever weapon comes to hand—including weapons of mass destruction—their goal is not to wipe out our secular democracy, but to deter us by military means from attacking the things they love. Bin Laden et al are not eternal warriors; there is no evidence that they are fighting for fighting's sake, or that they would be lost for things to do without a war to wage.
>
> . . . To understand the perspective of the [tens or hundreds of millions of] supporters of Bin Laden, we must accept that there are many Muslims in the world who believe that US foreign policy is irretrievably biased in favor of Israel, trigger happy in attacking the poor and ill-

defended Muslim countries, Sudan, Iraq, Afghanistan, Somalia, and so forth; rapacious in controlling and consuming the Islamic world's energy resources; blasphemous in allowing Israel to occupy Jerusalem and US troops to be based in Saudi Arabia; and hypocritical and cruel in its denial of Palestinian rights, use of economic sanctions against the Muslim people of Iraq, and support for the Muslim world's absolutist kings and dictators.

For holding essentially these views, Hitchens's leftist opponents are labeled apologists, rationalizers, and eager excusers of terror. A few moments' reflection and/or a few grains of knowledge would have saved him from indulging in these slurs, so damaging to his reputation for fairness and urbanity (insofar, that is, as anyone cares about slurs on leftists). But although his prose has retained its poise since 9/11, his thinking has not.

On and on Hitchens's polemics against the left have raged, a tempest of inaccuracy, illogic, and malice. Naomi Klein opines that since most Iraqis agree with the insurgents at least in wanting an end to the occupation, the US should end it. Without disputing her premise, Hitchens condemns her "nasty, stupid" conclusion as an "endorsement of jihad," "applause for the holy warriors," and "swooning support for theocratic fascism." He jeers repeatedly at the antiwar left for having predicted that Saddam would use WMD against a US invasion, conveniently forgetting that what the left actually said was: If, as the Administration insists without evidence, Saddam has WMD, then the most likely scenario for their use is against a US invasion. And that was true. He fiercely ridicules the antiwar argument that there was no contact and no sympathy between Saddam and al-Qaida—only that wasn't the argument. The argument was that it was so unlikely Saddam would entrust weapons of mass destruction to al-Qaida or any other uncontrollable agent that the United States was not justified in invading Iraq in order to prevent it. And that was true too. He continually deplores leftwing "isolationism," even though his opponents are, on the contrary, trying to remind Americans that the UN Charter is the most solemn international agreement ever made ("the first universal social contract," Hitchens's friend Erskine Childers once observed to him), embodying the deep, desperate hope of the weaker nations that the stronger ones will someday submit themselves consistently to the rule of law; while the Bush administration is—not reluctantly but purposefully—undermining it. "The antiwar left," Hitchens scoffs, "used to demand the lifting of sanctions without conditions, which would only have gratified Saddam Hussein and his sons and allowed them to rearm." Not quite true —all leftists agreed that import restrictions on military materials were justified. But more important, a gratified Saddam would not have been the "only" result of ending sanctions. Besides killing hundreds of thousands, the sanctions left Iraqi society helpless, disorganized, and dependent on the state, thus blocking the most likely and legitimate path to regime change—the path followed in Romania, Haiti, Indonesia, South Korea, the Philippines, and other dictatorships, all of them more broadly based, and all (except South Korea) ruling poorer and less-educated societies, than pre-sanctions Iraq. Really, one could almost get the idea that Hitchens thinks the antiwar left doesn't care every goddamned bit as much as he and the neocons about the sufferings of Iraqis.

About any sufferings that cannot serve as a pretext for American military intervention, moreover, Hitchens appears to have stopped caring. (Given how much he writes, and in how many places, if he hasn't mentioned something for several years, it doesn't seem unfair to assume he's stopped caring about it.) He is "a single-issue person at present," he wrote in endorsing President Bush for re-election. This issue, compared with which everything else is "not even in second or third place," is "the tenacious and unapologetic defense of civilized societies against the intensifying menace of clerical barbarism." The invasion of Iraq is a justified act of self-defense against clerical barbarism, and the Bush administration is to be praised and supported for undertaking it.

A lot of suffering people would disagree, I think—and not just the perennial ones, betrayed by every US administration: the tens of millions who die annually for lack of clean water, cheap vaccines, mosquito nets, or another thousand daily calories while the US devotes 0.2 percent of its GDP (one-thirtieth of its military budget and less than one-tenth the cost so far of invading Iraq) to international aid. These unfortunates are mostly not part of a "civilized society under attack from clerical barbarism," so they're out of luck. No, I mean a new class of suffering people, specifically attributable to the new tenacious and unapologetic compassionate conservatism. From its first days in office the Bush administration has made clear its determination to reverse as much as possible the modest progress made in the 20th century toward public provision for the unfortunate, public encouragement of worker, consumer, and neighborhood self-organization, public influence on the daily operation of government and access to the record of its activities, public protection of the commons, and public restraint of concentrated financial and corporate power—not only at home but also, to the (considerable, given American power) extent feasible, abroad. And from the first weeks after 9/11, as Paul Krugman and many others have documented, the Administration has found ways to take advantage of that atrocity to achieve its fundamental goals. The results, now and in the future, of this return to unfettered, predatory capitalism have been and will be a really vast amount of suffering. Enough, one would think, to be worth mentioning in the second or third place, after the dangers of clerical barbarism. Not a word from Hitchens, however, at least in print. Perhaps he is whispering a few words about these matters in the ear of the "bleeding heart" (Hitchens's description) Paul Wolfowitz and his other newly adopted neoconservative allies.

From Hitchens, this silence is very peculiar. Another of his silences is equally so. The South African critic and historian R. W. Johnson once alluded to George Orwell's "simple detestation of untruth." Hitchens—who has written very well about Orwell—was once thought (and not only by me) to feel the same way. *No One Left to Lie To*, his finely indignant critique of Bill Clinton's "contemptible evasions" about his sexual predations and even more contemptible efforts to intimidate potential accusers, convinced many of us that Clinton should have resigned and faced criminal prosecution or at least been served with a sealed indictment at the end of his second term. (Hitchens rightly didn't try to make a case that impeachment, properly limited to official misfeasance, was warranted.) It's a short book, though, pocket-size and with only 103 pages of text. But you would need more than that just for a preface to an adequate critique of the lies of the Bush administration. As the journalist Paul Waldman has remarked: "Bush tells more lies about policy in a week than Bill Clinton did in eight years." He has lied about taxes, budgets, and deficits; about employment statistics; about veterans' benefits; about the Social Security trust fund and the costs of privatization; about climate change; about environmental policy; about oil drilling in the Arctic; about the California electricity crisis; about stem-cell research; about Enron and Harken; about the Florida recount process in November 2000; about his National Guard service and his record as governor of

Texas; and about most of his political opponents. And then there are his lies about Iraq. The Bush administration is the most ambitiously and skillfully dishonest pack of liars in American history, probably by a large margin. And since 9/11, Hitchens has never said a mumbling world about it.

Why? What accounts for Hitchens's astonishing loss of moral and intellectual balance? I think there was a plausible and even creditable reason. Anyone intelligent enough to understand that there are institutional and structural, not merely contingent, constraints on the behavior of states will also understand how difficult it is to budge those constraints and produce a fundamental change in policy. To make the United States an effective democracy—to shift control over the state from the centers of financial and industrial power, now global in reach, to broadly based, self-financed and self-governing groups of active citizens with only average resources—will take several generations, at least. This is a daunting prospect for just about anyone. For someone of Hitchens's generous and romantic temperament, it is potentially demoralizing. The temptation to believe that this long, slow process could be speeded up if only he could find and ally himself with a faction of sympathetic souls close to the seat of executive power who really *understood*—i.e., the neoconservatives, the only ones, Hitchens has written, willing to take "the radical risk of regime change"—must have been overpowering.

And why not? It is hardly dishonorable to try to influence even arbitrary, undemocratic power in a more humane direction. Hitchens has rebuked the American left for its supposedly intransigent refusal to consider supporting the American government in any military undertaking "unless it had done everything right, and done it for everybody." He is mistaken. Here is Noam Chomsky, at the end of a lengthy essay on humanitarian intervention:

> The conclusions that a rational observer will draw about [the probable motives of] US-led "humanitarian intervention" do not answer the question whether such intervention should nevertheless be undertaken. That is a separate matter, to be faced without illusions about our unique nobility. We can, in short, ask whether the pursuit of self-interest might happen to benefit others in particular cases, or whether unremitting public pressure might overcome the demands of the principal architects of policy and the interests they serve.

I think this is exactly right. It was as plain as day to me (and no matter what Hitchens may say, I can't help suspecting it was equally plain to him) that the Bush administration's chief purposes in invading Iraq were: to establish a commanding military presence in the region where the most important natural resource in the world is located; to turn a large and potentially rich country into a virtually unregulated investors' paradise; to impress the rest of the world once again with America's insuperable lead in military technology; to exploit the near-universal hatred of Saddam to legitimize (by establishing a precedent for) the doctrine of unilateral American military intervention expounded in the National Security Strategy Document of September 2002; and to unify the electorate behind an administration that was making a hash of the economy and the environment in order to reward its campaign contributors. Still, this is not why I opposed the war. If I had not also believed that the invasion would strike a sledgehammer blow at most of the world's fragile hopes for international order and the rule of law, I might have calculated that, whatever the government's motives, the potentially huge expenditure of lives and money it contemplated would be better employed in removing Saddam than in, say, providing clean water, cheap vaccines, mosquito nets, etc. to the wretched invisibles, and so saving tens of millions of lives. Not likely, but it would have been a decision based on calculation rather than principle.

Even at their easiest, such calculations are excruciating. Weighing immediate costs and benefits is hard enough; figuring in the effects of setting a good or bad precedent, though often just as important, is devilish hard. The conscientious have always struggled with these difficulties, and sometimes lost patience with them. Randolph Bourne, criticizing the *New Republic* liberals of his era for supporting America's entry into World War I, wondered

> whether realism is always a stern and intelligent grappling with realities. May it not sometimes be a mere surrender to the actual, an abdication of the ideal through a sheer fatigue from intellectual suspense? . . .

> . . . With how many of the acceptors of war has it been mostly a dread of intellectual suspense? It is a mistake to suppose that intellectuality makes for suspended judgments. The intellect craves certitude. It takes effort to keep it supple and pliable. In a time of danger and disaster we

jump desperately for some dogma to cling to. The time comes, if we try to hold out, when our nerves are sick with fatigue, and we seize in a great healing wave of release some doctrine that can be immediately translated into action.

("War and the Intellectuals")

Compare Hitchens's widely quoted response to 9/11: "I felt a kind of exhilaration . . . at last, a war of everything I loved against everything I hated." More recently, explaining to *Nation* readers last November "Why I'm (Slightly) for Bush," he testified again to the therapeutic value of his new commitment: "Myself, I have made my own escape from your self-imposed quandary. Believe me when I say . . . the relief is unbelievable." I believe him.

Will Hitchens ever regain his balance? Near the end of his Bush endorsement, Hitchens defiantly assured his former *Nation* readers that "once you have done it"—abandoned cowardly and equivocating left-wing "isolationism" and made common cause with Republicans in their "willingness to risk a dangerous confrontation with an untenable and indefensible status quo"—there is "no going back." It certainly wouldn't be easy. After heavy-handedly insulting so many political opponents, misrepresenting their positions and motives, and generally making an egregious ass of himself, it would require immense, almost inconceivable courage for Hitchens to acknowledge that he went too far; that his appreciation of the sources and dangers of Islamic terrorism was neither wholly accurate nor, to the extent it was accurate, exceptional; that he was mistaken about the purposes and likely effects of the strategy he associated himself with and preached so sulfurously; and that there is no honorable alternative to—no "relief" to be had from—the frustrations of always keeping the conventional wisdom at arm's length and speaking up instead for principles that have as yet no powerful constituents. But it would be the right, and even the contrarian, thing to do.

Agonizing

Securus judicat orbis terrarum, says a maxim of Roman law; which means, for my purposes: the *New York Times*, the *New York Review of Books*, and the *Times Literary Supplement* can't all be wrong. Isaiah Berlin is a certified sage, an object of near-universal veneration. "Few writers and intellectuals command the awe and admiration accorded to Sir Isaiah Berlin, and with good reason," declared the *Economist* recently. "There is, arguably, no more admired thinker in the English-speaking world," began the Boston *Globe's* review of his latest book, *The Crooked Timber of Humanity*[1]. Berlin's career has been a rapid-fire sequence of academic honors: fellow of two Oxford colleges; Chichele Professor of Social and Political Theory at Oxford; President of Wolfson College, Oxford; President of the British Academy; the Erasmus, Lippincott, Agnelli, and Jerusalem prizes; and a knighthood for academic distinction.

The Crooked Timber of Humanity is a twilight volume: it revisits long-standing preoccupations and restates long-held positions, not in order to revise or synthesize but to clarify or embellish. As usual, Berlin's essays blend the history of ideas, the philosophy of history, political theory, and moral philosophy; his

[1]Edited by Henry Hardy, Knopf, 1991.

approach is relaxed and untheoretical (although sometimes almost dismayingly uncluttered with textual references); his prose style is weighty and graceful.

The unity of Berlin's thought is not far to seek: he has devoted his career to telling a single story. If the master narrative of modernity recounts the gradual progress of emancipation, the alternate, or anti-, narrative describes the costs of that progress: the blindness of enlightenment and the cruelties of emancipation. No sooner was the autonomy of reason secured than the adequacy of reason began to be questioned. Kant's and Hegel's challenges to Enlightenment rationalism are well-known; but Berlin has brought into view, more than any other historian, the full vigor and variety of the anti-Enlightenment tradition. In previous books he showed deep similarities among such marginal and apparently disparate figures as Vico, Herder, Sorel, the nineteenth-century Russian Slavophiles, and Tolstoy as a moral and political thinker. The longest and most substantial essay in *The Crooked Timber of Humanity* adds Joseph de Maistre to this number, though with due allowance for de Maistre's distorting extremisms.

What these thinkers have in common is epistemological and moral pluralism: a conviction that the aims of scientific method—predictiveness, universal applicability, logical simplicity, ontological parsimony—cannot be imported into the study of psychology, history, or politics. Individuals and cultures are radically diverse, ineffably deep, infinitely complex. Only imaginative identification, a renunciation of the urge to theoretical mastery, and a yielding to the sheer particularity of things can produce genuine understanding.

Even more important than this interpretive pluralism is ethical pluralism. Moral no less than aesthetic values are radically diverse. Both within and among human beings, conflict, or at any rate tension, is inevitable. Compromise is possible, but not perfect harmony. This "banality" (his own characterization) is Berlin's constant, almost obsessive, theme. An astonishingly high proportion of his essays, whatever their subject, employ something like the following formula. Enlightenment political thought is said to rest on three premises: first, that every meaningful, properly formulated question has a single correct answer; second, there exists a reliable method for discovering this answer; third, all these answers must be compatible, since truths cannot contradict one another. It follows from these premises that one (and only one) perfectly rational and harmonious way of life is discoverable. This conclusion is deemed to justify unlimited coercion by those who have attained to this discovery against those who have not. And so the tendency of every utopian movement is totalitarian: when perfectibility is the assumption, coercion must be the result.

Of course Berlin's pluralism has more flesh on its bones than this. In his finest essays—on Vico, Hamann, and Herder in *Against the Current*, on Herzen, Belinsky, Turgenev, and Tolstoy in *Russian Thinkers*, and on de Maistre in *The Crooked Timber of Humanity*—he depicts the rebellion against Enlightenment rationalism through marvelously vivid and dramatic intellectual portraits. But the actual arguments, even in his celebrated "Two Concepts of Liberty" and "Historical Inevitability," are thin.

By his own astute and engaging admission, Berlin is not an original thinker. He is, rather, a supremely effective exponent of the conventional moral and political wisdom. This is not entirely, or even in the main, a disparaging judgment. The conventional wisdom is genuine wisdom. Revolutionary, egalitarian, and utopian rhetoric has been put to deplorable uses in the twentieth century; now and for a long time we would do well to be suspicious of it. To have articulated this suspicion comprehensively and, so to speak, genealogically, with large resources of erudition and eloquence, as Berlin has done, is an important service. So is his lifelong admonition that (to quote his approving summary of Montesquieu's position) "durable and beneficial social structures are seldom simple, that large areas of political behavior always remain very complex and obscure, that a radical change of one part of it might easily lead to unpredictable effects in others, and that the end might be worse than the beginning."

This last, however, is a sentence that Michael Harrington or Rosa Luxemburg might have written—it is, at least, a sentiment they would have endorsed. The conventional wisdom had nothing to teach either of them about respect for individual liberty, and they had a great deal of unconventional wisdom to teach Berlin and the civilization that has lionized him. In every society, some truths are convenient and some are not. To those who expound convenient truths (especially with Berlin's incomparable verve), much is given and much forgiven.

Berlin's frequent animadversions on Marx and Marxism are, unfortunately, a contribution to conventional unwisdom. The notion that Marx is responsible for the Gulag is, of course, a terrible simplification. Berlin himself has warned more than once against it. Nonetheless, it's hard to see what other sense to give comments like this:

> [For Hegel and Marx,] a large number of human beings must be sacrificed and annihilated if the ideal is to triumph. . . . The path may lead to a terrestrial paradise, but it is strewn with the corpses of the enemy, for whom no tear must be shed, since right and wrong, good and bad, success and failure, wisdom and folly, are all in the end determined by the objective ends of history, which has condemned half mankind— unhistorical nations, members of obsolete classes, inferior races—to what Proudhon called "liquidation" and Trotsky . . . described as the rubbish heap of history (*The Crooked Timber of Humanity*).

Or this:

> Marx—and it is part of his attraction to those of a similar emotional cast—identifies himself exultantly . . . with the great force which in its very destructiveness is creative, and is greeted with bewilderment and horror only by those whose values are hopelessly subjective, who listen to their consciences, their feelings, or to what their nurses and teachers tell them. . . . When history takes her revenge . . . the mean, pathetic, ludicrous, stifling human anthills will be justly pulverized. . . . Whatever is on the side of victorious reason is just and wise; whatever is on the other side . . . is doomed to destruction (*Four Essays on Liberty*).

At one remove from Marx himself, "Marxist sociology" teaches:

> It is idle for the progressives to try to save their reactionary brothers from defeat: the doomed men cannot hear them, and their destruction is certain. All men will not be saved: the proletariat, justly intent upon its own salvation, had best ignore the fate of their oppressors; even if they wish to return good for evil, they cannot save their enemies from "liquidation." They are "expendable"—their destruction can be neither averted nor regretted by a rational being, for it is the price that mankind must pay for the progress of reason itself: the road to the gates of Paradise is necessarily strewn with corpses (*Crooked Timber*).

All this is superb prose, but as an account of Marx's historical materialism, it is tosh. Marx doubted—correctly, as the bloody history of the American labor movement demonstrates—that capitalists would give up without a fight or that they would (even by their own standards) fight fair. That's about all his infamous revolutionary amorality amounted to. To talk darkly of liquidating half of mankind or pulverizing human anthills—that is, to assimilate Marxism to Stalinism—is mere mischief.

I do not mean that Berlin tailored his rhetoric to flatter the prejudices of his Establishment audience, or anything of that sort. On the contrary, he seems to me all unselfconscious integrity, incapable of altering an adjective, much less an opinion, for the sake of the Erasmus, Lippincott, Agnelli, and Jerusalem prizes together. He obviously believes every word he has written about Marx, many of which are just and penetrating. But if Berlin didn't believe and hadn't frequently and eloquently expounded these damaging half-truths about Marx during the central decades of the Cold War, I doubt he would have been the object of so much institutional affection and gratitude.

The fervent gratitude he inspires is, in a way, the most remarkable thing about Berlin's career. He obviously strikes exactly the right chord. "People are pleased," observes Russell Jacoby (in "Isaiah Berlin: With the Current," *Salmagundi*, Winter 1982), "to find a man of learning who does not accuse them or their society of unspeakable crimes. . . . Berlin reassures his readers in a prose studded with the great names of Western culture that complexity is inevitable, solutions, impossible; the threat is from the utopians and artists who imagine a better world."

The critique of utopia is certainly the nerve of Berlin's writings. Like his critique of Marx, it is surprisingly simplistic for so renowned an evangelist of complexity. Sometimes it is not even minimally informative. Berlin frequently tries to make mere repetition or enumeration do the work of detailed analysis. By and large, his strictures are pronounced rather than proved.

Take this passage from "The Decline of Utopian Ideas in the West":

> Broadly speaking, western Utopias tend to contain the same elements: a society lives in a state of pure harmony, in which all its members live in peace, love one another, are free from physical danger, from want of any kind, from insecurity, from degrading work, from envy, from frustration, experience no injustice or violence, live in perpetual, even light, in a temperate climate, in the midst of infinitely fruitful, generous nature. The main characteristic of most, perhaps all, Utopias is the fact that they are static. Nothing in them alters, for they have reached perfection: there is no need for novelty or change; no one can wish to alter a condition in which all natural human wishes are fulfilled (*Crooked Timber*).

In short, the Garden of Eden minus original sin. But consider what are perhaps the five most influential utopian fictions in English: More's *Utopia*, Bellamy's *Looking Backward*, Morris's *News from Nowhere*, Wells's *A Modern Utopia*, and Ernest Callenbach's *Ecotopia*. No characteristic from Berlin's list applies categorically to all five, or indeed, arguably, to any of them. All members of all these utopian societies are liable to some danger, want, frustration, envy, violence, insecurity, and tedious work, however insignificant compared with present-day levels. They are cooperative, egalitarian, technically advanced commonwealths, not idylls of static perfection. *Pace* Berlin, no "metaphysical" theories of human nature are required to accept them (with whatever reservations) as inspiring models or programs, only a lively and discriminating moral imagination.

Similarly, in "The Apotheosis of the Romantic Will" Berlin declares that

> thinkers from Bacon to the present have been inspired by the certainty that there must exist a total solution: that in the fullness of time . . . the reign of irrationality, injustice and misery will end; man will be liberated, and will no longer be the plaything of forces beyond his control—savage nature, or the consequences of his own ignorance or folly or vice; that this springtime in human affairs will come once the obstacles, natural and human, are overcome, and then at last men will cease to fight each other, unite their powers, and cooperate to adapt nature to their needs . . . (*Crooked Timber*).

This Berlin regards as an absurdity, a Sorelian "great myth" of perfect harmony through a scientifically-arrived-at "total solution"—the sinister implications of that last phrase are almost certainly intended. To me, on the contrary, it seems an entirely reasonable and humane goal (though patronizingly and tendentiously formulated by Berlin, to be sure)—a goal that implies neither psychological nor intellectual nor moral uniformity, nor any perfect harmony, fortuitous or coerced.

A final example, from the same essay. According to Berlin, the Romantics have done well for humanity by dealing a "fatal blow" to the notion that

> rational organization can bring about the perfect union of such values and counter-values as individual liberty and social equality, spontaneous self-

expression and organized, socially directed efficiency, perfect knowledge and perfect happiness, the claims of personal life and the claims of parties, classes, nations, the public interest. If some ends recognized as fully human are at the same time ultimate and mutually incompatible, then the idea of a golden age, a perfect society compounded of a synthesis of all the correct solutions to all the central problems, is shown to be incoherent in principle.

If this passage is purged of exaggeration and caricature—or even if one merely removes the words "perfect" and "golden age"—then the incoherence vanishes, or at least requires a good deal more demonstration than Berlin provides, either in this essay or anywhere else. Would any of those to whom the above beliefs are ascribed—that is, the "many who put their trust in rational and scientific methods designed to effect a fundamental social transformation"— acknowledge them in the form here proffered by Berlin? I doubt it. Again and again—almost without exception, in fact—Berlin trivializes and dismisses utopianism by means of such phrases as "earthly paradise," "the perfect life," "a perfect and harmonious society, wholly free from conflict or injustice or oppression," "a static perfection in which human nature is finally and fully realized, and all is still and immutable and eternal." But has any utopian writer, no matter how deluded, ever really promised perfection? Any *influential* utopian writer? *Most* influential utopian writers? Even if the answer to that last question were "Yes" (and if it is not, then Berlin's central claim about utopianism is untrue), the important issue raised by the utopian tradition would not be "Is humankind perfectible?" but "How perfectible is it? How far can we go? And why can't we even make a start?"

Notwithstanding his famously varied interests and extraordinary range, Berlin has never found the occasion to raise, much less come to terms with, these urgent and obvious questions. He has instead devoted himself to addressing continual reminders about the unattainability of perfect harmony to a civilization that cannot rouse itself to legislate a decently progressive income tax or do more than gesture fitfully at homelessness, global hunger, and a score of other evils for which a doubtless imperfect posterity will doubtless curse and despise us. Berlin will not, I'm afraid, win the Scialabba Prize.

He will survive that disappointment; for all his frequent and graceful self-deprecation, he evidently enjoys, along with everyone else's, his own good opinion. Near the end of his splendid essay on Turgenev is a passage of what is unmistakably self-description:

> ... the small, hesitant, not always very brave band of men who occupy a position somewhere to the left of center, and are morally repelled both by the hard faces to their right and the hysteria and mindless violence and demagoguery on their left. Like the men of the [18]40s, for whom Turgenev spoke, they are at once horrified and fascinated. They are shocked by the violent irrationalism of the dervishes on the left, yet they are not prepared to reject wholesale the position of those who claim to represent the young and the disinherited, the indignant champions of the poor and the socially deprived or repressed. This is the notoriously unsatisfactory, at times agonizing, position of the modern heirs of the liberal tradition (*Russian Thinkers*).

This is a perfectly honorable position, but it is not, as far as I can see, an agonizing one. It seems, in fact, quite a comfortable one. Turgenev, it is true, was not comfortable. But then, he tried long and hard to find common ground with the "indignant champions of the poor," rather than merely informing them that not much, alas, can be done. Berlin is, of course, in favor of whatever *can* be done; but what in particular that might be, and why not more, never seems to be his immediate concern. "The concrete situation is almost everything," he advises, concluding an essay entitled "The Pursuit of the Ideal." The concrete situation is just what Berlin has rarely had a word to say about.

Forty years ago Irving Howe wrote: "But if the ideal of socialism is now to be seen as problematic, the problem of socialism remains an abiding ideal. I would say that it is the best problem to which a political intellectual can attach himself." So it was, and still is. And Berlin still hasn't.

Dying of the Truth

The argument over modernity is as old as modernity. Pascal could not forgive irony, self-consciousness, radical doubt. Kant labored to overcome Hume's skepticism. Kierkegaard railed at Hegel's cosmopolitan historicism. Dostoevsky stated the conservatives' ultimate misgiving: "If God does not exist, everything is permitted."

On the left, too, there is a tradition of ambivalence about the results of certain modern liberations. Mill fretted that virtue might not survive the decline of Christian superstition. Morris was sure that beauty and mass production could not coexist. Lawrence called industrialism "a black mistake." By now the modernist turn seems irreversible, yet thoughtful radicals like Christopher Lasch and Michael Walzer are still troubled by a sense of something lost as everything solid melts into the air.

What has worried opponents of modernism is its primarily critical, destructive character. Its chief strategies have been negative: dissolution (of supposedly fundamental distinctions), unmasking (of unconscious motives, class interests), debunking (of myths), stripping away (of gratuitous assumptions, superfluous first principles). In one perspective, modern intellectual history seems a kind of ascetic frenzy, a continual renunciation of consoling, structure-providing, community-creating illusions. And what, ask the anti-modernists, is left? Babel, chaos, anomie, nihilsm: unreal cities, a handful of dust. Something like this bleak picture describes contemporary religious and moral philosophy, according to Leszek Kolakowski and Alasdair MacIntyre. By and large in both fields, the center does not hold: there is little final or even preliminary agreement, and no agreement on how agreement might eventually be reached. Once *arbiter scientiarium*, philosophy has become an administrative convenience. What's more, this fragmentation of theoretical discourse mirrors the anarchy of our moral and political practice and the spiritual disunity of our culture.

All this profoundly disturbs Kolakowski and MacIntyre, who have written strikingly similar, or at least congruent, diagnoses of the modern condition.[1] Both men are former Marxists, transplanted Europeans, and distinguished academic philosophers. In both their voices, a crepuscular note sounds: beleaguered and disillusioned, but determined to outface the end, if this be the end, with a valiant, quixotic faithfulness to professional norms of rationality. Let us go reasoning into that good night.

Kolakowski quotes Ivan Karamazov's remark about everything being permitted if God does not exist and proposes that is "valid not only as a moral rule but as an epistemological principle." Reason and religion have fought each other to a standstill; and while there are no rational grounds for admitting any religious truth, we are not bound to accept any definition of rationality that, like scientific positivism, excludes religious possibilities altogether. Positivism's main line of attack has been to demonstrate that religious language doesn't do what plain, honest, everyday usage is expected to do: produce predictions, consensus, and other useful results. Normative statements, ultimate choices, and cosmic conjectures about how everything hangs together cannot be justified in empirical terms. But, Kolakowski argues, such norms, choices, and cosmic prejudices are exactly what is presupposed by the positivists' assumption that all genuine knowledge is publicly verifiable and that nothing else counts. In reality, he claims, what counts only counts within some epistemological/moral/cosmological framework, and such a framework cannot be justified, only chosen. Belief is

---

[1] *Religion: If There Is No God . . .* by Leszek Kolakowski. Oxford Univ. Press, 1982.
After Virtue: A Study in Moral Theory by Alasdair MacIntyre. Univ. of Notre Dame Press, 1981.

choice, and secular rationalists are believers, too. Not to choose is to drift, to define truth as whatever solves whatever problems are at hand. Hence our dilemma: "either an infinite regress or a discretionary decision . . . either God or a cognitive nihilism."

Of course, even discretionary decisions are not made in a void, so Kolakowski offers an account of how religious commitments come about. Certainly not by sheer force of argument: "Probably nobody has ever been converted to faith by philosophical discussion." Instead "people are initiated into the understanding of religious language and into worship through participation in the life of a religious community," in which "knowledge, the feeling of participation in the ultimate reality, and moral commitment appear as a single act." This faith-act is strictly ineffable: the inner life of the faith-community cannot be explained or communicated, but those inside understand one another as reliably as the most austere positivists. One is, it seems, chosen by faith almost as much as one chooses it. Nonbelievers call this a mystification; believers call it a mystery.

Kolakowski's defense of religion is peculiarly modern: all the standard objections are cheerfully admitted, then declared not to matter. Belief is a "logically arbitrary" option, but then so is unbelief. Believers and nonbelievers should not expect to convert one another, indeed should not even expect to understand one another. We shouldn't talk of "an 'escape into irrationality,'" but of the irreducibly different ways in which religious beliefs are validated in contrast to scientific propositions, of the incommensurable meanings of 'validity' in those respective areas." The sacred and the profane are equally coherent and equally compelling, each on its own terms, and may as well quit feuding and just nod stiffly at each other from opposite sides of the room.

It is a little too pat. What is really on Kolakowski's mind? One hint is that, despite his professed agnosticism, his references to skeptics are almost uniformly negative. Rationalists have "travestied" Christian notions like original sin. Free-thinking, once an instrument of tolerance, has degenerated into "fanatical rationalism." Science has "monopolistically" arrogated to itself the very notion of Reason. And so on. This may be the author's idea of sportsmanship, since religion is definitely the underdog in this matchup and needs all possible rhetorical support. But these jibes sound too genuinely enthusiastic; more likely, they are the product of Kolakowski's long-standing ambivalence. He once declared himself an "inconsistent atheist" and went on to observe wistfully that never-theless "men have no fuller means of self-identification than through religious symbolism" and that "religious consciousness . . . is an irreplaceable part of human culture, man's only attempt to see himself as a whole." In *Religion* he concludes forlornly that "human dignity is not to be validated within a natu-ralistic concept of man. The absence of God spells the ruin of man in the sense that it demolishes or robs of meaning everything we think of as the essence of being human: the quest for truth, the distinction of good and evil, the claim to dignity, the claim to creating something that withstands the indifferent destructive-ness of time." After a life extraordinarily full of both action (dissent and expulsion from Communist Poland) and thought (the massive and renowned *Main Cur-rents of Marxism*), here stands Kolakowski, head bloodied and only just unbowed, unable to take comfort but unwilling to renounce it altogether, at least for others. Perhaps—at least for others—there is some escape from modernity.

Alasdair MacIntyre is much less ambivalent: he is determined to deliver us from modernity. Though somewhat more practical than Kolakowski's, his concerns are no less sweeping, and *After Virtue* is a far more rigorous, ambitious, and original book than *Religion*. It is a reinterpretation of the entire history of West-ern moral philosophy, as decline, fall, and—possibly—rebirth.

To motivate this vast undertaking, MacIntyre begins by canvassing contem-porary moral philosophy. What he finds is an explicit and widespread disavowal of its perennial ideals: objectivity, impersonality, universality, proof. Emotivism, the view that moral utterances are at bottom functional (i.e., persuasive state-ments of one's own attitudes or preferences) has swept the field. Moral discourse is now framed almost exclusively in terms of interests. In the society at large, moral argument consists of asserting interests—often, to be sure, disguised in terms of "rights" or "justice," but less and less convincingly to the other protago-nists. Philosophers now mostly try to devise procedures for arbitrating among the claims of individuals whose interests and values, it is taken for granted, will be wholly disparate. For Aristotle and other premoderns, "justice" meant fidel-ity to a shared conception of cosmic or social order; now it means fair treatment of competing equals, who share no such conception. Since even this degree of procedural egalitarianism involves some prior consensus about values—how to weigh them, which to designate as within the political arena—public moral discussion verges on cacophony.

As a result, modern culture has produced a distinctive character-type, our equivalent of the Homeric warrior-hero, the Athenian gentleman-citizen, the Christian saint, the eighteenth-century *honnête homme*. The defining activity of this character-type is manipulation; its most common embodiments are the aesthete, the therapist and, above all, the manager. All three express their culture's understanding of social relations as primarily instrumental: through the consumption of other people as interesting sensations or through the deployment of morally neutral expertise to achieve organizational goals. In a developed society that has renounced the ideal of virtue, of universal, rationally justifiable norms, this is the form taken by the war of all against all, and these characters are its warrior-heroes.

Having sketched this chilling and plausible portrait, MacIntyre asks: how has it come to this? His answer is that we took a wrong turn, roughly at the Enlightenment. Classical and Christian morality was based on the concept of *telos*, which means variously "goal," "purpose," "perfection," or "essential nature." Homer, Aristotle, Aquinas, and Calvin all believed that virtues were qualities that enabled men and women to fulfill their essential nature and so achieve the goal of their existence. Of course, these writers described the goal of human existence differently, and so gave differing accounts of the virtues. But the form of moral reasoning was the same: from the *telos*.

Then it was discovered (perhaps the founding discovery of the modern era) that science could only be done by dispensing with the idea of essential natures. In the riot of liberation, teleological reasoning was banished from the—as yet only putative—human sciences. And that, according to MacIntyre, was our cardinal mistake. Physical science may be incompatible with *telos*, but there has never been and never will be a human or social science. MacIntyre devotes a scathing chapter to demonstrating the utter nullity and bogusness of contemporary social science and to arguing that the spurious fact-value distinction invoked to support its pseudoscientific pretensions is merely ideological camouflage. The modern rejection of normative rationality, the cliché that no "ought" may be deduced from an "is," is based on a mechanistic misunderstanding of human subjectivity and, consequently, of moral reasoning. So much for Weberian bureaucratic rationality. And so much for Marxism and all other theories which agree with Weber that values are created by human decisions and that conflicts between rival values cannot be rationally settled.

At this point one may begin to suspect MacIntyre of reactionary intentions. That would be a mistake. His few specific comments on politics are acute and evenhanded. In one deft, lethal paragraph, Burkean traditionalism is exposed as a fraud, an opportunistic yoking of market and hierarchy. In another, right-wing libertarianism, exemplified by Robert Nozick's *Anarchy, State and Utopia*, is shown to rest on absurdly unhistorical fiction: "justified original acquisition." Marxism is judged a failure, but not for the usual reasons: "the barbarous despotism of the collective Czardom which reigns in Moscow is as irrelevant to the question of Marxism's moral substance as the life of a Borgia pope was to that of Christianity's moral substance." MacIntyre is a neo-Aristotelian; he urges a thorough repudiation of modern ideologies, left or right, in favor of a commitment to . ... virtue.

A hundred years ago "virtue" meant "chastity." Today it hardly means anything. To reinstate this admittedly archaic concept, MacIntyre embarks on a dense and suggestive though finally unsatisfying attempt to prove that human life does indeed have a purpose, a *telos*. His argument weaves together notions of community, tradition, practices (i.e., skills, crafts, arts, intellectual disciplines), and narrative considered as the form of unity of a life. Virtues (e.g., honesty, prudence, diligence) make possible our participation in practices (e.g., physics, pottery, public service), each of which rests on a tradition (a history of development whose past merits allegiance and whose future is the responsibility of its virtuous practitioners). Practices are communal and narrative: they are the embodied history of a community of practitioners. Practices are teleological: they have intrinsic, characteristic goals, distinctive lines of development. And practices presuppose a larger community, or *polis*, which prizes and makes possible the common pursuit of those perfections aimed at by the practices (which is to say—though MacIntyre says so almost inaudibly—a society not based on competition and commodity production). All this sounds vaguely promising. But what's the cash value of this elaborate philosophical construction? What might the virtuous community actually look like? Isn't that species extinct, beyond reviving after centuries of modern barbarism? Addressing these questions, Mac-Intyre falters. "The good life for man," he concludes lamely, "is the life spent in seeking the good life for man, and the virtues necessary for the seeking are those which will enable us to understand what more and what else the good life for man is." This is not much help. The final gloomy pages of *After Virtue* compare the present to the Dark Ages after the fall of Rome. The partisans of virtue can do little but huddle together in unspecified sanctuaries, guarding the tradition. "What matters at this stage is the construction of local forms of community within which civility and the intellectual and moral life can be sustained through the new dark ages which are already upon us." Modernity cannot be repealed, but perhaps it can be survived.

Richard Rorty has, if possible, even less hope than MacIntyre, but doesn't seem to mind. His exquisitely witty, humane book is a *dernier cri* of modernist disillusionment. *Consequences of Pragmatism*[2], a collection of essays, announces that the history of philosophy is over, and a good thing too. Rorty presents that history as a series of enchantments or incantations which, as is now obvious to everyone, simply haven't worked. Our culture's trek to the present has been a Long March through one province after another of philosophical folly: Plato's Ideas, Aristotle's essences, Descarte's mind-body distinction, Kant's *Ding-an-sich*, Husserl's phenomenological method, the logical positivists' scientific method—all in quest of absolute, supra-historical Certainty. At last we have learned from the great antiphilosophers—James and Dewey, Nietzsche and Heidegger, Wittgenstein and Foucault—that this Certainty is not to be had, and that wanting it was all along a lack of maturity, a failure of nerve, a yearning for what Nietzsche called "metaphysical comfort."

There is no God, in other words, and no *telos*. "Is everything permitted, then?" ask Kolakowski and MacIntyre, anxiously. "Yes indeed," replies Rorty. "We must grow up or go under. Our culture's childhood is at an end."

[2]*Consequences of Pragmatism: Essays, 1972-1980* by Richard Rorty. Univ. of Minnesota Press, 1982.

Nietzsche and Foucalt suppose that this recognition must lead to lonely self-creation for the few and ubiquitous bureaucratic control for the many. But James and Dewey—Rorty's heroes—hope that a sense of our common predicament might lead to something else. "To accept the contingency of starting points is to accept our inheritance from, and our conversation with, our fellow-humans as our only source of guidance . . . In the end, the pragmatists tell us, what matters is our loyalty to other human beings clinging together against the dark, not our hope of [Certainty]."

A fragile idea, this community of despair, and Rorty knows it. His remarks about morality and politics are oblique, almost resigned. In the end, he endorses an ecumenical liberalism and recommends Dewey as the model contemporary moralist "simply because his vocabulary allows room for unjustifiable hope, and an ungroundable but vital sense of solidarity." That's something, surely. But is that all?

"Art and nothing but art," wrote Nietszche. "We have art in order not to die of the truth." How not to die of the truth is what both Kolakowski and MacIntyre are asking: the truth that everything is contingent, that no religious or moral system can compel assent, that purposes are not given in the nature of things. Kolakowski asks how belief is possible, and MacIntyre asks how virtue is possible; both answer, "through community." But neither can explain how community is possible without a willful suspension of the critical spirit. Rorty is more helpful but finally can offer only the hope that rigorous intellectual honesty will keep the delicate flowers of human decency and autonomy from being smothered by metaphysical weeds. About how we might nourish the life that this strenuous hygiene is supposed to protect, he has nothing to say. Does modernity hold out no more robust hope than this?

Perhaps it does. Tracing the decline of teleological reasoning and normative rationality, MacIntyre identifies Hume as the most powerful and destructive antagonist of the premodern tradition. After finishing off the Aristotelian philosophical fictions, Hume had somehow to account for altruism, to show how reason might be enslaved to benign passions. In a famous footnote to the *Enquiry Concerning Morals*, he fudged the issue: "It is needless to push our researches so far as to ask why we have humanity or a fellow-feeling with others: it is sufficient that this is experienced to be a principle in human nature. We must stop somewhere in our examination of causes; and there are, in every science, some general principles beyond which we cannot hope to find any principle more general." The irony of history's most consistent skeptic suggesting sheepishly that we take for granted the conceptual cornerstone of his positive moral theory does not escape MacIntyre, who exultantly declares Hume's whole project a failure.

But Hume's project was completed, or at least continued, by some very unlikely collaborators. Godwin enthusiastically accepted Hume's critique of traditional superstition and tried, crudely and uncertainly, to imagine an emancipated world. In Shelley, Enlightenment rationalism and Romantic imagination were harmoniously combined. *A Defense of Poetry* locates the cultivation of altruism (Hume's "fellow-feeling") among the effects of Art: "The great instrument of moral good is the imagination . . . a going out of our own nature, and an identification of ourselves with the beautiful which exists in thought, action, or person not our own."

Later, construction began on the ground Hume had cleared and on the foundations the Romantics had laid. The supposedly prosaic British political imagination produced an unrivaled burst of utopian art and theory, including Morris' *News From Nowhere* and "How We Live and How We Might Live"; Wilde's *The Soul of Man Under Socialism*; Russell's "The World As It Could Be Made" and *Principles of Social Reconstruction*; Shaw's "The Revolutionist's Handbook" and *The Intelligent Woman's Guide to Socialism and Capitalism*; Wells's *Men Like Gods* and "The Discovery of the Future"; and Lawrence's "Democracy," "The Education of the People," and *Reflections of the Death of a Porcupine*. Despite many extravagances, inconsistencies, and plain mistakes, these and other works in the utopian mode achieve something for human solidarity: not the metaphysical grounding that Rorty rightly mocks, but imaginative embodiment. They further our collective education in desire.

Modernity may be considered the joint accomplishment of skeptics and visionaries. The skeptics can be seen as clearing a space for the utopian imagination, for prophecies of a demystified community, of a solidarity without illusions. The skeptics weed, the visionaries water. Where the seed of generous, human sympathy comes from is as obscure as where genius comes from. "We can't make life," wrote Lawrence. "We can but fight for the life that grows in us."

With at least these two weapons: criticism and vision. In our culture, the great skeptical liberators of the Enlightenment have long been honored as (even christened) the party of humanity. If their project—the modern project—succeeds, it will be because we have also assimilated and surpassed the dreams of, among others, Godwin and Shelley, Morris and Wilde, Shaw and Wells, Russell and Lawrence—the visionary party, the party of hope.

Disenchantment and Democracy

"There is no God," James Mill confided to his son, "but this is a family secret." The utility of religion is a commonplace of Western discourse from Protagoras to *Habits of the Heart*. Educated nonbelievers, however unenthusiastic about contemporary political and economic arrangements, have nevertheless worried that widespread unbelief would make social cohesion impossible. In the capitalist democracies of the late twentieth century, unbelief is widespread; and though the bourgeois virtues may be less in evidence, anomie does not yet loom. But this may be in part because of the currency within these societies of secular substitutes for religion, especially the metaphysics of "human nature," "natural rights" and "objectivity." As long as *something* absolute, something transcendent, is believed to validate a society's rules, the necessary minimum of solidarity and self-discipline may be expected from its members.

Locke, Rousseau, and Kant—the church fathers of the Enlightenment—bequeathed us the philosophical doctrines that have come to underwrite liberalism: inviolable rights, moral autonomy and responsibility, the uniqueness and ineffability of each personality. All these doctrines rest on the traditional epistemology of "objective truth." Throughout two millenniums of classical philosophy, truth meant correspondence to something "out there," to the essential nature of reality, conceived variously as the mind of God, the Platonic Ideas, rational substances, and the realm of things-in-themselves. Likewise, justice meant treating human beings according to their essential nature, which, by definition, could not vary between cultures or epochs. Then came science, capitalism, and the French Revolution, and along with them philosophical modernity. "About two hundred years ago," Richard Rorty writes in *Contingency, Irony, and Solidarity*[1], "the idea that truth was made rather than found began to take hold of the imagination of Europe."

This idea—that "where there are no sentences there is no truth, that sentences are elements of human languages, and that human languages are human creations," as Rorty puts it—implies that individual and social moralities are human creations, not derived from our human essence or the nature of things. For there *is* no human essence, no nature of things; there are only alternative scientific and moral vocabularies, better or worse suited to our diverse purposes. And these purposes are themselves contingent, dependent on our socialization and our community's history.

The most compelling and influential account of morality yet produced is Nietzsche's. Rightly perceiving that the purpose of most moralities heretofore has been to suppress the self-assertion of exceptional individuals, Nietzsche concluded that every form of social solidarity is a mystification based on envy. In particular, democracy is merely the attempt of the masses—the "last men"—to secure their welfare by legislating universal mediocrity. Less explicitly, Nietzsche's successors—Shaw, Lawrence, Heidegger, Foucault, Adorno, and many others—have also assumed an opposition, at the level of individual psychology if not of social policy, between equality, compassion, and other liberal virtues, on the one hand, and on the other, the disenchantment and self-cultivation of the gifted few.

Few writers have tried to do justice to the claims of both disenchantment and democracy, both irony and solidarity, and none so successfully as Richard Rorty. One of his two previous books, *Philosophy and the Mirror of Nature*, interpreted the history of philosophy as an increasingly thorough emancipation from

[1]Cambridge Univ. Press, 1989.

metaphysical illusions, culminating in the utterly different but equally decisive critiques of Dewey, Wittgenstein, and Heidegger. *Consequences of Pragmatism*, an essay collection, filled in the details of this idiosyncratic narrative and speculated about the "post-philosophical" future. *Contingency, Irony, and Solidarity*, another collection, is also about the consequences of pragmatism: not, this time, for philosophy and other academic disciplines but for the soul of the pragmatist.

It is no longer possible to believe confidently, with Plato and the Christian or Enlightenment philosopher, that a proper conception of justice will fuse the public and the private, that individual perfection and common good must coincide. Instead we have to ask anxiously whether they may even—as a practical matter; as live, motivating concerns within a single person—coexist. "We would like," Rorty writes, "to be able to admire both Blake and Arnold, both Nietzsche and Mill, both Marx and Baudelaire, both Trotsky and Eliot, both Nabokov and Orwell." We would like, that is, to be both detached and committed, autonomous and connected, fastidious and fervent, subtle and savagely indignant. No theory, no philosophical formula, will enable us to strike an ideal balance. No theory can resolve this dilemma; Rorty offers only to describe it. But that's a help.

Rorty's description ingeniously plays off exemplary "public" and "private," political and antipolitical writers: Nietzsche against Proust, Habermas against Foucault, Nabokov's scorn for "topical trash" in literature against his horror of cruelty, and the first two thirds of 1984 against the last third. Rorty explicates Nietzsche's ("to become who one actually is") and Proust's ("the discovery of our true life") famous mottos, which name a similar project: "Both men wanted to create themselves by writing a narrative of the people who had offered descriptions of them; they wanted to become autonomous by redescribing the sources of heteronomous descriptions." But Proust accepted more fully the contingency of these previous, inherited descriptions and the consequent incompleteness of his own narrative. Nietzsche, in his ambiguous exposition of the will to power, sometimes "claims to see deeper rather than differently" and thus "betrays his own perspectivism and his nominalism." These occasional lapses from irony are the source of Nietzsche's adventitious antiliberalism. Of the two most original contemporary philosophers, Habermas is a liberal (Rorty borrows Judith Shklar's definition of liberals—those for whom "cruelty is the worst thing they do"—but his usage throughout embraces social democrats and even libertarian socialists) "who is unwilling to be an ironist" (i.e., someone who has come to terms with the contingency of all philosophical vocabularies and political ideas), while Foucault is "an ironist who is unwilling to be a liberal." Habermas insists on grounding his admirable politics on a new epistemology, the theory of "communicative reason," which will allegedly escape the fate of all previous epistemologies, and about which Rorty is, here and elsewhere, persuasively skeptical. Foucault demonstrates brilliantly that "the patterns of acculturation characteristic of liberal societies have imposed on their members kinds of constraints of which older, premodern societies had not dreamed." But he fails to see—or refuses to acknowledge—that liberal societies have also evolved humane values and institutions roughly equal in strength and flexibility to the manipulative discourses he expertly analyzes.

The chapters on Nabokov and Orwell in *Contingency, Irony, and Solidarity* are superb. Chief among the consequences of pragmatism is that philosophy makes nothing happen: it is politically useless. No political order, including liberalism, can be theoretically grounded. Progress depends rather on extending our—"we" being the politically competent citizens of the rich democracies—imaginative range, identifying with those who are unnecessarily suffering. And this is a task not for philosophers but for social scientists, journalists, and, above all, novelists. Nabokov and Orwell were, temperamentally, poles apart. But both of them, according to Rorty, "warn the liberal ironist intellectual against temptations to be cruel"; both of them "dramatize the tension between private irony and liberal hope."

Nabokov notoriously despised the "sociological side" of literature and was scathing about writers who aspired to be "teachers" and "reformers" rather than "enchanters." But as Rorty shows, Nabokov's aesthetic pronouncements are irrelevant; his "best novels are the ones which exhibit his inability to believe his own general ideas." Although Nabokov asserted the moral sufficiency of pure art, *Lolita* and *Pale Fire* are actually "reflections on the possibility that there can be sensitive killers, cruel aesthetes, pitiless poets—masters of imagery who are content to turn the lives of others into images on a screed, while simply not noticing that these other people are suffering." For all his mockery, Nabokov understood that "the pursuit of autonomy is at odds with feelings of solidarity," and that this antithesis might, at times, yield a moral problem. Without the liberal virtues, the ironic intelligence may turn inhuman.

Nabokov's Humbert and Kinbote are apolitical genius-monsters. O'Brien in 1984 is a political genius-monster; he lacks the liberal virtues not because he is indifferent to other people—he is anything but that—but because in his society solidarity is no longer possible. Many critics have not seen the point of Orwell's extended portrait, supposing it a specimen of his unfortunate "mysticism of cruelty." But in this case, the mysticism is all on his critics' side: the assumption that an atemporal, noncontingent human nature endows us with at least some measure of inner freedom and rationality and will prevent the permanent disappearance of liberal institutions. O'Brien is plausible—not because sadism or power hunger is innate, but because nothing is innate. O'Brien illustrates the truth to which the failure of classical philosophy points: socialization goes all the way down.

Orwell offered no consistent program, and certainly no theoretically-based program, for avoiding the extinction of freedom. What he offered instead was a sometimes infuriatingly vague advocacy of "decency" and, far more important, a terrifyingly explicit description of where the lack of such solidarity had led and might yet lead. Both as a journalist and a novelist, Orwell worked on his readers' moral imagination, showing them suffering they had failed to notice and then showing them what the best, the most intelligent, of them would turn into if this moral obtuseness overwhelmed the fragile culture of liberalism. Rorty believes with Shelley, an earlier radical pragmatist, that "the great instrument of moral good is the imagination" (*A Defense of Poetry*); or, in his own formulation, that "detailed descriptions of particular varieties of pain and humiliation (in, e.g., novels or ethnographies), rather than philosophical or religious treatises, are the modern intellectual's principal contribution to moral progress." So Orwell is, for him, a paradigmatic example of the responsible intellectual.

But Rorty respects the prerogatives of irresponsible intellectuals. Nietzsche, Proust, Heidegger, and Derrida should obviously be encouraged to pursue their idiosyncratic projects of self-creation. How can a democratic society avoid either alienating or privileging its spiritual elite?

One can ask these men to *privatize* their projects, their attempts at sublimity—to view them as irrelevant to politics and therefore compatible with the sense of human solidarity which the development of democratic institutions has facilitated. This request for privatization amounts to the request that they resolve an impending dilemma by subordinating sublimity to the desire to avoid cruelty and pain.

Such a request will be based not on a theory of justice but on

> nothing more profound than the historical facts which suggest that without the protection of something like the institutions of bourgeois liberal society, people will be less able to work out their private salvations, create their private self-images, reweave their webs of belief and desire in the light of whatever new people and books they happen to encounter. In ... an ideal society, discussion of public affairs will revolve around 1) how to balance the needs for peace, wealth, and freedom when conditions require that one of these goals be sacrificed to one of the others, and 2) how to equalize opportunities for self-creation and then leave people alone to use, or neglect, their opportunities.

Rorty would be the first to acknowledge that these prescriptions are little more than banalities. They are, however, the best that philosophy can do. Rorty's accomplishment has been to help liberate us from the illusion that things are otherwise, that we can turn away from terrestrial pain toward political truths inscribed in the heavens or in our inmost nature. The tradition of all the dead generations of philosophers weighs a little less on those who have read Rorty's books, which free us to turn toward those who need a more than philosophical liberation.

Only Words

"Poetry makes nothing happen," as Auden wrote; and neither does philosophy, as Richard Rorty has shown. You'd never know it, though, from the last decade or so of all-out cultural polemics. The sky is falling, warns the right, and it's the fault of tenured radicals and trendy *artistes*. Racism, sexism, and imperialism remain unsmashed, complains the left, and it's the fault of the dominant cultural/ideological formations and of the literary/artistic canon that underwrites their hegemony. Along with several grains of truth, a certain amount of chaff has found its way into the arguments on both sides, as Rorty has pointed out with unfailing, almost excessive tact and Stanley Fish has pointed out with unflagging, almost excessive energy.

One can identify a master argument on each side. The right declares: Judgments about merit, desert, responsibility and liberty—whom to admit, hire, elect, promote, aid, or punish; what to teach, what to prohibit—should be made according to permanent, neutral, objective, universal criteria, which will be acknowledged as valid and relevant by all rational, disinterested persons. This is only fair; it is, in fact, the definition of fairness. Past unfairness cannot justify present unfairness; two wrongs do not make a right. Ergo, away with affirmative action, racial redistricting, hate-speech codes, rainbow curriculums, diversity requirements, administration-subsidized campus separatism, and all other violations of formal equality.

The left rejoins: Beings who are always and necessarily partial, local, temporal, embodied and purposive—that is, *human* beings—cannot attain universality, disinterestedness, or "pure" rationality. Principles and definitions are empty until interpreted, and every interpretation rests on a chain or network of assumptions and stipulations, which cannot all simultaneously be examined. Criteria and values do not come from nowhere (or from God or the nature of things) but from their proponents' histories and interests. Since the latter must differ, so must the former, fundamentally and irreducibly. Ergo, to invoke objectivity, formal equality, and other purportedly nonpartisan, noncontroversial principles is bad faith, an effort to place one's perspective or goal above criticism.

This rejoinder—"antifoundationalism"—is true and important. But to explain why would be to review Stanley Fish's last book rather than his new one. *Doing What Comes Naturally: Change, Rhetoric, and the Practice of Theory in Literary and Legal Studies*[1] comprehensively maps the consequences of antifoundationalism, which only sounds like an arcane project until one reflects that antifoundationalism is another name for philosophical modernity. Along with Rorty's *Consequences of Pragmatism* (1982), *Doing What Comes Naturally* is the best available guide to where we are now, to our current understanding of (in my favorite definition of philosophy) "how things, in the largest sense of the term, hang together, in the largest sense of the term." Where we are now is where we've always been—still in base camp, civilizationally speaking—but with the metaphysical mists dissolving. We've just about got rid of God, reason, freedom, dignity, and even, *pace* Nietzsche, grammar; nearly dispensed with the illusion of salvation by theory (or antitheory); and at last acknowledged the primacy (not quite the right word, since it implies a distinction—between theory and practice—that Fish deconstructs) of the practical. And having repeatedly and epistemologically demonstrated that progress requires getting down to cases, Rorty and Fish have lately begun getting down to cases—i.e., getting political.

[1]Duke Univ. Press, 1989.

For Rorty this has meant eloquent, wistful essays in the quarterlies on feminism, human rights, the responsibilities of intellectuals, and the hollowness of liberal hope. For Fish, who is about as wistful as the twelve-cylinder engine of his infamous Jaguar, it has meant barnstorming the country in campus debates with Dinesh D'Souza and browbeating William F. Buckley Jr. on *Firing Line*. *There's No Such Thing As Free Speech*[2] collects the D'Souza debates and assorted essays, reviews, and addresses. Though more topical and less focused than *Doing What Comes Naturally*, it displays the same dazzling facility—Fish's stock in trade—for making apparently solid and fundamental distinctions melt into air: e.g., direct versus indirect evidence (in contract law), original intent versus non-originalism (in constitutional law), determinate versus indeterminate, neutral versus partisan, principled versus self-interested, logical versus rhetorical, persuasion versus force, autonomy versus authority, individual versus community. The book's title and much of its salience derive from yet another, and perhaps the politically weightiest, of these deconstructive gambits: speech versus action.

What is freedom of speech for? To have no answer at all to this question is, in a democratic society, to have nothing to say for ourselves. On the other hand, any answer undermines First Amendment absolutism. The standard answers in liberal political theory and First Amendment jurisprudence are, as Fish writes: "(1) the emergence of truth as the product of public discussion, (2) the self-fulfillment of individuals, who are best served if they have access to as many views and arguments as possible, and (3) the maintenance and furtherance of democratic process, of the serious business of self-government by an informed population." Whatever one thinks of these reasons (I think they're perfectly adequate, and so, it appears, does Fish), they all presuppose—as will any other imaginable reason—that speech has consequences and that we protect and encourage speech not for its own sake (whatever that might mean), regardless of the consequences (again, an empty and incoherent notion), but for the sake of those consequences. In ethics and politics, we are all consequentialists rather than absolutists, whether we know it or not.

---

[2] *There's No Such Thing As Free Speech . . . and It's a Good Thing Too* by Stanley Fish.
    Oxford Univ. Press, 1994.

To put this argument another way: what is free speech supposed to be free from? Political and legal restrictions, presumably. But commercial fraud, libel, perjury, declaiming in a stranger's living room, and shouting "Fire!" in a crowded theater are all uncontroversially restricted forms of speech, whose boundaries are nevertheless sometimes contested. Those contests are resolved—and hence the boundaries of "free" speech are determined—legally and politically: not once and for all, through metaphysical discovery, but contingently and revisably, through democratic deliberation. And so, if free speech is conceived (as it is in much contemporary liberal and conservative rhetoric) as a pristine and protected region, founded on and defined by abstract, immutable rights, then there's no such thing as free speech.

Why is that a good thing, too? What's good is not contingency; contingency is just the way things are. What's good, at least potentially, is the recognition that ahistorical abstractions like free speech (reason, equality, merit, tolerance, etc.) are, as currently deployed by neoconservatives, a swindle. "When such words and phrases are invoked," Fish charges, "it is almost always as part of an effort to deprive moral and legal problems of their histories so that merely formal calculations can then be performed on phenomena that have been flattened out and no longer have their real-world shape." This (which is, by the way, exactly the form and function of capitalist economic theory as well) is how efforts to correct for the limitations and vulnerabilities bequeathed by a history of disadvantage come to be stigmatized as discrimination, a reaction that is analogous to maiming or poisoning a rival and then inviting him to compete with you on equal terms, or to degrading and insulting someone from birth and then being surprised that she is easily intimidated or offended. That is plainly bad faith; and that, Fish demonstrates, is what the standard, "principled" arguments against affirmative action, hate-speech codes, etc., amount to.

There are, however, nonstandard, pragmatist arguments against affirmative action, hate-speech codes, etc., and one wishes Fish had spared a little time from pulverizing Lynne Cheney, Arthur Schlesinger Jr., and Dinesh D'Souza to ponder them. "I am persuaded," he concludes, judiciously enough, "that at the present moment . . . the risk of not attending to hate speech is greater than the risk that by regulating it we will deprive ourselves of valuable voices and insights or slide down the slippery slope toward tyranny." By all means, let us attend to hate speech, but we cannot very well do that if we suppress it. Hate speech is invaluable; it is the best indicator we have of hate. And like any other pathology, hate should not merely be officially and symbolically disapproved of but rather understood and addressed—I would even say alleviated. Hate does not come from nowhere. It comes from aggrieved, resentful people who deserve, as citizens, to have their grievances and resentments considered, even if they cannot articulate them properly. The racism of economically secure whites does not issue in hate speech but in tax revolts. Hate speech is (I suspect; I have no data) more often than not the last refuge of the beleaguered.

Similarly, it is unworthy (and uncharacteristically obtuse) of Fish to equate opposition to affirmative action with bigotry and crass selfishness. He remarks offhandedly, apropos the *Miss Saigon* episode, that "in the 1990s being sensitive to the sensibilities of Asians and blacks is a higher priority than being sensitive to the sensibilities of whites, who have been, and continue to be, doing quite well in the theater and everywhere else." Actually, many of them haven't been. Moreover, whites who *are* doing quite well are (again, I'm speculating) less often hostile to affirmative action than are working-class ethnics and nonblack minorities, whose livelihoods, neighborhoods, and moral identities are anything but secure.

There is another relevant argument, not exactly against affirmative action but aslant it. The purpose of affirmative action is to change the current distribution of jobs and educational credentials, since that is what determines the distribution of status, leisure, medical care, retirement security, and most other social and individual goods. But why should the former determine the latter? There is an intrinsic connection between medical, managerial, or any other kind of skill and the supreme pleasure one may feel practicing that skill and being esteemed by fellow practitioners. But there is no intrinsic connection between practicing any kind of skill and driving a Jaguar, flying first-class, owning a summer home, having state-of-the-art consumer electronics, or sending one's children to private schools. Now let's face it: affirmative action is about spreading around Jaguars and private schools rather than spreading around the satisfactions of removing brain tumors or explicating Milton. The latter are not for everyone; and besides, usually only those with a reasonable chance of attaining them even want them. Why not, then, distribute sports cars and summer homes at random, by lot, so that cardiology, poetry, and investment banking will be practiced only by those attracted to and capable of their peculiar pleasures?

This ought to be Stanley Fish's program. Recently in the *London Review of Books*[3] there appeared an extraordinary essay, "Why Literary Criticism Is Like Virtue," in which Fish expounded, fervently and convincingly, the joys of explicating Milton. The writer of that essay would obviously have become an inspired interpreter and inspiring teacher of *Paradise Lost* even if condemned to drive a Volvo or a tricycle. Which suggests, to me at least, yet another distributive scheme: why not pay the hardest, dullest, meanest jobs the most, letting the gaudy baubles serve as consolation prizes for those who are incapable of moral or intellectual *jouissance*?

Behind these admittedly flippant questions lurk some dauntingly grave and complex ones, which Fish is exceptionally well qualified to elucidate. In *There's No Such Thing As Free Speech*, he exuberantly trounces *New Criterion*ism (and occasionally deals *Nation*ism a box on the ear). This is amusing, and it needed to be done—once. Let's hope he will now apply his cherubic wit and diabolical dialectical prowess to another "great Argument" (*Paradise Lost* I, 24): not merely deconstructing but also completing and reconciling the fragmentary, conflicting political intuitions of his earnest and confused fellow citizens.

[3]June 10, 1993.

Privilege and Its Discontents

A specter is haunting conservatism, and always has. "All we can do," wrote Burke, "and that human wisdom can do, is to provide that change shall proceed by insensible degrees." In *The Conservative Mind*, Russell Kirk expounded Burke's deepest fear: "Men's appetites are voracious and sanguinary, Burke knew; they are restrained by this collective and immemorial wisdom we call prejudice, tradition, customary morality. . . . Whenever the crust of prejudice and prescription is perforated at any point, flames shoot up from beneath, and terrible danger impends that the crack may widen, even to the annihilation of civilization. If men are discharged of reverence for ancient usage, they will treat this world, almost certainly, as if it were their private property, to be consumed for their sensual gratification; and thus they will destroy in their lust for enjoyment the property of future generations, of their own contemporaries, and indeed their very own."

In the generation after Burke's, the "crust of prejudice" was shattered, a process described in *The Communist Manifesto* in language whose rhetorical power equals—and whose tropes strikingly parallel—Burke's own. That capitalism is subversive of "prejudice, tradition, customary morality" is something thoughtful conservatives have generally understood and honest conservatives generally admitted. William F. Buckley has done neither, a failure that is at the center of gravity of his career and an important part of John Judis's new biography[1].

That the center of gravity of a life and the narrative core of a biography should coincide is more or less the definition of a successful biography. Judis just misses. Buckley's life has been so crowded, so colorful, that to do justice to the details while keeping the center properly central would have required exceptional mastery. Judis at least does justice to the details. Buckley's unusual childhood is fully, often amusingly, rendered, and the sources of his famously ferocious argumentativeness (for instance, that he adored his parents but was sixth among ten children and so had to compete for their attention) are shrewdly, though not heavy-handedly, suggested. The internal life of *National Review* over the decades—including continual skirmishing, principled and merely personal, among Willmoore Kendall, James Burnham, Whittaker Chambers, Brent Bozell, Garry Wills, George Will, and William Rusher—is a dependably interesting motif. And Buckley's gradual transformation from voice in the wilderness to celebrity generates some piquant quotes and anecdotes, like Kevin Phillip's attack on "Squire Willy and his Companions of the Oxford Unabridged Dictionary" and several episodes in his friendship with David Niven.

From the mid-1950s through the early 1970s, Buckley was not only the most visible conservative public intellectual in America, he was founder and editor of our only halfway respectable conservative journal of opinion and creator of television's most successful political talk show. He has had nearly unlimited access to, and in some cases longstanding friendships with, Goldwater, Nixon, Kissinger, Reagan, and Bush. His brother was a United States senator, and his brother's successor, Daniel Moynihan, is a friend. He launched the Young Americans for Freedom and the American Conservative Union. He ran for mayor of New York in 1965 and got more than 13 percent of the vote. He is a member of the Council on Foreign Relations and the ultra-élite Bohemian Grove. He served briefly in the CIA and became friendly with Howard Hunt, who told him the full truth about Watergate before it was known to anyone except the co-conspirators and

---

[1]*William F. Buckley: Patron Saint of the Conservatives* by John Judis. Simon and Schuster, 1988.

their lawyers. He has carried on public friendships with Norman Mailer and John Kenneth Galbraith and public feuds with Gore Vidal and Arthur Schlesinger Jr. He's written several best-selling novels whose hero (a CIA agent) seems to be modeled on himself; and his sailing memoirs are frequently excerpted in the New Yorker. Even a minimally competent biography could hardly be dull, and *Patron Saint* is more than competent.

Judis devotes a chapter and several passages to the "big book" that Buckley long projected but never finished, a theoretical work that would reformulate and extend the insights of his intellectual heroes: Oakeshott, Ortega, Voegelin. This crucial failure was surely overdetermined—by Buckley's temperament and by the contradictions of contemporary conservatism. Although Judis mentions both causes, only his discussion of the former is satisfactory. It was by no means merely the pleasures of celebrity that distracted Buckley; it was also, and chiefly, the demands of an extraordinarily full and fruitful life, "a life, as he saw it," Judis writes, "of steady, unremitting good works": three columns a week, seventy speeches and a novel each year, much occasional writing, *National Review* and *Firing Line*, fund-raising, an enormous correspondence, and a fair amount of private charity. It begs the question to suppose (and Judis does not) that all this activity served mainly to insulate Buckley from a devastating recognition of his own philosophical inadequacy. That recognition came, and was acknowledged with admirable, even affecting, grace, in *Cruising Speed*:

> ... the theoretical depth is *there*, and if I have not myself dug deep the foundations of American conservatives, at least I have advertised their profundity. How can I hope to do better against positivism than Voegelin has done? Improve on Oakeshott's analysis of rationalism? ... What does it take to *satisfy*, to satisfy *truly*, *wholly*? ... A sense of social usefulness ... How will I satisfy those who listen to me today, *tomorrow?* Hell, how will I satisfy *myself* tomorrow, satisfying ... myself so imperfectly, which is not to say insufficiently, today; at cruising speed?

He appears to have had (to coin a Buckleyesque phrase) a vocation for the quotidian. And, in all humility, to have accepted it.

But the larger project was futile, anyway. In its "theoretical depths," modern conservatism affirms values that cannot be reconciled: on the one hand, social stability, sustained by an immutable moral order and religious orthodoxy; on the other, the minimal state and the unregulated market. Competition creates new needs, which undermine old solidarities and deferences. Buckley celebrates capitalist abundance but frets over the lack of popular militancy in America vis-à-vis the welfare state and the Communist threat. It seems not to have occurred to him, or to many of his ideological comrades, to consider seriously whether these two phenomena are related. (This is perhaps the specific difference between traditionalist conservatives and neoconservatives.)

Curiously, the *National Review* colleague whom Buckley loved and admired most came very near to rubbing his nose in this insight. In December 1958 Whittaker Chambers wrote in a letter to Buckley: "I claim that capitalism is not, and by its essential nature cannot conceivably be, conservative. . . . Conservatism is alien to the very nature of capitalism, whose love of life and growth is perpetual change . . . Capitalism, whenever it seeks to become conservative in any quarter, at once settles into mere reaction." And in May 1959 (quoted in Buckley's *Odyssey of a Friend*):

> As I have said ad nauseam, I hold capitalism to be profoundly anticonservative. I have met capitalists who thought otherwise; would, in fact, be outraged by such a statement. I have concluded that they knew their craft extremely well, but not its implications; and that what they supposed to be a Conservative Position was chiefly a rationalization rooted in worry. The result is the oddest contradiction in terms. But, then, the world is full of august contradictions.

Unlike Buckley's writings, which, for all their wit and rigor, are, as Chambers gently hinted in another letter, utterly undialectical.

Buckley might have learned a similar lesson from an essay in his anthology of twentieth-century conservatism. *Did You Ever See a Dream Walking?*, despite its odd title, was a splendid achievement, certainly no less useful than Buckley's projected treatise would have been. One of the cardinal essays in this collection is Michael Oakeshott's "The Masses in Representative Democracy." (Buckley's "big book" had been tentatively entitled *The Revolt Against the Masses*.) Introducing this essay, Buckley praised Oakeshott's writings as "trenchant . . . exhilarating . . . sublime . . . the finest distillate I know of traditional conservatism" and endorsed his argument that "the discovery of the individual was the pre-eminent fact of modern European history" and "conservatism is . . . the politics of the individual."

It's remarkable that Buckley failed to notice the implications of Oakeshotts's argument. According to Oakeshott, European individuality began to emerge in the fourteenth century "as a consequence of the collapse of a closely integrated manner of living." For the first time, "men examined themselves and were not dismayed by their own lack of perfection." Gradually but inexorably, "the old certainties of belief, of occupation, and of status were being dissolved." By the middle of the sixteenth century, "not all the severity of the Calvinist *régime* in Geneva was sufficient to quell the impulse to think and behave as an independent individual. The disposition to regard a high degree of individuality in conduct and belief as the condition proper to mankind and as the main ingredient of human 'happiness'" had established itself: a "moral revolution" that appears in retrospect as "the event of supreme and seminal importance in modern European history."

Buckley's fervent and wholly orthodox Catholicism is his deepest commitment, his essential identity, as he has often made clear. Did he really not understand that Oakeshott is describing the decline of religious orthodoxy as a precondition for the emergence of individuality? In its terms and stages, Oakeshott's account virtually *is* the classical liberal account of modernity: emancipation from communal faith and customary morality, defiance of temporal and spiritual authority, the desacralization or "disenchantment" of the world. What could Buckley have supposed was meant by "the old certainties of belief" that were being "dissolved," or by Oakeshott's reference to the new individualism's "conflict with [sixteenth-century] moral sentiment, still fixed in its loyalty to the morality of communal ties"? Individualism and secularism are inseparable, are aspects of the same historical development, as orthodox churchmen from the sixteenth century to the twentieth century have recognized (and deplored), even if Buckley does not. "The Church did well to mistrust Roger Bacon," Chambers once reminded him. What did Buckley make of *that*?

Another former *National Review* colleague—Buckley's college debating partner and brother-in-law, Brent Bozell—recently argued forcefully (in the theologically conservative but politically radical Catholic journal *New Oxford Review*) that "unmitigated capitalism" means "war against the development of virtue as the goal of public life," that is, against the Catholic ideal of society. (There's currently a lively debate in conservative Catholic circles on this question, of interest even to unbelievers. Soon after Bozell's article, an editor of *New Oxford Review* chimed in: "How can the [conservative] defend tradition while ignoring one of its prime destroyers? Industrial capitalism simply cannot be squared with the values he cherishes.") The relationship between Buckley and Bozell has apparently been a complicated and poignant one, as Bozell's emotional instability drove him from conservatism to monarchism to theocracy to mental illness. Although they started out as acknowledged intellectual equals, and from virtually identical premises, Buckley's temperament and his opportunities—to perform all those "steady, unremitting good works"—have kept him clear of the various personal hells into which Bozell's unchecked dogmatism has led him. But Bozell has evidently not returned from hell with empty hands.

Commenting in 1970 on his ambivalence toward then-President Nixon, Buckley admitted: "It's always . . . more difficult to be rhetorically ruthless with somebody with whom you spend time." The same goes for the subject of a biography. It is difficult to loathe someone whose press conferences, during his campaign for mayor of New York, contained exchanges like this:

> Q.: Do you want to be Mayor, sir?
> A.: I have never considered it.
>
> Q.: Do you think you have any chance of winning?
> A.: No.
>
> Q.: How many votes do you expect to get, conservatively speaking?
> A.: Conservatively speaking, one.

Or whose column on Election Day, 1970, was a good-natured but quite persuasive defense of the early Beethoven against an intemperate critique in the previous issue of *National Review*. Or who can unexpectedly end a lengthy and bitter account of his feud with Gore Vidal with a qualified but genuine apology.

On the other hand, it is difficult not to loathe someone who can write, in *Up from Liberalism*, his most substantial philosophical defense of conservatism:

> It is a part of the conservative intuition that economic freedom is the most precious temporal freedom, for the reason that it alone gives to each one of us, in our comings and goings in our complex society, sovereignty . . .

—this in bland disregard of the familiar and extensive literature on the economic hardships, in both the United States and Europe, of industrialization under capitalist auspices, hardships mitigated only (apart from the prosperity induced by the self-destruction of America's international competitors in two world wars) by the social-welfare legislation that Buckley has devoted his career to disparaging. Or who can remark, in an interview with *Playboy* (May 1970):

> I can't think of any country that we've "dominated" or "imperialized" . . . that is worse off as a result of its experience with America than it would have been had we not entered into a temporary relationship with [i.e., invaded or subverted] it.

By 1970, the United States bore substantial responsibility for large-scale massacres in Indonesia, Guatemala, and El Salvador; for intense repression, often accompanied by torture, in Iran, Paraguay, Nicaragua, and Brazil; and for horrifying poverty in Honduras, the Dominican Republic, Haiti, and the Philippines. Buckley's apparent assumption is that preventing a government not hospitable to American economic penetration (the operative definition of Third World "communism") justifies any quantity of suffering inflicted on a country's population. This is a common enough assumption among American intellectuals, but usually implicit. It's the explicitness, the relentlessness, the enthusiasm with which Buckley has enforced this assumption that is hard to forgive.

Judis's portrait, for all its historical and psychological acuity, is not a critical biography; it does not explore the question: what, ultimately, do conservatives like Buckley seek to conserve? If one disbelieves their own answer—"traditional morality and individual freedoms"—the most plausible remaining answer is "privilege." And although that is a less restrictive, and even a less discreditable, purpose than it may sound, it is unworthy of the decent, intelligent man with whom we spend time in *Patron Saint of the Conservatives*.

Demos and Sophia: Not a Love Story

Allan Bloom's *The Closing of the American Mind*[1] has met with enormous popular, though not much critical, success. At least four major reviews—by Martha Nussbaum in the *New York Review*, Alexander Nehamas in the *London Review*, George Levine in *Raritan*, and Benjamin Barber in *Harper's*—have suggested persuasively that Bloom's understanding of classical thought is deficient, his account of modern intellectual history implausible, and his willingness or ability to argue his opinions, rather than merely announce them, no better than intermittent. In the *Times Literary Supplement*, David Rieff was less polite: *Closing*, he concluded, is "a book decent people would be ashamed of having written." But inasmuch as half a million Americans have not been ashamed to read, or at any rate buy, Bloom's book, it seems worth considering why *Closing* has spoken so compellingly, if misleadingly, to so many. Even a mediocre book may ask excellent questions.

Closing has two strains: contemporary culture criticism, based largely on Bloom's observations of college students and including a long *maledizione*

---

[1] *The Closing of the American Mind: How Higher Education Has Failed Democracy and Impoverished the Souls of Today's Students* by Allan Bloom. Simon and Schuster, 1987.

directed at the Sixties; and underlying the first, though at a great distance, a disjointed meditation on the history of political philosophy. The culture criticism, which undoubtedly accounts for most of those half-million buyers, is often shrewd, but just as often glib, even mean-spirited. Occasionally Bloom sounds like Christopher Lasch, who is, surprisingly, not mentioned in *Closing*. But Lasch is a vastly more discriminating, profound, and original critic, incapable of such simplifications as: "The bad conscience they [i.e., the "radicals in the civil rights movement"] promoted killed off the one continuing bit of popular culture—the Western [movie]" or "*All* literature up to today is sexist" or "As I have said many times and in many ways, most of the great European novelists and poets of the last two hundred years were men of the Right" or "The July 14 of the sexual revolution was really only a day between the overthrow of the Ancien Regime and the onset of the Terror." (The "Terror" is feminism.) My favorite Bloomism: "I cannot forget the Amherst freshman who asked in naïve and good-natured bewilderment, 'Should we go back to sublimation?' I was charmed by the lad's candor but could not regard him as a serious candidate for culture." This is harmless, almost engaging malice. Not so amusing are Bloom's references to "the Nietzscheanization of the American left" during the Sixties, meaning that a new existentialist discourse of "commitment," "will," and "values," allegedly displaced the traditional radical language of rights, justice, and equality. To anyone familiar with the theory and practice of participatory democracy within the New Left, or who has read its founding document, the Port Huron Statement, Bloom's notion is a half-truth, all the more irritating for his condescension toward so much honest, earnest confusion.

Still, there is much insight and even pathos in Bloom's characterization of students at elite universities, who often arrive jaded at adolescence, for whom "survivalism has taken the place of heroism as the admired quality," and who display the early, poignant effects of what Lasch has called "the narcissistic personality of our time." In particular, *Closing* contains a fine evocation of naiveté as a desirable educational disposition. Bloom points out that the capacity to be transformed by new knowledge is not a constant capacity, automatically triggered by encounters with great books, but is a fleeting and easily aborted developmental stage. Premature exposure to advanced ideas, like too-early exposure to sexual or emotional complexities, may generate defenses against hyperstimulation. The typical form of this defense is a flattening of affect, manifested at present, according to Bloom, in a too-easy tolerance, an unreflective cultural relativism—what he calls "openness" and describes ironically as "our virtue."

It is not, he acknowledges, that such openness is not valuable, but only when earned by living down one's prejudices. And prejudices presuppose myths, which enlightened educational theory proscribes. Bloom's argument about education is parallel—though he seems unaware of it—to a now-familiar psychoanalytic one: just as emotional maturity requires the mastery of illusions about an internalized omnipotent father, so intellectual maturity requires gradual emancipation from inherited political and religious myths. In both cases, eliminating these painful struggles also eliminates the possibility of depth, emotional or imaginative. Bloom's extrapolation of his observations about education to marriage and family life, contemporary literature, attitudes toward death, and practically every other aspect of present-day American culture is a little indiscriminate, even reckless. But here, too, *Closing* has its moments. For example, concluding a paragraph of otherwise simplistic anti-feminism, Bloom asks: "What substitute is there for the forms of relatedness that are dismantled in the name of the new justice?" It is clear that Bloom himself will be no help in answering this question; yet it is an urgent question, and it could hardly be formulated better.

Now, it is not obvious that the arguments considered above actually has the conservative political implications generally drawn from them—for Christopher Lasch, among others, the reverse is true. One reason for this disagreement among cultural conservatives may be methodological: while Lasch provides a subtle, synthetic account of the rise of narcissism and its relation to mature capitalism, dense with historical detail and analytic interconnections, Bloom insists that the source of the cultural relativism he deplores "is not social, political, psychological, or economic, but philosophic." Bloom himself claims, dubiously, to be not conservative but antipolitical: the root of all contemporary troubles, he contends, is our neglect or misunderstanding of the wisdom of the Greeks. Only they rightly understood "the relationship of the philosopher to the political community"; and this relationship is the really important thing, the alpha and the omega of political theory.

For Plato and Bloom, the ideal form of this relationship is straightforward enough: "Unless philosophers rule as kings, or those now called kings and chiefs

genuinely and adequately philosophize . . . there is no rest from ills for the cities
. . . nor, I think, for human kind" (*The Republic*). Since this fortunate or unfortunate condition never has been or will be realized, the responsibility of intellectuals, according to Bloom, is to look out for themselves:

> The toleration of philosophy requires its being thought to serve
> powerful elements in society without actually becoming their servant.
> The philosopher must come to terms with the deepest prejudices
> of men always, and of the men of his time. The one thing he cannot
> change and will not try to change is their fear of death and the whole
> superstructure of beliefs and institutions that make death bearable, ward
> it off or deny it. . . . Changing the character of his relationship to [other
> men] is impossible because the disproportion between him and them
> is firmly rooted in nature. . . . [I]n antiquity all philosophers had the
> same practical politics, inasmuch as none believed it feasible *or salutary*
> to change the relations between the rich and poor in a fundamental or
> permanently progressive way.
>
> (Italics added)

Neither, it appears (despite much hedging), does Bloom. It would be interesting to know whether Saul Bellow, who wrote an admiring foreword to
Closing, and Secretary of Education William Bennett, who has championed the
book, also endorse these profoundly illiberal—indeed, downright un-American—sentiments.

Epithets, however richly deserved, are not arguments. To dismiss Bloom out of
hand as elitist, authoritarian, antidemocratic, regressive, and a crank would be,
in a way, to repeat the error of our noble democratic and modernist forebears, the
citizens of fourth-century Athens. Bloom is indeed all those unpleasant things;
so was Socrates.* But by making a clever and influential, though specious, case
against popular sovereignty, they offer its defenders an opportunity to refine and
deepen the case for equality.

---

*For the sorry truth about Socrates, see I.F. Stone, *The Trial of Socrates*.

By now, if not already by the fourth century B.C., it is apparent that refinements are necessary. For modernity has not turned out altogether well. To the pioneers of Enlightenment, it appeared that false certainties and artificial hierarchies were the chief obstacles to general happiness. To many the suspicion has by now occurred that there are no true certainties and no natural hierarchies, yet also that individual and social well-being require *some* certainties, some hierarchies. The rapid increase in mobility and choice, in the sheer volume of stimuli that followed the erosion of traditional ways of life and thought, has taxed and occasionally overwhelmed nearly every modern man or woman. This no longer seems, even to the most optimistic partisans of modernity, merely a phenomenon of transition. It may be that, just as in any generation there are broad limits to physical and intellectual development, so also there are psychological limits, which likewise alter slowly. "Human nature," in short, though in an empirical rather than a metaphysical sense; not eternal and immutable, but with enough continuity—inertia, to be precise—to generate illusions of essence and a need for roots.

Bloom repeatedly invokes Nietzsche, whose lifework was a supremely effective demonstration that humankind—most of us, at any rate—cannot bear very much reality. Like Socrates, Nietzsche believed that only those who could endure complete disillusionment ought to rule. But since, like virtually every other modern thinker, he could not take Socratic/Platonic metaphysics seriously, he assumed that Socrates was motivated by spite, by resentment of aristocratic exuberance, which could dispense both with democratic solidarity and with metaphysical mysticism. To this perennial exuberance of the few, incarnated henceforth in the warrior/artist/statesmen/seer, Nietzsche ascribed political sovereignty, warning that self-rule by the unheroic, uninspired many must result in universal mediocrity. "The happiness of the last man" (a prosaic contemporary translation might be "the welfare of the average citizen") was Nietzsche's name for the goal of democratic regimes, with social tolerance, rough material equality, and other policies designed to minimize suffering and risk. But though suffering and risk may crush ordinary natures, they stimulate great natures; and the latter alone produce culture, which makes life worth living.

Equality or excellence: what sounds like the stale formulation of educational bureaucrats was an anguished dilemma for Tocqueville, Carlyle, Nietzsche, even

John Stuart Mill. If it is now no longer a live question, that is only because belief in equality has triumphed completely in the United States, has become what Bloom would call a democratic dogma, along with our near-reflexive cultural relativism. It is thus open to gadflies to gibe that the question has been buried, not answered. Apart from pointing out that (with a few glorious exceptions, like classical Athens) democracy is a rare and recent experiment, fully entitled to the benefit of doubts like Bloom's, what can a non-dogmatic democrat reply?

He or she might reply with Shelley that the moral and the aesthetic or theoretical faculties have the same source: "Poetry strengthens the faculty which is the organ of the moral nature of man, in the same manner as exercise strengthens a limb. . . . A man, to be greatly good, must imagine intensely and comprehensively; he must put himself in the place of another and of many others; the pains and pleasures of his species must become his own. The great instrument of moral good is the imagination." (*A Defense of Poetry*). A passionate democrat, Shelley would have denied the incompatibility, which Bloom assumes, between creativity and happiness as cultural imperatives, between the needs of the philosopher and the needs of the many. In this, Shelley was relying on the eighteenth-century doctrine of "sympathy": that fellow-feeling is innate, grounded (by mechanisms still imperfectly understood) in human physiology. As expounded by Ferguson, Hume, Adam Smith, and others, this doctrine seems to me true and its implications egalitarian.

But suppose Socrates, Nietzsche, and Bloom are right, and the truth about our moral psychology is less benign? Suppose that solidarity does inhibit sublimity? Democrats must face this possibility. Fortunately, one of the greatest already has. Around the time Nietzsche was writing *Thus Spoke Zarathustra*, throwing down the gauntlet to democratic humanism, Walt Whitman wrote *Democratic Vistas*, which met the challenge:

> America . . . must, for her purposes, cease to recognize a theory of character grown of feudal aristocracies, or form'd by merely literary standards, or from any ultramarine, full-dress formulas of culture, polish, caste, &c., and must sternly promulgate her own new standard, yet old enough, and accepting the old, the perennial elements, and combining them into groups, unities, appropriate to the modern, the democratic, the west, and to the practical occasions and needs of our own cities and the agricultural regions. Ever the most precious in the common.

The genius or splendor of the few may afford the rest of their society a sense of participation in infinity and immortality. But if the maturation of a people requires the sacrifice of this vicarious experience for the direct experience by the many of their own, more limited individuality, then such an exchange should—with a proper sense of the genuine loss that maturation always involves—be accepted. Growing up (remember Kant's definition of Enlightenment: "humankind's emergence from its self-imposed minority") has its compensations. Whitman describes those of democratic society with incomparable verve:

> I can conceive a community, today and here, in which, on a sufficient scale, the perfect personalities, without noise, meet; say in some pleasant western settlement or town, where a couple of hundred best men and women, of ordinary worldly status, have by luck been drawn together, with nothing extra of genius or wealth, but virtuous, chaste, industrious, cheerful, resolute, friendly, and devout. I can conceive such a community organized in running order, powers judiciously delegated—farming, building, trade, courts, mails, schools, elections, all attended to; and then the rest of life, the main thing, freely branching and blossoming in each individual, and bearing golden fruit. I can see there, in every young and old man, after his kind, and in every woman after hers, a true personality, develop'd, exercised proportionately in body, mind, and spirit. I can imagine this case as one not necessarily rare or difficult, but in buoyant accordance with the municipal and general requirements of our times. And I can realize in it the culmination of something better than any stereotyped *éclat* of history or poems. Perhaps, unsung, undramatized, unput in essays or biographies—perhaps even some such community already exists, in Ohio, Illinois, Missouri, or somewhere, practically fulfilling itself, and thus outvying, in cheapest vulgar life, all that has been hitherto shown in best ideal pictures.

And in an essay written shortly before the appearance of Bloom's book, a contemporary democrat with a sensibility that could hardly be more different from Whitman's, the incomparably subtle Richard Rorty, dotted the last i and crossed the last t:

> From Plato through Kant down to [Habermas and Derrida], most philosophers have tried to fuse sublimity and decency, to fuse social hope with knowledge of something big. . . . My own hunch is that we have

to separate individual and social reassurance, and make both sublimity and *agape* (though not tolerance) a private, optional matter. That means conceding to Nietzsche that democratic societies have no higher aim than what he called "the last men"—the people who have "their little pleasures for the day and their little pleasures for the night." But maybe we should just make that concession, and also concede that democratic societies do not embody anything, and cannot be reassured by anything, larger than themselves (e.g., by "rationality"). Such societies should not aim at the creation of a new breed of human being, or at anything less banal than evening out people's chances of getting a little pleasure out of their lives. This means that citizens of those societies who have a taste for sublimity will have to pursue it in their own time, and within the limits set by *On Liberty*. But such opportunities might be quite enough.

Plato is a peerless philosopher-poet. But Whitman is a better poet; and Rorty, though less original than Plato, is a better philosopher. Their efforts, seconding and supplementing each other (a fitting relation for democratic thinkers) can help emancipate the rest of us from Plato's and Bloom's radical doubts about our capacity for autonomy and solidarity. Bloom would "open" a few American minds by chilling a great many American hearts. Unfortunately, a great many Americans, including some very influential ones, appear to be tempted by this proposition. That is a reminder—and here is the chief value of Bloom's book—that democracy really is still an experiment.

Living By Ideas

"'Lord, enlighten thou our enemies,' should be the prayer of every true reformer," wrote Mill in his essay on Coleridge. "Sharpen their wits, give acuteness to their perceptions, and consecutiveness and clearness to their reasoning powers. We are in danger from their folly, not from their wisdom: their weakness is what fills us with apprehension, not their strength." Over the last three decades, those of us who share these sentiments have had our prayers answered in the shape of *The Public Interest, The National Interest, Commentary,* and *The New Criterion.* True, neoconservatism may have sometimes seemed to consist mainly of superficially plausible arguments for profoundly pernicious policies—a blessing we would perhaps rather do without. But for such ingratitude Mill had an answer:

> Even if a Conservative philosophy were an absurdity, it is well calculated to drive out a hundred absurdities worse than itself. Let no one think that it is nothing to accustom people to give a reason for their opinion, be the opinion ever so untenable, the reason ever so insufficient. A person accustomed to submit his fundamental tenets to the test of reason will be more open to the dictates of reason on every other point. Not from him shall we have to apprehend the owl-like dread of light, the drudge-like aversion to change, which were the characteristics of the old unreasoning race of bigots.

And anyway, not all the neoconservatives' opinions are untenable. In its crusade against the politicization of contemporary culture, the *New Criterion* is—on the whole, in the main, and not to put too fine a point on it—right. Notwithstanding the importance of legal and social equality for women, homosexuals, and members of racial minorities, most of the cultural (as opposed to political and legal) strategies employed in the service of these ends have been—again, on the whole, and with many exceptions, not always duly acknowledged by conservative critics—misguided and counterproductive. Multiculturalist pedagogy; the promotion of "cultural diversity" through arts administration, philanthropy, and public policy; academic departments of Women's Studies and Afro-American Studies; the project of "critical theory"; and in general, the greatly increased weight—in teaching and research, hiring, programming and grant-making—given to explicitly political considerations: altogether these things have done more harm than good. They have undoubtedly made possible some valuable work and attracted some people to culture who would otherwise have been lost to it. But they have also generated a staggering amount of mediocre and tendentious work. And not only do these ideological priorities make for less accomplished artists and scholars; they also make for less effective citizens. Gratuitously politicizing one's professional or artistic activity can distract from—can even serve to rationalize the avoidance of—everyday democratic activity, with all its tedium and frustration. As Richard Rorty has pointed out: "One of the contributions of the [radical-academic] left has been to enable professors, whose mild guilt about the comfort and security of their own lives once led them into extra-academic political activity, to say, 'Sorry, I gave at the office.'"[*]

This, at any rate, is my interpretation of (admittedly a very small sample of) the vast literature on the contemporary culture wars. It is a view formed in not insignificant measure by reading *The New Criterion*. Along with books and essays by Richard Bernstein, Russell Jacoby, Christopher Lasch, Diane Ravitch, Robert Hughes, David Lehman, Frederick Crews, Harold Bloom, Helen Vendler, Camille Paglia, Irving Howe, Katha Pollitt, Harold Fromm, Robert Brustein,

*Richard Rorty, "Intellectuals in Politics" (*Dissent*, Spring 1992).

and others, the magazine's steady documentation of absurdity and outrage, its chronicling of intellectual sins both grave and venial, has worn down and finally worn away my initial sympathy with the cultural program of my political comrades. Of course, excruciating firsthand experience with the writings of Edward Said, Houston Baker, bell hooks, Donna Haraway, and other leading cultural radicals has also done its part.

Against the Grain[1], forty-five selections from the *New Criterion*'s first thirteen years, is a less polemical volume than one might expect—that is, it is less than wholly polemical. Much of it is simply very good critical writing; John Simon on Nabokov, Joseph Epstein on Cavafy, Guy Davenport on Gertrude Stein, Brooke Allen on Shaw, Brad Leithauser on Housman, John Gross on Beerbohn, Samuel Lipman on Walter Gieseking, James Tuttleton on Frederick Douglas. In one of the book's more programmatic pieces, Hilton Kramer calls for a return to connoisseurship—that is, "the close, comparative study of art objects [and literary texts] with a view to determining their relative levels of aesthetic quality." It is cogent formulation, which the above-mentioned essays and others in *Against the Grain* well exemplify.

The more contentious selections are less consistently satisfying. Plenty of points are scored, but the point is sometimes missed. According to Roger Kimball, for example, Foucault was nothing more than a con man. Certainly he was a con man, but nothing more? A short chapter in Michael Walzer's *The Company of Critics* carefully and dispassionately analyzes Foucault's theory of politics, past its occasionally brilliant insights down to its fundamental incoherence. The result is no less devastating and vastly more illuminating than Kimball's hatchet job. Similarly, Gerald Graff's debatable suggestion that radicals and conservatives argue out their differences before students becomes, in James Tuttleton's account, a devious stratagem preparing the way for academic totalitarianism. The golden rule of polemics is: state your antagonist's view as persuasively as possible. This rule is frequently broken in *Against the Grain* (as well as in every issue of the *New Criterion*). Still, some pieces in this vein are undeniably fine, like

---

[1] *Against the Grain: The New Criterion on Art and Intellect at the End of the Twentieth Century*, edited by Hilton Kramer and Roger Kimball. Ivan Dee, 1995.

Kramer's fierce, gloomy, eloquent, and heartfelt vindication of traditional high culture as the proper content of undergraduate education, and a characteristically witty and penetrating address by Christopher Ricks, "What Is at Stake in the 'Battle of the Books'?"

There is an essay by Immanuel Kant (not found in *Against the Grain*) entitled "On the Old Saw: That May Be True in Theory, But It Doesn't Hold in Practice." Contrariwise, I find the *New Criterion* generally right in practice—in its judgments about "relative levels of aesthetic quality" and intellectual merit—but mistaken on what it identifies as the crucial theoretical issue in the culture wars: that is, relativism. The politicization of culture, Kramer and Kimball write, "rests on the contention that nothing is meaningful or valuable *in itself*: that everything, from literary texts and paintings to personal relations, must be understood as an interchangable token for the exercise or expression of power." They cite as the purest statement of this execrable doctrine a sentence by Stanley Fish: "There is no such thing as intrinsic merit." This, they thunder, is "a version of nihilism and a license for sophistry."

> For if there is no such thing as intrinsic merit, then no judgment of quality can be anything more than a veiled political commendation or a statement of personal partisanship. Without the idea of intrinsic moral, intellectual, and artistic value, criticism and scholarship degenerate into a species of propaganda, and morality becomes little more than a cynical calculus aimed at increasing personal advantage. *The New Criterion* takes categorical exception to such beliefs. We proceed on the conviction that there *is* such a thing as intrinsic merit, that it can be discerned and rationally argued for, and that its rejection is a prescription for moral and cultural catastrophe.

Well, then, what *is* intrinsic merit? "Intrinsic" can't mean "universally agreed upon," since no aesthetic criteria are. It can't mean "independent of inherited, unconscious, or other local determination," since no beliefs are. It can't, in short, mean supra-historical and noncontingent, since nothing whatever is. What Fish, Rorty, and other pragmatists contend is that all criteria start out equal and must be justified to those who would be affected by their adoption—that democracy, in other words, is prior to philosophy. Beyond this, as Fish never tires of pointing out, antifoundationalism has no consequences. In any case, if Kramer and Kimball believe there are objective, irrefragable, rationally demonstrable aesthetic and moral criteria, they ought by now to have offered the rest of us a fairly precise idea of what they are, or in whose writings they can be found.

They haven't, and they can't. But then, they needn't. They need only muddle along, employing and occasionally articulating the criteria that have emerged from our culture's conversation since the Greeks initiated it, and showing that what used to and still usually does underwrite our judgments about beauty and truth is inconsistent with giving Robert Mapplethorpe a one-man show, or Karen Finley a National Endowment for the Arts grant, or Toni Morrison a Nobel Prize. More than that, no one can do.

The patron saint of *The New Criterion* is Matthew Arnold; and rightly, for no one has written better about the proper relation between culture and politics. Arnold's notions of "disinterestedness" and "the free play of mind" are an excellent corrective for contemporary left-wing cultural practice. All values may be political in an ultimate, metaphysical (or rather, anti-metaphysical) sense. But that—as Fish would be the first to acknowledge—is a null, an empty sense. In the ordinary, everyday, practical sense, there are indeed nonmoral and nonpolitical values. The hunger for beauty, for perfection of form, is as organic as the hunger for justice. To subordinate one to the other, or ignore one for the sake of the other, is, as Kramer and Kimball warn, a prescription for universal mediocrity.

Quite possibly, however, if the shade of Matthew Arnold returned to preside over the contemporary debate, he would have a word or two to say to his disciples at *The New Criterion* as well. For one thing, Arnold's polemical manners were impeccable, while Kramer's and Kimball's are atrocious. He never wrote a rancorous word, and they seem never to have written a gracious one. "Sourness and light" is their critical formula, *toujours attaquer* their polemical maxim. "We have discovered," they assert, "that a more delicate phraseology is not so much conciliatory as feckless: an invitation to discount the seriousness of the issue." One can imagine Arnold's (or, for that matter, Trilling's) astonishment and disgust at this pronouncement.

For another thing, the *New Criterion*ists sometimes boast that they and not the multiculturalists are the true democrats, applying to themselves Arnold's words in *Culture and Anarchy*: "The men of culture are the true apostles of equality. [They] are those who have a passion for diffusing, for making prevail, for carrying from one end of the society to the other, the best ideas of their time." But it is a hollow boast. Arnold freely acknowledged, as Kramer and Kimball do not, the dependence of spiritual equality on at least a rough, approximate material equality. Here are a few words from *Culture and Anarchy* (with my helpful interpolations in brackets):

> Culture, or the study of perfection, leads us to conceive of no perfection as being real which is not a *general* perfection, embracing all our fellow-men with whom we have to do. . . . Individual perfection is impossible so long as the rest of mankind are not perfected along with us. . . . So all our fellow-men, in the East of London [today, the South Bronx] and elsewhere, we must take along with us in the progress towards perfection, if we ourselves really, as we profess, want to be perfect; and we must not let the worship of any fetish, any machinery, such as manufactures or population [today, "economic growth" or "national security"]—which are not, like perfection, absolute goods in themselves, though we think them so—create for us such a multitude of miserable, sunken, and ignorant human beings, that to carry them all along with us is impossible, and perforce they must for the most part be left by us in their degradation and wretchedness. But evidently the conception of free-trade [today, "freedom from government interference"], on which our Liberal [today, Republican] friends vaunt themselves and in which they think they have found the secret of national prosperity—evidently, I say, the mere unfettered pursuit of production of wealth, and the mere mechanical multiplying, for this end, of manufactures and populations threatens to create for us, if it has not created already, those vast, miserable masses of sunken people—one pauper, at the present moment, for every nineteen of us [today, one in six worldwide]—to the existence of which we are, as we have seen, absolutely forbidden to reconcile ourselves, in spite of all that the philosophy of *The Times* [today, the *Wall Street Journal*] . . . may say to persuade us.

In *Culture and Anarchy*; in "Democracy," where he argued against the anti-government party that "the action of a diligent, an impartial, and a national government . . . can really do much, by institution and regulation, to better the condition of the middle and lower classes"; and in "Equality," with its affirmation that "certainly equality will never of itself alone give us a perfect civilization. But with such inequality as ours, a perfect civilization is impossible"—in these and other passages Arnold demonstrated his humane moral imagination and democratic good faith. Kramer and Kimball have yet to demonstrate theirs.

Finally, there is the complicated matter of disinterestedness, or intellectual conscience. That both Kramer and Kimball would sooner die than fake a fact or twist a quote, I do not doubt. But disinterestedness is something larger, finer, rarer than that. To perceive as readily and pursue as energetically the difficulties of one's own position as those of one's opponents; to take pains to discover, and present fully, the genuine problems that one's opponent is, however futilely, addressing—this is disinterestedness as Arnold understood it.

Arnold thought he had found a splendid example of it in Burke who, at the close of his last attack on the French Revolution, nevertheless conceded some doubts about the wisdom of opposing to the bitter end the new spirit of the age. In "The Function of Criticism," Arnold cited this passage and commented:

> That return of Burke upon himself has always seemed to me one of the finest things in English literature, or indeed any literature. That is what I call living by ideas: when one side of a question has long had your earnest support, when all your feelings are engaged, when you hear all round you no language but one, when your party talks this language like a steam-engine and can imagine no other—still to be able to think, still to be irresistibly carried, if so it be, by the current of thought to the opposite side of the question, and, like Balaam, to be unable to speak anything "but what the Lord has put in your mouth": I know nothing more striking, and I must add that I know nothing more un-English.

I wish I could imagine someday praising Kramer and Kimball in such terms. But alas, I know nothing more un-*New Criterion*-ish.

A Ravaged History

For anyone who believed that humankind had, morally speaking, emerged from the primeval slime and now walked upright on terra firma, the twentieth century was a terrible shock. Thanks to progress in military technology and administrative practice (among other things), the production of violence, coercion, and want assumed heavy-industrial proportions. Everyone knows the main episodes: two world wars, the Armenian genocide, the Great Depression, Stalinism, Nazism, Maoism, the partition of India, the Indochina war, the Soviet-Afghan war, the Iran-Iraq war, bloodbaths in Manchuria, Indonesia, Biafra, Bangladesh, Cambodia, Central America, East Timor, Bosnia, Rwanda, Chechnya, Sierra Leone, Kurdistan. What is there to say about this catastrophic century, and who is qualified to say it?

Surely Robert Conquest is. His minor credentials include a trans-Atlantic and pan-European family background, a literary education in several languages, lengthy government service in war and peace, long friendships with Kingsley Amis, Philip Larkin, and Anthony Powell (hilariously recounted in Amis's *Memoirs*), and several books of light verse, which Amis, editor of *The New Oxford Book of Light Verse*, claimed to have found "nothing better or more congenial in the language."

Conquest's major work has been more sobering. He is perhaps the world's leading historian of Stalinism. Among his weighty and influential books (much praised and widely reprinted in post-Communist Russia) are: *The Great Terror*, *The Nation Killers*, *Kolyma: The Arctic Death Camps*, *Inside Stalin's Secret Police*, *The Harvest of Sorrow*, and nearly a dozen others. It is a body of writing that, in scope, detail, and literary power, ranks with Solzhenitsyn's.

One might have expected from this supremely civilized and accomplished man, surveying so much and such intense suffering, such demonically inventive and energetic evildoing, a tone of subdued melancholy and abashed curiosity. Surely he must acknowledge some mystery, some intractable conflict of deepest human propensities, behind the century's ravages? It can't all simply have been wickedness and delusion, can it? And one party (the author's party) can't have been wise and virtuous throughout—can't have emerged with clean hands and a clear conscience from the whole bloody epoch?

Actually, yes, in Conquest's view. The villain of his twentieth century is Ideology. "All the major troubles the world has had in our era have been caused by people who have let politics become a mania." Utopianism is our Black Plague. Conquest quotes the anti-rationalist political philosopher Michael Oakeshott to the effect that "the conjunction of dreaming and ruling generates tyranny." Those who govern should not exercise too much imagination. "Totalitarianism," according to Conquest, "can be seen as an extreme of ideological subjectivism, in which the machinery of state is primarily a means of enforcing the Ideas of the ruler or ruling group on a recalcitrant or refractory society."

The virus of ideology is spread by intellectuals who try to apply system, method, theory to human affairs, where such notions are out of place. The ambition to reform or restructure society is, at bottom, an ambition to push people around. A regime based on a theory will naturally be managed by professional theory-expounders, who will tend to regard resistance not as a phenomenon to be accommodated but as an error to be corrected—i.e., repressed. Marxism was the most common form of the ideological virus (social democracy and welfare-state liberalism are weaker strains), and the Soviet Union and its spawn were the leading examples of the "long, bitter, and murderous . . . confrontation between ideology and reality." Nationalism is a related disease, and the combination of nationalism and socialism made for a particularly deadly plague, above all in its German form.

The opposite of an ideological (or "ideocratic") culture is a civic culture. In a civic culture, voluntary associations flourish, localism and individual self-reliance are the norm, markets are unfettered, goods, labor, and ideas are mobile, laws are enforced and contracts observed, corruption is rare, government functions are limited, and centralized power is suspect. Experience, tradition, and continuity are the primary guides to political action, not ideas. The English-speaking countries (through historical accident and not, of course, racial superiority) are the chief repositories of this "culture of sanity." Burke, Tocqueville, and Oakeshott are its great exponents and, in our time, Thatcher and Reagan its exemplary practitioners.

If one is determined to draw a short and simple lesson from the twentieth century, this one is plausible enough. Revolution is indeed always and everywhere a bad idea. Stability and continuity are as vital to every social organism as to every physical one. Markets work—most of the time. Bureaucracies tend to grow and perpetuate themselves. The politicization of everything is regrettable: much better—when possible—to persuade or shame others than to sue them. Intellectuals are feckless, unworldly, resentful, and power-hungry. People who shout (or write) slogans should be politely ignored. This much of neoconservatism cannot be gainsaid.

But this is not enough for most neoconservatives, and it is nowhere near enough for Conquest. What ought to have been a somber meditation turns out to be an angry fulmination. Rather than gentle counsels of restraint we get urgent warnings against attempting much of anything. Instead of nuanced musings about the limitations of human wisdom we get scoffing rejection of the very possibility of understanding social structure and dynamics. *Reflections on a Ravaged Century*[1] is less a philosophical reflection on the human prospect and retrospect than a Tory/Republican harangue.

Nowhere is this indiscriminate partisanship more misleading than on the subject of Marxism. Conquest has no use for it whatever—it has been falsified in theory, and in practice it leads straight to the Gulag. But the latter claim is simply

---

[1] *Reflections on a Ravaged Century* by Robert Conquest. Norton, 2000.

untrue. As another historian puts it, there was "no inherent connection between the philosophy Marx developed in Berlin, Paris, Cologne, and London and the economic-political apparatus imposed upon Russia and China by revolutionary leaders primarily motivated by a resolve to seize and entrench themselves in power." Revolutionary leaders, one should add (and as Conquest acknowledges), themselves steeped in the despotic traditions of those unhappy countries.

The former claim is more complexly untrue. Conquest writes that "by the end of the nineteenth century, the Marxist predictions of a capitalist failure to expand production, of a fall in the rate of profit, a decrease in wages, of increasing proletarian impoverishment and the resulting approach of revolutionary crisis in the industrial countries had all proved false." Case closed. But Marx did not predict that all or any of these things would occur to some precise degree by some precise date. They all certainly did occur, in one form or another and to one degree or another, throughout the nineteenth century and again throughout the twentieth. Whether Marx's explanation for them is at all plausible is a question for a more dispassionate judge than Conquest. What is not in doubt, though, is that Marx's identification of the main historical tendencies of our era—the concentration of capital within and then across industries; the dwindling importance of the entrepreneur, the artisan, the small farmer, the shopkeeper, and all other instances of economic self-sufficiency; the encroachment of market relations and market logic on family life, social life, culture, and the professions; the erosion of local identities, traditions, and allegiances through the irresistible penetration of the world economy—places him among the greatest modern thinkers.

But never mind Marx. He was a genius, but even so Marxism may well prove a gigantic dead end. What is hardest to forgive Conquest, and what undermines his book's moral seriousness, is his unwillingness to play fair with the revolutionary and utopian impulses—to admit that they might have any sources except a lust for domination. That lust, it is true, eventually corrupts the most generous impulses. But what gives rise to such impulses is the fact that in (nearly) all times and places, the rich grind the faces of the poor. It may be a delusion, as Conquest repeats endlessly, to imagine that state power can ever create a just society. But one reason some people are perennially tempted to try is that private power is generally so comfortable with unjust ones.

Even the "civic," English-speaking cultures have been usefully leavened by ideology-driven agitators and unruly masses, without whose pressure the progressive income tax, universal suffrage, labor unions, the New Deal, and other moderate and pragmatic reforms might still be opposed as "premature" and "imprudent" by propertied conservative gentlemen. Conquest has scarcely a good word to say for these or any other liberal measures. His silence on this score is loud enough to make one wonder whether any democratic collective action (except self-defense against totalitarian enemies) would qualify for him as benign. If not, then he should not be surprised if the young and the disadvantaged mumble approvingly when rash intellectuals preach revolution at them.

In effect, Conquest is denying that the twentieth century was tragic. A tragedy cannot be merely sordid or merely contingent. Someone or something noble must come to grief, and his (its) essential qualities must contribute to this downfall. Conquest's century resembles instead a tale told by an idiot—a vast misfortune or a vast crime, but not the ruin of an honorable impulse and an inspiring vision. As the preeminent chronicler of twentieth-century barbarism, Conquest will (let us hope) be read forever. But we are still awaiting its interpreter.

"No, in thunder!": Christopher Lasch and the Spirit of the Age

I.

One of the bittersweet pleasures of American intellectual life over the last twenty-five years has been to follow the curious evolution of Christopher Lasch, our premier social critic. It is not, however, a widely shared pleasure. A lot of people have stopped paying attention. Lasch's comradely hectoring has long since alienated most of the left, while the right has never overcome its (well-founded) suspicion that wherever he ended up, he would remain radically anti-capitalist. His antipathy to liberalism, in both its "compassionate" and "pragmatic" versions, to feminism and other varieties of cultural radicalism, and even to the new "communitarianism," has been unflagging. By now, virtually every political and cultural tendency in recent American history has smarted under Lasch's criticism. But the breadth of his displeasure has, to some extent, blunted its sting—he is often written off as merely a scold or a grouch. "What does Christopher Lasch want?", a question once plaintively or exasperatedly posed by thousands of nonetheless admiring readers, has been heard less frequently—in my experience, at least—over the last half decade or so.

Those of us who have persevered now have our reward. *The True and Only Heaven*[1] is a landmark work of social and cultural criticism. The scope and complexity of its central argument, and the ingenuity with which a vast range of evidence is brought to bear, are phenomenal. Even if you remain, as I do, unconvinced—"unconverted" might be more appropriate—you cannot be unimpressed.

In the first phase of his career, Lasch published three collections of historical and political essays: *The New Radicalism in America* (1965), *The Agony of the American Left* (1969), and *The World of Nations* (1973). Though clearly a product of the New Left, with its attractive but unstable blend of Marxist analysis and anti-authoritarian impulse, Lasch differed from other radical historians in at least two respects. Most of them studied American foreign policy, labor movements, or slavery, while Lasch's interests were mainly cultural and psychological. And perhaps as a consequence, he had a far more ambivalent attitude toward authority. Militant, unqualified opposition may have been an adequate response to imperialism, economic exploitation, and slavery; but mass culture and the rise of "the intellectual as a social type" (the subtitle of *The New Radicalism in America*) inevitably evoked more complicated judgments and diagnoses.

By the mid-1970s, the civil rights, antiwar, and anti-poverty movements within the New Left had largely faded from public view, leaving behind only the counterculture. The personal became virtually the whole of the political. Lasch had always had reservations about the New Left's cultural politics; and as the carnival turned into a riot, his disenchantment deepened.

But instead of turning rightward, like many other disaffected intellectuals, he turned inward. Under the influence of Max Horkheimer, Theodor Adorno, and the rest of the Frankfurt School, who combined a philosophically sophisticated Marxism with psychoanalytic theory, Lasch produced three studies of "the socialization of reproduction": *Haven in a Heartless World* (1977), *The Culture of Narcissism* (1979), and *The Minimal Self* (1984). He tried to show that the pressures of competition and commodification had gradually transformed education, medicine, psychotherapy, social work, entertainment, journalism, and

[1]*The True and Only Heaven: Progress and Its Critics* by Christopher Lasch. Norton, 1991.

even scholarship, into agencies for the formation of a specific character type, one which fit the requirements of twentieth-century capitalism. This character type—"the narcissistic personality of our time"—is morally pliant, emotionally and aesthetically voracious, and ingratiating but wary of intimate, permanent relationships, in contrast with its nineteenth-century "bourgeois" predecessor, which was rigid, self-righteous, austere. To simplify: the bourgeois character suited a culture of production; the narcissistic character, a culture of consumption. These two types, in more general form, as the "ethos of production" and the "ethos of consumption," are the twin suns around which Lasch's conceptual system revolves in *The True and Only Heaven*.

II.

The ur-text of modernity, by Lasch's account, is Adam Smith's argument in *The Wealth of Nations* that the creation and satisfaction of new needs in the course of economic development is a process potentially without limit. From this claim flows nearly every belief and value at the core of the modern outlook: the primacy of efficiency and economic growth, the perception of nature as resource, the ethical priority of individual welfare, the definition of the good life in terms of leisure and abundance, and most important, the image of history as continuous moral and material progress, made possible by the spread of scientific and social rationality. This is the worldview of the Enlightenment, Marx's no less than Adam Smith's. The quarrel between democratic socialism and liberal capitalism is not over whether these values should be realized, but how.

Adam Smith's originality lay in grasping the implications of what was then a relatively new development: the division of labor. So persuasively did he argue its advantages that it came to be considered, along with secularization, the sovereignty of the individual, and the scientific revolution, one of the essential preconditions of modernity, a cornerstone in the ideology of progress. True, the costs of progress were soon enough evident. Secularization frequently threatened psychic stability and morale. Enhanced individual freedom meant diminished social cohesion and solidarity. The predominance of science diverted imaginative energies from non-quantifiable forms of inquiry and expression, and made possible a purely instrumental view of the natural (eventually also the human) world. But for all these ills the defenders of modernity had a plausible diagnosis: growing pains. As Kant remarked on the French Revolution: one learns to exercise freedom by exercising it, and in no other way.

The disadvantages of the division of labor (about which Smith was candid, even eloquent, unlike subsequent champions of capitalism) were famously summed up by Marx in a single word: alienation. The division of labor meant the concentration of production, and this meant the loss of economic autonomy, of the freedom to work where one lived, to choose one's own materials, style, rhythms, and perhaps most important, one's customers, if any. Wage labor meant forced mobility, the decay of local communities and loyalties, monotonous and unhealthy work, and economic vulnerability. All of which Marx (like all subsequent champions of socialism) accepted as a necessary evil. Through the sheer immensity of its wealth-creating powers, mass production would at length bring into being a population capable of rationalizing and humanizing it. As with other historic innovations, so too with this one: through many trials, tears, and woes, Progress will lead us home.

III.

I hope this description of the modern weltanschauung sounds banal. It's meant to. However inchoately, the ideology of progress is as obvious to most of us as the shape of the earth. Whether radical, liberal, or conservative, we would no more think of denying the necessity of industrialism or the eventual triumph of reason and science over traditional dogma and local prejudice than the desirability of a rising standard of living or the right of everyone to plan her own life. Wars, depressions, and other typical twentieth-century disasters may retard progress but cannot ultimately reverse it. Even what is to count, fundamentally, as progress— a fuller, freer (i.e., more mobile and abundant, leisured and cultivated) life for ever more individuals—is generally agreed on.

To all this, the spirit of the age, Lasch replies (like Thomas Carlyle, one of the heroes of *The True and Only Heaven*), "No, in thunder!" Modernity is a mistake. Progressive ideology in all its aspects—optimism, individualism, rationalism, humanitarianism, internationalism, efficiency, growth, centralization—rests on a misunderstanding of history and human nature. Of course no single book, however ambitious, could fully argue such a claim. So diffuse and pervasive is the progressive outlook that merely to articulate it is an achievement. But Lasch's critique cuts deep.

It is, first of all, historical. According to progressivism, capitalist development created an increasingly educated, militant, unified working class, whose challenge to wage labor and private ownership of the economy became more and more radical. The Russian Revolution derailed (or fulfilled, depending on one's viewpoint) this socialist dynamic, which is currently in historical limbo. But whatever radical opposition to capitalism there's been has come from industrial workers, together with a few professionals and intellectuals, and has been oriented to the future—to the fulfillment of capitalism's stunted potential by new, non-capitalist institutions.

Wrong, Lasch counters. The working class and its socialist or social democratic leaders have fought hard, but never over fundamentals. The only challenge to capitalism per se—to wage labor, the factory system, and the concentration of credit—came from movements of independent small producers threatened with extinction: farmers, craftsmen, shopkeepers, and others usually disparaged by Marxists as politically naive or reactionary "populists." Socialist struggles were about wages and working hours; only the "reactionary" populists, rooted in a vanishing way of life, raised questions about self-management, the effect of work on the worker, or the control of investment.

The historical scholarship of the last two decades supports this claim of Lasch's, along with another: that the political philosophy of the American Revolution was not Lockean liberalism or "possessive individualism," i.e., an ideological precursor of liberal capitalism, but an older, "republican" philosophy of civic virtue. The Revolution was less about property rights than about citizenship. And once again, it was small producers and proprietors who were the main bearers of this ideology and the source of the most effective and radical opposition.

These historical reinterpretations lead on toward a deeper moral and psychological revisionism. The ideology of progress assumes that maturation involves moving away from narrow and particular affections toward abstract and universal ones. Family, ethnic, regional, and religious loyalties are something we supposed to grow out of, or at least subsume in a wider sympathy. When such loyalties are exclusive, we call them "chauvinistic" or "fanatical"; and we usually assume that the more intense one of these particularistic commitments is, the more likely it is to be dangerously exclusive.

For Lasch, this devaluation of the local and traditional is a radical error. It is not enlightenment but memory, not breadth of sympathy but intensity of identification, that makes for inner strength. In *The Culture of Narcissism* and *The Minimal Self,* Lasch argued that to achieve secure selfhood an infant must experience love and discipline from the same source; otherwise the child, and eventually the adult, will feel for everyone in authority the same combination of rage and terror that the infant feels for whomever it depends on. And more: he showed that it was the advent of wage labor and mass production, which removed the father's work from the child's experience, thereby drastically altering his role in the child's psychic development, that has produced the characteristic neurosis of our time, along with a culture of consumption.

In *The True and Only Heaven* he takes a further step. What does it mean, he asks, that the democratic movement of the eighteenth century and the anti-capitalist movement of the nineteenth, like the civil rights movement of the 1960s, were wrought not by the "universal class" of Marxist theory, not by enlightened rationalists liberated from local attachments and traditional beliefs, but by people very much committed to such attachments and beliefs, people loyal to the "archaic" creeds, crafts, and communities under attack from the forces of "progress"? Not, that is, by people looking toward the future, but by people looking toward the past?

It means, he answers, that "the victory of the Enlightenment," with its unwillingness to accept limits on human aspiration and its promise that in a rational society the traditional virtues would be obsolete, "has almost eradicated the capacity for ardor, devotion, and joyous action." On moral even more than environmental grounds, "the basic premise of progressive thought—the assumption that economic abundance comes before everything else, which leads unavoidably to an acceptance of centralized production and administration as the only way to achieve it—needs to be rejected." Not rational optimism but supra-rational hope is true wisdom and succor:

> Popular initiative . . . has been declining for some time—in part because the democratization of consumption is an insufficiently demanding ideal, which fails to call up the moral energy necessary to sustain popular movements in the face of adversity. The history of popular movements

... shows that only an arduous, even a tragic, understanding of life can justify the sacrifices imposed on those who seek to challenge the status quo. The idea of progress alone, we are told, can move men and women to sacrifice immediate pleasures to some larger purpose. On the contrary, progressive ideology weakens the spirit of sacrifice. . . . Hope does not demand a belief in progress. . . . Hope implies a deep-seated trust in life that appears absurd to those who lack it. It rests on confidence not so much in the future as in the past. It derives from early memories in which the experience of order and contentment was so intense that subsequent disillusionments cannot dislodge it. Such experience leaves as its residue the unshakable conviction, not that the past was better than the present, but that trust is never completely misplaced, even though it is never completely justified either . . .

IV.

These passages probably make clear why it has proved so easy to dismiss, even ridicule, *The True and Only Heaven*. Scorn for an errant people, its rulers, and its false gods, and stern insistence on a complete change of heart and mind—this is the tone of a prophet. In fact, Lasch does declare his allegiance (or seems to) to "the tradition of Judeo-Christian prophecy." The "heart" of that tradition is belief in

the power and majesty of the sovereign creator of life; the inescapability of evil in the form of natural limits on human freedom; the sinfulness of man's rebellion against those limits; the moral value of work, which at once signifies man's submission to necessity and enables him to transcend it.

This "tragic understanding of life" Lasch also finds, more or less secularized, in the thought of Carlyle, Emerson, Orestes Brownson, William James, Georges Sorel, and Reinhold Niebuhr, as well as in eighteenth-century republicanism, nineteenth-century populism, and the Southern black culture from which Martin Luther King emerged. Lasch's reconstruction of this sensibility, the "ethos of the small producer," proceeds in step with, and as a kind of counterpoint to, his critique of progressivism and its ethos of abundance. As intellectual and social history, it is a tour de force.

Lasch is of course less interested in historiographical virtuosity than in civic virtue. He wants his critique and reconstruction to contribute to the transformation—he would probably say "redemption" or "conversion"—of our culture. But toward what? Populism "has generated very little in the way of an economic or political theory," he admits. "Its advocates call for small-scale production and political decentralization, but they do not explain how these objectives can be achieved in a modern economy."

Neither has anyone else, so populists should not be faulted too harshly. There is, though, another, more plausible objection to Lasch's radical anti-modernism. At one point he attributes William James's chronic ambivalence about modernity to "the difficulty of carrying on an essentially theological controversy without its theological context." But surely this is Lasch's difficulty, too? Or does he propose to resurrect "the theological context"—the existence of God, the freedom of the will, the immortality of the soul? The Covenant and the Incarnation? Must we believe in order to be saved? If so, then we are lost. We cannot believe the unbelievable, even to salvage our culture.

V.

Critics have complained, and readers will demur, over the length of *The True and Only Heaven*. But the change to small-scale production and political decentralization is so drastic, so urgent, and so unlikely that the case needs to be made decisively. It is hard to imagine a more rigorous and comprehensive argument than Lasch has made in the last two and a half decades. Even so, he will probably remain, like other critic-prophets, a voice crying in the wilderness.

Throughout history, the pain of everyday life has elicited a promise of happiness: first of Paradise, then of Progress. To have shown that Paradise is a myth, that supernatural religion is the opium of the people, is the enduring legacy of the Enlightenment. To show that Progress is a myth, that historical optimism is the opium of the intellectuals, is the aim of the Enlightenment's critics. About which a chronically ambivalent modern reviewer might say that these critics, from Carlyle and Emerson to James to Niebuhr to Lasch, have in a sense carried on the Enlightenment's own work: opposing the displacement of our hopes and the distancing of our fulfillment, forcing humanity's attention back to the limits and glories of our un-ideal world, reminding us that the kingdom of heaven is within.

A Whole World of Heroes

"The history of modern society, from one point of view," Christopher Lasch observed in *Haven in a Heartless World* (1977), "is the assertion of social control over activities once left to individuals and their families." This, at any rate, is the point of view from which Lasch constructed his ambitious and provocative critique of American society. From another point of view, of course, modernity is identified with, even defined by, the rise of individualism: economic, political, and ethical. The latter perspective is the once and probably still dominant ideology of progress: of history as the story of freedom, as a narrative of individual emancipation from the trammels of communal prescription and superstition.

Whether these two points of view are antagonistic or complementary is not clear, to me at least. It may be that individual freedom and social control have, in different areas or aspects of experience, simply grown up side by side; or that they are intimately and paradoxically (that is to say, dialectically) related. Typically the left has endorsed and the right opposed individualism in the progressive or Enlightenment sense, which denotes the lessened authority of traditional beliefs and practices. But what are the political implications of non-traditionalist anti-modernism—Lasch's brand?

Lasch himself offered little help in answering that question; he was notoriously, exasperatingly wary of programmatic statement and ideological self-definition. He did, for what it's worth, affirm in response to critics (albeit fifteen years before his death):

> Once and for all: I have no wish to return to the past, even if I thought a return to the past was possible. The solution to our social problems lies in a completion of the democratic movement inaugurated in the eighteenth century, not in a retreat to a pre-democratic way of life. Socialism, notwithstanding the horrors committed in its name, still represents the legitimate heir of liberal democracy. Marxism and psychoanalysis still offer the best guides to an understanding of modern society and to political action designed to make it more democratic.

In his last decade, Lasch's alarm and disgust deepened, his tone soured, and his allegiance to socialism faltered. But although his complaints about contemporary society sometimes sounded like the neoconservatives', their origin and import was radically different. To see why—to reconstruct Lasch's intricate and wide-ranging cultural critique and connect it with the neo-populism of *The Revolt of the Elites*—will require a lengthy detour through the labyrinth of psychoanalytic theory.

According to Freud, a newborn infant cannot distinguish between itself and the rest of the world, and therefore between the source of its needs (its own body) and the source of its gratifications (other people, especially its mother). Hence its first mental experience is a sense of omnipotence. Inevitably, some of its needs go unmet, at which time it becomes aware, more or less traumatically, of its separation from the rest of the world. It reacts with rage against the source of its frustration (its parents), but since the source of its frustration is also the source of its gratification and the sole guarantee of its continued existence, the infant cannot tolerate its own impulses of rage and aggression, which would, if realized, annihilate it along with its parents.

This dilemma is unique in the animal world, since only humans are so helpless for so long after birth. The infant's response is fateful—indeed, virtually defines the human condition. The infant represses its rage. But repressed emotions always return. The infant's rage is converted into a variety of fantasies: the fantasy of primal union, in which the irreversibility of separation and dependence is denied; the idealization of the parents, which denies that the parents sometimes frustrate the child and also that it wishes to punish them in return; and the splitting of parental images into all-good and all-bad, which denies the incomprehensible discovery that gratification and frustration come from the same source.

These fantasies have one crucial thing in common: they are all outsized, out of scale. The infant is pictured as either omnipotent or helplessly persecuted, the parents as either perfectly benevolent or implacably threatening. And the fundamental truth of the infant's situation—its separation from and dependence on the rest of the world—arouses alternating panic and denial.

According to psychoanalytic theory, the repression of infantile rage and the fantasies that result are universal and unavoidable. It is what happens thereafter that determines the degree of the child's—and adult's—maturity or pathology. What must occur, if emotional health is to be achieved, is a gradual scaling down of the superhuman size that the parents have assumed in the infant's fantasies, as well as a gradual softening and displacement ("sublimation") of the intense, overwhelming feelings they have called forth. How?

In Lasch's account, there are several ways. First, through the child's continual experience of love and discipline from the same source, i.e., its parents. The actual experience of discipline—of limited but not token punishment—slowly breaks down the archaic fantasy that the parents' displeasure means the infant's annihilation. Next, through what Lasch called "optimal frustrations." In sharp contrast to the awkward and excessive solicitude of the contemporary over-anxious mother, the instinctive confidence of a woman immersed in a kin community or "biological stream" allows the child to experience simultaneously the lessening of its mother's attentions and its own modest, growing mastery of its immediate environment. Then there is the child's encounter with what Lasch (following the British psychoanalyst D.W. Winnicott) called "transitional objects": playthings, games, and other objects and activities that symbolically express unconscious attachments but at the same time provide the child with reliable links to a stable, comprehensible external world. And finally, there is everyday contact with the father, whom infants of both sexes formerly envied, hated, and feared because of his superior access to the nurturing mother. When the child is part of the father's work environment, it observes two things: first, that he is fallible; and second, that he possesses important and satisfying skills, which he is able and willing to pass on to the child, thus earning its gratitude. Both insights help reduce him to human size in the child's psyche.

To the extent that these several experiences occur, the child can overcome its archaic terror at the discovery of its separateness from the world as well as its unconscious fear and hatred of those who forced this discovery upon it. It can also abandon its chief defense against those feelings: the fantasy of overcoming separateness and regaining primal, undifferentiated union with the world. In other words, it can become a self, distinct from others and comfortable with the distinction. It can grow up.

But if these maturational experiences do not occur, no secure self emerges. The growing child's unconscious mental life is still haunted by boundless rage over infantile helplessness, by the fear of parental retaliation that this rage induces, by the simultaneous idealization and demonization of the parents, and by the infant's only available defense against these impulses and fears: the fantasy of a return to oneness and omnipotence.

The result is a neurotic adult. Neurotic, Lasch asserted, in specific and predictable ways: wary of intimate, permanent relationships, which entail dependence and thus may trigger infantile rage; beset by feelings of inner emptiness and unease, and therefore ravenous for admiration and emotional or sexual conquest; preoccupied with personal "growth" and the consumption of novel sensations; prone to alternating self-images of grandiosity and abjection; liable to feel toward everyone in authority the same combination of rage and terror that the infant feels for whomever it depends on; unable to identify emotionally with past and future generations and therefore unable to accept the prospect of aging, decay, and death. This constellation of symptoms is known within psychoanalytic theory as narcissism: the lack of an autonomous, well-defined self. It is currently, as Lasch claimed and the clinical literature attests, the most common form of emotional pathology—the neurotic personality of our time.

It was not always so. The neurotic personality of Freud's time was quite different—acquisitive, fanatically industrious, self-righteous, sexually repressed. Then the typical symptom was obsessional (an inexplicable compulsion, e.g., incessant handwashing) or hysterical (chronic excitability or, conversely, nonsomatic paralysis of a limb or faculty, e.g., frigidity). These symptoms stood out in sharp relief against the background of a stable personality, something like a "bug" in an otherwise well-functioning computer program. To simplify for the sake of contrast: the Victorian/Viennese neurosis was localized and discrete;

contemporary narcissism is systemic and diffuse. To simplify even more dramatically: the character of selfhood has changed, from a strong (often rigid) self, in secure possession of fundamental values but riddled (often crippled) with specific anxieties, to a weak, beleaguered self, often full of charms and wiles, and capable, but only fitfully, of flights of idealism and imagination.

Why? What can account for this subtle but immensely significant shift? Lasch formulated an answer in *Haven in a Heartless World* (1977), *The Culture of Narcissism* (1978), and *The Minimal Self* (1984). He posited a connection between two of the deepest, broadest phenomena of modern history: the change in personality described above, and the change from early, developing capitalism (relatively small-scale, still permeated with pre-industrial values and work practices, and largely concerned with expanding production to satisfy basic needs) to mature capitalism (dominated by huge, bureaucratic organizations, "rationalized" by the reduction of workers' initiative, autonomy, and skills, and concerned with expanding consumption through the creation of new needs). Modernization, according to Lasch, is the introduction of new, parallel forms of domination into work life and family life. In a sweeping but closely argued passage he makes the central link in his complex argument:

> The socialization of reproduction completed the process begun by the socialization of production itself—that is, by industrialization. Having expropriated the worker's tools and concentrated production in the factory, industrialists in the opening decades of the twentieth century proceeded to expropriate the worker's technical knowledge. By means of "scientific management," they broke down production into its component parts, assigned a specific function on the assembly line to each worker, and kept to themselves the knowledge of the productive process as a whole. In order to administer this knowledge, they created a vastly enlarged managerial apparatus, an army of engineers, technicians, personnel managers, and industrial psychologists drawn from the same pool of technical experts that simultaneously staffed the "helping professions." Knowledge became an industry in its own right, while the worker, deprived of the craft knowledge by which he had retained practical control of production even after the introduction of the factory system, sank into passive dependence. Eventually, industry organized management itself along industrial lines, splitting up the production of knowledge into routinized operations carried on by semiskilled

clerical labor: secretaries, typists, computer card punchers, and other lackeys. The socialization of production—under the control of private industry—proletarianized the labor force in the same way that the socialization of reproduction proletarianized parenthood, by making parents unable to provide for their own needs without the supervision of trained experts.

How does industrialization produce a culture of narcissism? Lasch argued that the evolution of capitalism has affected family structure and the socialization of children in a number of ways. In reorganizing the production process, it has removed the father from the child's everyday experience and deprived him of the skills that formerly evoked the child's emulation and gratitude. This means that the child's archaic, punitive fantasies about the father persist unchecked. In encouraging geographic mobility, it has uprooted families from kin communities and replaced intergenerationally transmitted folk wisdom about child rearing with social-scientific expertise dispensed by professionals. This undermines parental confidence and replaces face-to-face authority over the child with the impersonal, bureaucratic authority of schools, courts, social-welfare agencies, and psychiatrists. In promoting mass consumption, advertisers (like social-science professionals) have convinced parents that their children are entitled to the best of everything but that, without expert assistance, parents are helpless to determine what that might be. In generating a mass culture glutted with rapidly obsolescing commodities and transient images, it blurs the distinction between reality and illusion and renders the world of objects unstable and bewildering. This makes it difficult for the child to locate "transitional objects" that would help it find its way from infantile attachments into the external world of culture and work. And in promising an endless supply of technological marvels, it evokes grandiose fantasies of absolute self-sufficiency and unlimited mastery of the environment, even while the quasi-magical force that conjures up those marvels— i.e., science—becomes ever more remote from the comprehension or control of ordinary citizens. This is a recipe for regression to psychic infancy: fantasies of omnipotence alternating with terrified helplessness.

One of the prime tenets of psychoanalysis is that pathology and normality are not sharply demarcated but continuous. So these secular developments—the sundering of love and discipline in the child's experience, the invasion of family life and work life by professional and corporate elites, the blurring of distinctions by mass culture—not only produce more narcissistic individuals than formerly but also create a new psychic environment. A world populated by rigid selves is a world of sublimation and its derivatives: aggression, greed, cruelty, hypocrisy, unquestioning adherence to inherited values and restraints. A world of weak selves is more fluid, corruptible, blandly manipulative, sexually easygoing, un-comfortable with anger and rivalry, and leery of defining constraints, whether in the form of traditional values or future commitments. The distinction between the early capitalist self and the late capitalist self is, roughly, the distinction be-tween Prometheus and Narcissus, the Puritan and the swinger, the entrepre-neur and the corporate gamesman, the imperial self and the minimal self. That these distinctions bespeak profound change is obvious; that they represent prog-ress is less so.

For Lasch, then, modernization was not the solution but a new form of the problem—the problem, that is, of domination. This belief was the source of his longstanding quarrel with his fellow socialists and feminists. Much, perhaps most, of the left has always been convinced that industrialization, technological development, and the erosion of traditional forms of authority are intrinsically progressive. Modernization has had its costs, admittedly, but the answer to the problems of modernity was usually held to be more of the same, preferably under democratic auspices. In socialism's glorious youth, Marx called for "a ruthless criticism of everything existing"; few of his successors doubted that the decline of Christianity, patriarchy, possessive individualism, and everything else existing would be followed directly by something better. But, Lasch argued, these things have by and large declined; the result is not a radical extension of political and sexual autonomy but rather a bureaucratically mediated war of all against all.

Lasch's most intimate and intense disagreements were with cultural rad-icals: critics of education, sports, religion, sexuality, the family, and the work ethic, and proponents of a new, "liberated" ideal of expressiveness and self-re-alization. What these radicals ignore, Lasch charged, is that Christianity, com-petitive individualism, and the patriarchal family are already obsolescent, at least in those social strata where modernization is most advanced. These values and institutions have been undermined not by leftist opposition but by capital-ists themselves, for their own purposes: to promote mass consumption and to regiment the work process. By espousing an ideal of personal liberation largely confined to leisure time and heavily dependent on the consumption of goods and services, cultural radicals have conceded defeat. Instead of adapting to industrialization and mass culture, Lasch contended, the left should oppose them. Only a change to human scale—to local, decentralized control in workplaces, communities, and families—can halt the spread of commodity relations and the bureaucratization of the self.

But what, if anything, can motivate so drastic a reversal of the direction of modern history? *The True and Only Heaven* (1991), Lasch's *chef d'oeuvre*, addressed this question.* In that book Lasch opposed the philosophy of "progress" to the tradition of "virtue," a universalistic moral psychology to a particularist one, the "ethos of abundance" to the "ethos of the producer." It was the latter, he argued—the ethos of the artisan, the small proprietor, the yeoman farmer; of civic virtue, civic equality, and a broad diffusion of wealth, culture, and competence—that sustained the "moral economy"—the character, worldview, and social relations—that mass production and political centralization have decisively undermined. "The history of popular movements," he concluded, "shows that only an arduous, even a tragic understanding of life can justify the sacrifice imposed on those who seek to challenge the status quo."

To the majestic edifice of argument in his previous books, *The Revolt of the Elites*[1] adds numerous elegant flourishes, though no new structural features. Lasch's death last year at sixty-one was, in the obvious sense, sadly premature; in another sense, this posthumous collection nicely rounds off his oeuvre. Forcefully written, erudite, and topical, it achieves a public voice, while those who have followed Lasch's long and complex intellectual development will be glad of a few more clues to what, in the end, his thought comes to politically.

The title essay and its companion, "Opportunity in the Promised Land," are a critique of two pillars of progressive ideology: meritocracy and social mobility. Though frequently considered essential features of a democratic society, they are best understood, Lasch argues, as an efficient method of elite recruitment and

*See the preceding essay in this volume, "No! in thunder."
[1] *The Revolt of the Elites and the Betrayal of Democracy* by Christopher Lasch. Norton, 1995.

legitimation. Meritocratic elites, he points out, are in some ways even less publicly accountable than hereditary ones. The latter usually had local roots and loyalties, and their caste ideology emphasized civic responsibility and *noblesse oblige*. Even more important, their superiority was obviously, savingly arbitrary. They were therefore far less prone to the pernicious delusion—which Lasch, drawing on the work of Robert Reich and Mickey Kaus, shows is alarmingly prevalent among the newer managerial/cognitive elites—that they deserved their relative immunity from social ills.

A high degree of upward mobility is in fact quite compatible with sharp social stratification. Nor does it have much historical connection with democracy in the United States. That anyone with enough energy, talent, cunning, and ambition could become President, or become rich, or otherwise escape the common lot is not at all what most eighteenth- and nineteenth-century Americans meant by democracy. What "defined a democratic society, as Americans saw it, [was] not the chance to rise in the social scale so much as the complete absence of a scale that clearly distinguished commoners from gentlemen." The egalitarianism that so profoundly impressed generations of European visitors derived "not merely from the distribution of wealth or economic opportunity but, above all, from the distribution of intelligence and competence."

> Citizenship appeared to have given even the humbler members of society access to the knowledge and cultivation elsewhere reserved for the privileged classes. Opportunity, as many Americans understood it, was a matter more of intellectual than of material enrichment. It was their restless curiosity, their skeptical and iconoclastic turn of mind, their resourcefulness and self-reliance, their capacity for invention and improvisation that most dramatically seemed to differentiate the laboring classes in America from their European counterparts.

Readers who are not professional historians may wonder whether this is an idealized portrait, though enough evidence is included in *The True and Only Heaven* and *The Revolt of the Elites* to place the burden of proof on those who would reject it. If it is even approximately accurate, it argues powerfully for Lasch's contention that we can aim either at maximum economic efficiency (conventionally defined) or robust democracy, but not at both.

Lasch's dissatisfaction with present-day political culture is intense and comprehensive. It extends to the supplanting of neighborhoods by networks and "lifestyle enclaves"; of public parks, cafes, taverns, general stores, community centers, and other informal gathering places that "promote general conversation across class lines" by shopping malls, health clubs, and fast-food chains; of schooling based on patriotic myths and stories of heroic virtue by a sanitized, ideologically innocuous curriculum "so bland that it puts children to sleep instead of awakening feelings of awe and wonder"; of the torchlight parades and oratorical eloquence, the impassioned debates before vast audiences, the scrappy, partisan newspapers and high voter turnout associated with nineteenth-century politics by the apathy and gullibility of the contemporary electorate and the intellectual and moral poverty of contemporary political speech. Of course, lots of people complain about such things. But without a plausible account of their origins, that sort of complaint merely exasperates and demoralizes. It is just because Lasch convincingly connects these phenomena with the rationalizing imperatives of the market and the state that, even though the latter seem all but irresistible, his criticism energizes.

Lots of people talk about "virtue," too. The preaching of virtue to the poor and beleaguered by such court philosophers as William Bennett, Gertrude Himmelfarb, and George Will has unfortunately done much to discredit the word among the friends of equality. Lasch's conception strikes a better balance than theirs between self-denial and self-assertion. It includes an emphatic lack of deference toward wealth, office, and professional credentials; contempt for luxury and greed; a strong preference for economic independence and for face-to-face relations in business and government; a sense of place; a lively curiosity about science, art, and philosophy; and perhaps most of all, a passion for vigorous debate and splendid rhetoric. A lot more, in short, than diligence and chastity, which seems to be mainly what the neoconservatives have in mind. Lasch's notion of virtue is strenuous and classical; his ideal of a democratic society is, in a magnificent phrase of Carlyle's that he quoted often, "a whole world of heroes."

A whole world of heroes—this ideal has at least two radical implications. The first is that democracy requires a rough equality of condition. Dignity and virtue cannot survive indefinitely amid extremes of wealth and poverty; only someone with a paltry conception of virtue could believe otherwise. The second is that the democratic character can only flourish in a society constructed to human scale. Just as modern war has made military valor more or less superfluous, a world dominated by large corporations and bureaucracies offers little scope for the exercise of civic virtue; nor even, in the long run, for psychic autonomy and integrity—i.e., for selfhood, as we currently understand it.

It may very well be, as Lasch recognized, that these and other prerequisites of full, rather than merely formal, democracy cannot be reestablished. The "assertion of social control" that Lasch identified as the thrust of modern history may not be reversible. It certainly will not be reversed unless more people begin to think as passionately, rigorously, and imaginatively about democracy as Christopher Lasch—and very few others in our time—have done.

Requiem for the Enlightenment

From time immemorial the prime agency of individual and social reproduction has been inertia, the biological form of which is instinct and the cultural form, tradition. That is to say, things were done because they had been done before—an efficient, though not infallible, way to achieve organismic and societal stability. Modernity is, in one of its numerous definitions, the progressive attenuation of inertia by consciousness. Where tradition was, there shall reason be.

In the classical account, science, democracy, market relations, and ethical individualism were born and grew up together, the offspring of modernity. The first modern generations looked upon what these phenomena had wrought, pronounced them good, and called for their indefinite continuation and extension. But subsequent developments have not been altogether satisfactory, notably environmental spoliation, advanced weaponry, totalitarian social organization, the destruction of peasant societies and folk cultures, widespread anomie, and an altered rhythm of daily life that has arguably produced toxic levels of stress and epidemic psychopathology. Many writers, from Pascal to Lasch, have rehearsed these ills and proposed that modernity be reconsidered. *Enlightenment's Wake*[1],

[1]*Enlightenment's Wake: Politics and Culture at the Close of the Modern Age* by John Gray. Routledge, 1995.

a collection of recent writings by English political philosopher John Gray, takes its place in this antimodernist tradition.

Gray defines the Enlightenment project as a combination of rationalism, or the criticism and reconstruction of morality and politics by means of reason alone; universalism, or the supercession of fundamental cultural differences, which will eventually dwindle and disappear; humanism, or the technological subjugation of nature for human purposes; and scientism, the neglect or disparagement of informal, tacit knowledge. Each of these beliefs and hopes is, he argues, an illusion. Reason cannot resolve fundamental conflicts among values. It cannot define a universal human identity, or specify a universally valid set of rights, or formalize all local knowledge. Following Michael Oakeshott and Isaiah Berlin, Gray maintains that rights and values are frequently incompatible, even incommensurable. Our identities are inherited rather than created, the product of contingency and circumstance rather than choice. Much of our knowledge is embedded in traditions, in whole ways of life, and cannot be judged or even understood apart from them. This pluralism, powerfully and insistently stated, frames Gray's historical and political arguments. In particular, it motivates his rejection of contemporary liberalism, especially the Rawlsian, rights-based variety predominant in the United States. Because political philosophy in the Anglo-American mode remains for the most part animated by the hopes of the Enlightenment, above all by the hope that human beings will shed their traditional allegiances and their local identities and unite in a universal civilization grounded in generic humanity and a rational morality, it cannot even begin to grapple with the political dilemmas of an age in which political life is dominated by renascent particularisms, militant religions, and resurgent ethnicities.

So far we may imagine Gertrude Himmelfarb and Irving Kristol nodding approvingly, perhaps with a murmured reservation or two. What lifts Gray's work far above neoconservatism in intellectual and moral seriousness is his forthright acknowledgment that unregulated market relations may ultimately be destructive of everything worth conserving. It is not that Gray underrates the merits of the free market. On the contrary, his previous book, *Beyond the New Right*, contained a strongly affirmative account of the moral foundations of market institutions; and his essay in *Enlightenment's Wake* on "Post-Communist Societies in Transition" is withering in its depiction of the legacy of central planning. But Gray understands, as many British and American conservatives do not, that the market is merely a means of promoting human welfare, one that must be adapted and modified by each community, not an immutable ordinance of suprahistorical Reason. It is true that self-reliance, self-restraint, and the other virtues fostered by market relations are indispensable, and that markets are far superior epistemically to any alternative yet proposed. It is also true that humans flourish only in the shelter of families, neighborhoods, tribes, traditions, and well-known and loved places, and only with a minimum of economic security; and that all these things are threatened by the spread of market relations. To hold these discordant truths in tension, as Gray does, is an uncommon and valuable achievement.

In opposition to "market fundamentalism," which countenances levels of unemployment, forced mobility, deskilling, urban real-estate speculation, and so on, that are destructive of stable, healthy communities, Gray proposes a "social market" perspective. First elaborated in post-World War II Germany, social market theory views the market not as an ideal type that each society should strive to approximate but as one element in a society's ensemble of institutions and folkways, which it is policy's job to harmonize. The market should not command automatic legitimacy. Instead, as Gray puts it in a formulation that discloses vast common ground with democratic socialists: "In all those cultures where democratic institutions are themselves elements in the common conception of legitimacy, market institutions will be stable and flourishing only in so far as their forms and workings are acceptable, ethically, culturally, and economically, to the underlying population."

What's heartening about this proclaimed subordination of abstract economic efficiency to actual human well-being is that he means it. In *Enlightenment's Wake* and in even more detail in *Beyond the New Right*, Gray argues that although competition, risk, and inequality are inevitable and in fact desirable, many people will nonetheless be entitled to public help. He proposes an "enabling welfare state"—a happy phrase, which strikes exactly the right note. His principle is that those who have fallen out of the market economy or never been part of it should be helped to enter it, and that such assistance should, whenever feasible, be provided through the market (though funded publicly, for example, with vouchers). Education, health care, day care, job training are all on the table and must, he insists, be funded not grudgingly but generously. Moreover, "enablement" (a decided terminological advance over "empowerment") mandates not only individual entitlements but also public goods (again, provided to the extent feasible through a market): clean streets, parks, urban transport, the arts, noncommercial scientific research, and so on. With gratifying impatience Gray waves aside objections from the doctrinaire libertarian right. The proper goal of policy is to preserve healthy—according to our admittedly fallible and changeable contemporary judgment—communities, not to maximize economic freedom and economic growth, abstractly conceived.

On similar grounds Gray waves aside objections from the doctrinaire libertarian left to state action in defense of traditional morality. Although a self-described "ultra-liberal" in this area, he is scathing about the invention of "fundamental rights" by defenders of abortion, homosexuality, and pornography. All such controversies should be resolved through debate, negotiation, compromise—in short, politics—rather than by defining new and presumably unalterable constitutional rights. In the essay "Toleration: A Post-Liberal Perspective," Gray argues persuasively that the core proposition of rights-based liberalism—that the state should be neutral among all ways of life or ideas of the good—is incoherent. The right attitude for the majority in a morally divided community is tolerance, which is a solicitude for social peace arising in equal measure from self-confidence and self-doubt. Peaceableness and humility are not, however, the same thing as a refusal to make moral judgments.

In "The Undoing of Conservatism" Gray mounts a harsh critique of free-market extremism—from the right. The post-World War II social compact in Britain and America provided for full employment and a welfare state financed by the proceeds of economic growth. Faced with stagflation in the late 1970s, conservative parties scrapped the social compact but retained the assumption that political legitimacy depends on economic growth. The resulting feverish pursuit of growth has, predictably, generated social instability. Now, Gray writes, "the dystopian prospect—not so far, perhaps, from the present reality—is of a highly dynamic but low-growth economy in which a permanent revolution in technologies and productive arrangements yields large-scale structural unemployment and pervasive job insecurity." The stability of communities and families—the highest conservative value, one would have thought—has been sacrificed to "microeconomic flexibility, productivity, and low labour costs." GATT (General Agreement on Tariffs and Trade) and global free trade are pernicious policies, likely to entail "costs in human suffering that may come to rival those of twentieth-century experiments in central economic planning." Gray's summary indictment should be tattooed on Newt Gingrich's forehead:

> The social and cultural effects of market liberalism are, virtually without exception, inimical to the values that traditional conservatives hold dear. Communities are scattered to the winds by the gale of creative destruction. Endless "downsizing" and "flattening" of enterprises foster ubiquitous insecurity and makes loyalty to the company a cruel joke. The celebration of consumer choice, as the only undisputed value in market societies, devalues commitment and stability in personal relationships and encourages the view of marriage and the family as vehicles of self-realization. The dynamism of market processes dissolves social hierarchies and overturns established expectations. Status is ephemeral, trust frail and contract sovereign. The dissolution of communities weakens, where it does not entirely destroy, the informal social monitoring of behavior which is the most effective preventive measure against crime. ... The incessant change promoted and demanded by market processes nullifies the significance of precedent and destroys the authority of the past. Indeed it is not too much of an exaggeration to say that market liberal policy delivers the *coup de grace* to practices of authority and of subscription to tradition already severely weakened during the modern period.

Burke, thou should'st be living at this hour!

"Enlightenment's Wake," the book's last and longest essay, is a masterly attempt to think through the problem of modernity. The problem is that critical rationality, as propagated by the Enlightenment and modeled on the natural sciences, has (along with market rationality) undermined the cultural authority of virtually all moral values, norms, customs, and beliefs in virtually all modern societies. The moral foundations of Western culture have been hollowed out. To the question "why be good?" there is now no philosophically compelling answer, even if most people don't know it yet. The name of this condition is nihilism; the eventual result may be spiritual paralysis or, worse, a war of all against all and of all against nature.

Trenchantly and lucidly, Gray canvasses our alternatives. One course, advocated uncritically by religious fundamentalists and with great subtlety and rigor by Alasdair MacIntyre, is to return to premodernity. The Enlightenment, according to MacIntyre, was not merely a misfortune but a mistake: about moral. theory, Aristotle and Aquinas were right all along. Gray disagrees and argues cogently that modernity represents not the abandonment but the consummation of classical and Christian thought. Together they form one tradition, which is now exhausted. No return is possible.

It is not, of course, everyone's tradition. Gray alludes frequently to the East Asian industrial nations, especially Japan, who appear to have achieved economic modernization without undergoing cultural Westernization. He hopes fervently that they never do Westernize, lest they suffer our nihilist fate. I think he underestimates the vulnerability of East Asian cultural traditions to the inroads of individualism and the blandishments of consumer culture. To paraphrase Freud: the voice of appetite is a soft one, but it does not rest till it has gained a hearing. In any case, as Gray recognizes, Western liberal societies can no more import the Confucian ethos than they can recreate the Christian one.

Perhaps we can muddle through? Why not retain liberal values but abandon the hope of giving them a philosophical justification? Why not, as Richard Rorty has suggested, affirm "Enlightenment humanism without Enlightenment rationalism"? That makes good sense to me, and Gray allows that Rorty's is "perhaps the most powerful attempt we are likely to see to reformulate liberalism in explicitly post-Enlightenment terms." Nevertheless, he rejects it as parochial and excessively sanguine. Public and private cannot be kept separate, as Rorty recommends. Political institutions are the expression of a culture and a cosmology. The institutions of bourgeois liberal democracy are no exception, and the culture they express is, Gray repeats, ephemeral and exhausted.

Well then . . . what? Gray's reply is unflinching and not in the least melodramatic: the human race, he concludes, may very well destroy itself or suffer increasing, and finally irreversible, cultural entropy. Even more likely, and no less tragic, we may deplete and disfigure the nonhuman world beyond recovery.

Unless . . . Here Gray's accustomed lucidity fails him, or at any rate fails me. He finds some saving intimations in the later Heidegger, particularly the notion of *Gelassenheit* or "releasement," derived from Meister Eckhart and other

German mystics. "Releasement," according to Gray, is a disposition to "wean ourselves from willing and open ourselves to letting things be"; to attend calmly "to beings, to the things of the earth, in all their contingency and mortality"; to embrace "the groundless contingency that makes and unmakes the world." In Heidegger's words: "Releasement toward things and openness to the mystery belong together. They grant us the possibility of dwelling in the world in a totally different way. They promise us a new ground and foundation upon which we can stand and endure in the world of technology without being imperiled by it."

Out of respect for Gray, I will suppress my usual shallow, logocentric exasperation with Heidegger and merely observe that I don't find the above very helpful. I wish that Gray had, at the crucial juncture, not ascended into philosophical mysticism but instead descended into social criticism. I wish he had gotten down to cases, had said to his readers, humbly and prosaically, citizen to citizen: "Look, we can't all—all human being, that is—have air conditioning, safari vacations, automatic dishwashers, cars that go faster than forty or fifty miles an hour, meat every day (or every week), high-definition television with scores of channels, and bulgeless, odorless, wrinkle-free bodies. We'll spoil the planet if we try; and besides, those things are not all that important. What's important is [my own list follows; I would have liked to see Gray's]: singing in harmony at least once a week; having a body practiced in graceful movement; taking part in frequent and lively political (or aesthetic or metaphysical) argument; knowing many poems and prose passages by heart; having wilderness nearby or at a moderate distance; and above all, having useful and (at least part of the time) stimulating work. What's more, everyone could have all these things without spoiling the planet."

There's something to "releasement"; I don't deny it. But I suspect we'll get a better sense of it by hearkening to Wallace Stegner, Wendell Berry, or Seamus Heaney than to Heidegger. Philosophy as practiced by Gray and Rorty can lead us out of the modern wilderness; but only imagination and social criticism can lead us (if anything can) into the postmodern promised land.

Puny Expectations

"If you can't say anything nice," my mother used to admonish, "don't say anything at all." Presumably Russell Jacoby's mother told him the same thing—all mothers do. Fortunately, he disobeyed her and has written some of the most useful, tactless, and entertaining cultural criticism of recent decades. *Social Amnesia* (1975) traced the Americanization of psychoanalysis, in the course of which it lost sight of how society constrains subjectivity and hence lost its critical edge. *Dialectic of Defeat* (1981) surveyed the "Western Marxist" tradition of Lukács, Korsch, et al. *The Last Intellectuals* (1987), his best-known book, deplored the extinction of independent intellectuals, with wide interests and a broad general readership, and their replacement by academics and journalists housed in institutions and writing primarily for peers. *Dogmatic Wisdom* (1994) blasted both sides in the culture wars—militant multiculturalists and apocalyptic neoconservatives—for "litigating over property lines when the house is on fire"; that is, squabbling while liberal education "shatters under the weight of commercialism" and while "the irresistible power of advertising and television" produces a "monoculture of clothes, music, and cars." Jacoby's arguments were often original and were unfailingly astute, though not always couched in the gentlest, most collegial tones. One finished these books with a heightened appreciation of many intellectuals' capacity for vapidity, trivialization, and self-importance.

The End of Utopia[1] continues Jacoby's broadside against contemporary intellectuals, particularly those on the left. Their horizons have shrunk, he charges; explicitly or implicitly, they have acquiesced in the general conviction that "this society is the only possible one." Critics of the political economy take for granted competition and commodity production, timidly suggesting only minor modifications in the operation of markets. Multiculturalists absurdly equate their demands for increased turf, pelf, and status with a program for radical social transformation. The "idiom of pluralism and rights" bounds the imagination of philosophers. Whether or not the "end of ideology" and the "end of history" correctly describe the world, they all too aptly characterize the left's worldview.

> Today socialists and leftists do not dream of a future qualitatively different from the present. . . . Almost everywhere the left contracts, not simply politically but, perhaps more decisively, intellectually . . . at best radicals and leftists envision a modified society with bigger pieces of pie for more customers. They turn utilitarian, liberal, and celebratory. The left once dismissed the market as exploitative; it now honors the market as rational and humane. The left once disdained mass culture as exploitative; now it celebrates it as rebellious. The left once honored independent intellectuals as courageous; now it sneers at them as elitist. The left once rejected pluralism as superficial; now it worships it as profound. We are witnessing not simply the defeat of the left but its conversion, and perhaps inversion.

Much grapeshot follows, trained on an impressively wide range of targets for so short a book: Robert Kuttner's *Everything for Sale*, Michael Sandel's *Democracy's Discontent*, Michael Tomasky's *Left for Dead*, Ralph Miliband's *Socialism for a Skeptical Age*, John Roemer's *A Future for Socialism*, Michael Albert's *Looking Forward*, Lawrence Levine's *The Opening of the American Mind*, Charles Taylor, Nancy Fraser, Homi Bhabha, Gayatri Spivak, Jonathan Culler, Tony Judt, Edward Said, Stanley Fish, Clifford Geertz, bell hooks, *Social Text*, Toffler-style futurism, mass-culture studies, and sundry other persons, texts, and discourses. Here, in Jacoby's mordant asides, is the chief fun and profit of the book. Some

[1] *The End of Utopia: Politics and Culture in an Age of Apathy* by Russell Jacoby. Basic Books, 1999.

comfortably tenured leftists, he remarks, "see themselves as outsiders, blasting the establishment. Like uptown executives cruising around in pricey jeeps and corporate lawyers in luxurious utility trucks, they pose as rugged souls from the back country; they threaten the seats of power as they glide into their reserved parking spots." The radical program on multiculturalism "might be characterized as jargon attached to an air compressor." Three bemused paragraphs contemplating a Foucaultian critique of the Santa Cruz municipal anti-discrimination ordinance are a stitch. Like Dwight Macdonald (one of the few intellectuals he admires), Jacoby is important above all as a cultural hygienist, scouring verbal plaque and conceptual decay with his high-powered electric-sarcastic drill.

To deal the Zeitgeist a box on the ear is one thing, however; to account for it is another. What explains the eclipse of utopianism? In a sense, the answer is obvious: utopia lies buried in the rubble of Communism. As Jacoby points out, Cold-War thinkers consistently equated utopia with totalitarianism and liberal pluralism with democracy, and they carried the day. There were undoubtedly good counterarguments: in particular, that Stalinism was not in the least a utopian experiment but was more like Czarism plus electricity. But arguments are no defense against plausible and politically convenient simplifications. For every pundit, editorialist, and politician in America since roughly World War II, the automatic qualification of "utopia" as impractical and/or dangerous, and probably un-American, saved thought.

Still, one must give the Zeitgeist its due: what most people believe is not invariably false. There is a rational kernel within the shell of anti-utopian prejudice. It is simply this: we all want to see the plans. And there are no plans. A century or more of resonant but empty slogans urging revolution, liberation, the abolition of money, the end of scarcity, a world without work (or conflict or hierarchy or alienation or authority or force) have at last produced widespread skepticism about all fundamental criticism and exalted aspiration.

Utopian slogans have worked much mischief. (Jacoby himself is not wholly innocent: scoffing at mundane social democratic talk about full employment and retraining the workforce, he reminds us loftily that "once upon a time leftists and radicals talked of liberation and the abolition of work." So they did; but what, if anything, did they mean by it?) The remedy is not to give up on utopia but to stop sloganizing. To begin with, what does "utopia" mean? Jacoby, like the "negative thinkers" of the Frankfurt School, whom he quotes approvingly, is not generous with specifics, apparently as a matter of principle. But he does offer a helpful definition. The core utopian conviction is "that the future could fundamentally surpass the present . . . that the future texture of life, work, and even love might little resemble that now familiar to us . . . that history contains possibilities of freedom and pleasure hardly tapped."

Utopia, then, is in the *future*. Why is this worth emphasizing? Revolutionists and abolitionists, utopia's false friends, insist that it can be constructed out of present materials through a heroic act of will. This is to underestimate recklessly the depth and subtlety of the necessary changes and the intricacy and inertia of every moral culture. Utopia is impossible unless, among an overwhelming majority, solidarity and trust are nearly instinctive; responsibility, self-reliance, initiative, honesty, and other civic virtues are practiced much more widely than now; and democratic habits of self-confidence, candor, and tact are far better developed. Channels of communication and public information are as yet rudimentary. And let's not forget rhetorical skills like wit, fluency, and concision: without a vast improvement in the general level of these, attendance at all the necessary meetings on the way to utopia will result in an epidemic of premature brain death. With all these moral and psychological changes in place, we can make a start on the technical problem—no less complex, probably—of reconciling equity and efficiency in production and distribution.

Obviously such drastic and intimate changes, on the requisite scale, without undemocratic coercion or divine intervention, cannot be accomplished in a generation, or probably even in a few generations. Carrying off a general strike may be a fine thing, but creating a new moral ecology is an infinitely more difficult and valuable thing. In the *Fabian Essays*, defending gradualism against the revolutionists and abolitionists of his day, George Bernard Shaw wrote:

> The right is so clear, the wrong so intolerable, the gospel so convincing, that it seems to them that it must be possible to enlist the whole body of workers, soldiers, policemen, and all—under the banner of brotherhood and equality; and at one great stroke to set Justice on her rightful throne. Unfortunately, such an army of light is no more to be gathered from the human product of nineteenth century civilization than grapes are to be gathered from thistles.

Ditto for the human product of twentieth-century civilization. And even an army of light won't be enough, if a majority or a substantial minority remain benighted. The whole society, more or less, must see the light, or it isn't utopia.

The foregoing would be a counsel of despair if the human race were only going to last for a few generations. But utopia's enemies must, if they're logical, deny that such changes are possible in *any* number of generations; must assert, in essence, that humankind has already attained its farthest point of moral development and that our present level of social virtue cannot be substantially improved on *in saecula saeculorum*. This is even more implausible than revolutionism. The wisdom and generosity of the corporate boardroom and the *Wall Street Journal* editorial page may be the best we can do in 1999. But by 2500? Surely it's more likely that we'll all be as gods by then than that we won't have evolved beyond Robert Bartley and Steve Forbes. Today half the human race has no sanitation, one-fourth has no clean water, one-fifth no adequate housing, and one-sixth no basic health services, while the amount Americans and Europeans spend annually on pet food, cosmetics, and ice cream would supply all those necessities, plus basic education, to everyone in the world who lacks them, with a great deal left over. Do anti-utopians really believe that this vile state of affairs, or its moral equivalent, will persist until 2500 and beyond? It's too fantastic.

Moral progress is not inevitable, but it is not impossible. It is slow, painful, and uncertain; this is another way of putting the tragic view of life. That view is noble and true, but it is not the same as the lazy, self-serving assumption that things can never be radically better and so there's no point racking one's brains to come up with any possible steps in that direction.

What steps, then? Here I have some differences with Jacoby. He thinks modest reform schemes like Kuttner's and Roemer's—involving corporate tax incentives, citizen "policy juries," asset redistribution by means of coupons, and the like—are part of the problem and warms instead to the turgid deliverances of Bloch and Marcuse and the inspired rant of Fourier. I think there's no harm in the latter but find the former more useful by a long shot. Kuttner, Roemer, Alec Nove, et al. leave you feeling that they understand capitalism every bit as rigorously as its defenders—see the point of it, so to speak—yet are convinced it's a long way from the best that can be had, even if they can't quite articulate that "best." Suitably modest but sufficiently roused: this seems the right frame of mind just now for twenty-fifth-century utopianism.

I think, too, that a return to metaphysics, which Jacoby seems to favor, is not a step in the right direction. He finds in Rousseau, Whitehead, Marcuse, and other thinkers a "logic of negativity," according to which oppressive empirical reality is denied and transcended by means of a liberating metaphysical ur-reality. "Metaphysical universals inhere in the world, but transcend it," he explains. "An individual event may be 'untrue' in that it is contradicted by reality, but this untruth expresses its achievement or different truth, its basis in metaphysical principles." Hmm. Jacoby and his postmodern, anti-metaphysical antagonists seem to be making symmetrical arguments. His syllogism runs: Only metaphysical principles can generate utopian ideals; utopian ideals are indispensable; ergo, metaphysical principles are valid. Their syllogism runs: Only metaphysical principles can generate utopian ideals; metaphysical principles are invalid; ergo, utopian ideals are a fraud. But the shared major premise is wrong. Utopian ideals are indeed indispensable, but metaphysical principles are indeed invalid, and this is possible because the ideals don't depend on the principles. Ideals are not propositions; they are expressions of what the eighteenth century called "sympathy" or "benevolence" and what we may simply call moral imagination. The capacity to envision a more decent world is like the capacity to imagine beautiful forms. Both require a native endowment of sensibility, moral or aesthetic, cultivated by training and experience and not choked off by pressing personal burdens or insecurities. Bugger "metaphysical principles." Besides, the historical evidence is mostly the other way. Priestley and Diderot, Hazlitt and Shelley, Mill and Morris, Shaw and Wells, Russell and Dewey were all metaphysical skeptics and utopian radicals. Were they all merely confused?

One of my favorite utopians is Matthew Arnold, to whom Jacoby devotes several eye-opening pages. Though hijacked by conservatives, Arnold belongs in the pantheon of the left. He championed high culture: nearly everyone knows that, and that is all nearly everyone knows. But he was also, consistently and emphatically, an egalitarian. He thought the most important thing in life was the free development of one's highest faculties, to which everyone had a right; that this was only possible in a society without gross material and educational inequality; and that the best way to correct such inequality was democratic state action. His defense of tradition was not in the least anti-democratic; on the contrary.

Arnold kept his distance from contemporary politics. He called himself a "Liberal of the future." It was essential, he believed, to keep alive a sense of large and distant possibilities and to leaven the quotidian with it. A gracious life, a life of "sweetness and light," with ready access to "the best that has been thought and said in the world" and the resources and leisure to assimilate it: no society could be considered just in which all this was not universally available. The "secret of the life of the future," he wrote, is "civilization made pervasive and general." But that will require much slow effort, as he reminded radicals, and a lot of money, as he warned conservatives.

Arnold's "Liberalism of the future" seems to me the very pattern of an intelligent utopianism. If alive today he would, I have no doubt, sympathize with single-payer universal health care and a rise in the minimum wage and strongly deprecate a reduced capital-gains tax and across-the-board deregulation. But mainly, he would gently insist that this society is not "the only possible one." To cowed leftists and smug rightists he would repeat, in the name of the best that has been thought and said in the world, that "the ideal life is, in sober and practical truth, none other than man's normal life, as we shall one day know it."

Our Ancestors . . .

For a generation or more, schoolchildren in West Africa and Southeast Asia learned French from a reader that began: "Our ancestors, the Gauls . . . " Actually, this seems no more incongruous to me than my memory of first grade in East Boston in the 1950s: fifty little Italian-American savages bawling the Pledge of Allegiance. Two paradigmatic instances of cultural imperialism, I suppose. And yet, what lodged deepest—with me and, I suspect, with the Africans and Asians—was not the patriotic sentiment but the verbal music: "*Nos ancêtres, les Gaulois . . .*" and " . . . with liberty and justice for all."

On the evidence of Richard Bernstein's *Dictatorship of Virtue*[1], not much of either—patriotism or eloquence—survives in the contemporary American curriculum. Bernstein, formerly the national cultural correspondent of *The New York Times*, spent a couple of years following up several of the cultural controversies that flared briefly or chronically in the last decade: curricular innovation in schools and colleges; speech and harassment codes; Afrocentrism; canon revision and critical theory; workplace diversity. It's a dreary tale. Whatever may

[1] *Dictatorship of Virtue: Multiculturalism and the Battle for America's Future* by Richard Bernstein. Knopf, 1994.

once have been fresh and vital about multiculturalism is now evidently stale. The new courses and programs Bernstein describes, from Austin to Minneapolis to Brookline to New York, sound vapid and tendentious. Campus wrangles over discrimination or harassment seem motivated as often as not by opportunism or mere contentiousness. The current chairman of the National Endowment for the Humanities, a recent president of the Modern Language Association, and quite a few college presidents, professors, schoolteachers, and principals are plausibly depicted, largely in their own words, as horses' asses. And in the lowest circle of hell swarms

> a growing multicultural bureaucracy, a heavy rank of assistant deans and assistant provosts, of diversity programmers and social equity directors and affirmative action officers, of educational consultants who give full-day seminars on "understanding differences," of people with master's degrees in psychology and social work whose vocabulary is chock-full of expressions like "internalized oppression" and "psychological captivity," of specialists in multicultural education, people who use words like "problematize" and use "impact" as a verb.

Bernstein is as unhappy about all of this as Allan Bloom and William Bennett are, but his complaint is not theirs. His objections are not metaphysical and a priori but practical and ad hoc. A liberal and a pluralist, he was (he claims) inclined to give multiculturalism the benefit of the doubt. But instead of livelier, more imaginative pedagogy, more frank and frequent communication between the races of genders, and a steady growth of fairness, tolerance, and informed sympathy, he encountered a plague of mediocrity, conformism, and rancor, of "mandatory sanctimony" and "stale, simpleminded Manichean[ism]." Emasculated textbooks, the frantic pursuit of an artificial inclusiveness, neglect or even suspicion of intellectual mastery, subtle or unsubtle disparagement of classical ideals and achievements, reflexive accusations of racism, sexism, and elitism—it sounds a little like an earlier Cultural Revolution; though this time, fortunately, the promised hundred flowers have turned out to be not poisonous but merely plastic.

Actually, that analogy holds in another respect as well. Like Leninism, militant multiculturalism is primarily attributable—*pace* neoconservative apocalyptics—not to anything so profound as the "Utopian temptation," the dark side of the Enlightenment, or the Puritan strain in the American character, but to simple (or, if you prefer, complicated) careerism. The opportunism Bernstein describes—both among the diversity consultants and affirmative-action advocates and their clients—is dismaying. "My experience," he concludes, "leads me to believe that insofar as culture is involved in multiculturalism, it is not so much for me to be required to learn about other cultures as for me to celebrate myself and for you to celebrate me, and, along the way, to support my demand for more respect, more jobs, more foundation support, more money, more programs, more books, more prizes, more people like me in high places." It's not, in other words, genuine pluralism—any more than Leninism was genuine socialism—but rather, at bottom, business as usual: product innovation and marketing.

What children need, Bernstein contends—at any rate, poor and minority children, who, unlike their wealthier and whiter fellows, are stuck with the public schools—is not this newfangled pedagogy, but more and better old-fashioned pedagogy.[2] Self-esteem is indeed a worthy educational goal, but "a strong self-conception does not come from being informed that other people of your race have done well as much as it comes from seeing that you can accomplish things." Real educational equality consists in everyone's being held—and, if necessary, helped—to the same high standards.

Which standards? Bernstein makes a modest and pragmatic case—which is therefore much more persuasive than the neoconservatives' strident and dogmatic case—for Americanism and Eurocentrism. One main premise of multiculturalism is that assimilation has not worked. The proof is the allegedly pervasive and intensifying racism, sexism, and homophobia of contemporary America. Bernstein glances skeptically at the evidence for this charge, which indeed seems rather flimsy: several widely-cited recent studies are convicted of hyperbole and selectivity, and a good deal of evidence of steady, and sometimes dramatic, progress by women and minorities is cited. Even more effective is his extended portrait of a community remarkable for its ethnic diversity over several generations, whose Asian, African-American, Caribbean, and Southern and Eastern

---

[2]Emphasis on "better." As Katha Pollitt has pointed out, if all students ever read is what they read in school—which is usually the case now—then it doesn't matter much what they read in school. ("Canon to the Right of Me . . .," *Nation*, 23 September 1991). .

European denizens seem notably unalienated from the American dream. As it happens, this *echt*-multicultural community—Queens—came to national attention a few years ago as a focus of opposition to the New York State "Rainbow Curriculum," a circumstance that lends extra poignancy to Bernstein's account.

Demystifying this country's mainstream political tradition is one thing, and (as I wish Bernstein had affirmed a bit more emphatically) a very good thing— certainly Howard Zinn's *A People's History of the United States*, for example, ought to be required reading for every American child and adult. But impugning and abandoning that tradition, in the manner of doctrinaire multiculturalists, rather than insisting on the fulfillment of its promises, seems to me, as it does to Bernstein, foolhardy—though, I admit, I may have been brainwashed by thousands of repetitions of " . . . with liberty and justice for all."

Russell Jacoby is a radical social critic in the line of Bourne, Macdonald, and Mills: an intellectual generalist of the sort whose obsolescence he chronicled in his previous book, *The Last Intellectuals*. He too is unhappy about multiculturalism, not because it's a menace but because it's a distraction. *Dogmatic Wisdom*[3] argues that education in America is endangered less by leftist zealotry or rightist bigotry than by the fraying, even crumbling, of the social fabric.

> The "culture wars" are diversionary. . . . Conservatives, liberals, and radicals argue over which books should be taught in schools; meanwhile few books are read and a liberal education shatters under the weight of commercialism. Faculty and students dispute which words violate the rights of which groups; meanwhile society turns increasingly violent. Psychologists preach the virtues of a healthy self-esteem; meanwhile the world of the self—education and jobs—collapses. Citizens wrangle over multiculturalism, arguing how, when, and if diverse cultures should be studied; meanwhile the irresistible power of advertising and television converts multiculturalism into a monoculture of clothes, music, and cars.

On the one hand, Jacoby claims, the spread of multiculturalism in the elementary and secondary schools will be limited by the fact of local control,

---

[3]*Dogmatic Wisdom: How the Culture Wars Divert Education and Distract America* by Russell Jacoby. Doubleday, 1994.

exercised by elected school boards. (Bernstein's account of the protracted struggle between parents and the school system in Brookline casts some doubt on
this plausible-sounding notion.) On the other hand, American higher education is sharply divided between a thin layer of elite schools, where ideological
conflicts swirl, and a mass of state, community, and small private colleges with
other preoccupations. He quotes the author of a large-scale study: "The curriculum of students at elite colleges"—Stanford, Penn, Michigan, Berkeley, Duke,
etc.—"is so different from that followed by the other 97% that it is irrelevant to
[such] discussions." For that matter, something similar may be true of the primary and secondary schools, judging from Jonathan Kozol's *Savage Inequalities*
(1991)—a book that should be read, or re-read, in connection with Jacoby's and
Bernstein's—which documents the vast disparity in resources typically available
to suburban and inner-city school districts.

The sabotage of public finances by Reaganism; the de-industrialization of
the American economy; the effect on students of thirty hours a week of television plus (for a distressingly high percentage of them) ten or fifteen hours of
unskilled, low-wage work—compared with these, multiculturalism, even on the
most alarmist view of it, is barely a blip on the screen. More than half of all undergraduates major in vocational or occupational fields. Twenty-five percent of
all bachelor's degrees are in business; roughly one-half of one percent are in philosophy. Even before multiculturalism arrived on the scene, only one student in
twenty took any course at all in modern European history; only 22% of four-year
colleges (and even fewer two-year colleges) had a Western Civilization require-
ment. Reports of the death of liberal education in America have not been exag-
gerated, but the cause of death has been misidentified. This is not surprising:
the right has dominated the education debate, outside the academy at least, so
naturally the depredations of the free market and the blandishments of consumerism have largely escaped blame. Unlike their morally and intellectually
more serious predecessors, contemporary conservatives, Jacoby notes, "worship
the market and bemoan the education it engenders. They blast BMW radicals,
not a BMW society."

As for the left, there may not be much that multiculturalist kindergarten
teachers or cutting-edge literary theorists can do about the political economy,
but they can at least stop deceiving themselves. Richard Rorty has shrewdly

observed that "one of the contributions of the newer [i.e., the radical-academic] left has been to enable professors, whose mild guilt about the comfort and security of their own lives once led them into extra-academic political activity, so to say, 'Sorry, I gave at the office.'"[4] The traditional modes of democratic activity—organization, information, legislation, and donation—may seem tedious and unpromising. They may offer little scope for the enthusiasms and expertise of cultural radicals. But they are indispensable in a way that curricular innovation and diversity-enhancement programs are not. None of the poor children or parents Jonathan Kozol talked to seemed to feel that recovering their racial or ethnic heritage was their most pressing educational need. Instead, "they ask for . . . fairly obvious improvements: larger library collections, a reduction in the size of classes, or a better ratio of children to school counselors." No doubt, once such things can be taken for granted, the poor will soon come to appreciate advances in critical theory and multiculturalist pedagogy. But first things first.

George Bernard Shaw, at once the leading socialist and the leading music critic of his time, was asked whether in the interest of cultural diversity and popular empowerment, something ought to be done about the elitist and Eurocentric bias of the contemporary music scene. What about music for the people? Shaw's reply is still to the point:

> What we want is not music for the people, but bread for the people, rest for the people, immunity from robbery and scorn for the people, hope for them, enjoyment, equal respect and consideration, life and aspiration. When we get that I imagine the people will make tolerable music for themselves.

[4]"Intellectuals in Politics," *Dissent,* Spring 1992.

Critical Imperialism

Connoisseurs of book-jacket blurbs will likely award the palm for 1993 to Edward Said's *Culture and Imperialism*[1]. "The most distinguished cultural critic now writing in America" (Cornel West). "Brilliant, lucid, learned, humane" (Henry Louis Gates). "A classic of contemporary criticism" (Richard Poirier). "Splendidly eloquent and inspiring" (Basil Davidson). High praise also from Frank Kermode and Noam Chomsky, although slightly less expansive, as befits their greater age and eminence.

Said is the leading token leftist on *Nightline*, MacNeil-Lehrer, and the *New York Times* op-ed page, and, specter-like, haunts the pages of *Commentary*, *The New Republic*, and the *TLS*. *Raritan*, *Critical Inquiry*, the *Nation*, and the *London Review of Books* are home turf. He has received not one but two offers from Harvard, and God knows how many others from elsewhere. There'll be a MacArthur in his mailbox one of these years. For all these reasons, some envious and mean-

---

[1]Random House, 1994.

spirited comrade is undoubtedly even now preparing to sneak up and jab him in his (relatively) undefended left flank. Me, actually.

Culture and Imperialism is an inexhaustibly tiresome book. The writing is clumsy, stilted, verbose, imprecise, and marinated—pickled—in academic jargon. It is larded with superfluous qualifiers and synonyms, there only to add syllables. If needless words were omitted, the text would be roughly a third shorter. "In greatly disparate post-colonial regions one sees tremendously energetic efforts to engage with the metropolitan world in equal debate so as to testify to the diversity and differences of the non-European world and to its own agendas, priorities, and history. The purpose of this testimony is to inscribe, reinterpret, and expand the areas of engagement as well as the terrain contested with Europe.... There is thus both a stubborn confrontation and a crossing over in discussion, borrowing back and forth, debate." This is on page 30. By page 100, one's jaw is slack. Does Harvard really want its graduate students to write like this?

Worse, Said's polemical manners, here as elsewhere, are atrocious: sneering, overweening, *ad hominem*. Too often, he innocently misinterprets or not-so-innocently misrepresents other people's arguments. Bernard Lewis, for example, did not exactly claim that changes in Stanford's core curriculum would bring about the return of slavery, polygamy, and child marriage. Conor Cruise O'Brien did not peevishly dismiss the entire subject of imperialism with "Why don't they appreciate us, after what we did for them?" John Corry's controversial *New York Times* review of PBS's *The Africans* was not "insensate," "semi-hysterical," or written in "turbulent and disorderly prose." Said quotes a passage from Mill's *Principles of Political Economy* and observes sternly: "In Mill we have the ruthless proprietary tones of the white master used to efface the reality, work, and suffering of millions." Rubbish. The passage in question is about the meaning of the word "capital"; the West Indies are mentioned by way of illustration, nothing more. No one who ever lived was less capable of colossal insensitivity and self-deception than Mill. An only slightly less flagrant tendentiousness is inflicted upon Ruskin, Camus, Habermas, and many others who wander into Said's sights.

Still, all these are not reasons for disagreeing with *Culture and Imperialism*, merely for disliking it. Actually, it's impossible to disagree with the book's argument in its widest, most general sense, because taken in that sense it is a truism: every work of art is produced in some political, social, economic, and biological circumstances or other, which will have some effect or other on its style, structure, and atmosphere. But which circumstances and which effects? The ideological proof is in the critical pudding.

Although *Culture and Imperialism* is a pretty unappetizing pudding—soggy here, lumpy there, overspiced throughout—it is not utterly lacking in nutritional value. Said introduces us to some interesting and unfamiliar history; he's a good quoter, at least. And there are some sensible observations about contemporary politics. But about literature, which is his main subject, though he's sometimes thought-provoking, more often he's just provoking.

"The extraordinary formal and ideological dependence of the great French and English realistic novels on the facts of empire," Said announces, "has never been studied from a general theoretical standpoint." This is an understandable omission, because there is no such extraordinary dependence. There is not even an ordinary dependence. The facts of empire go virtually unmentioned in the major works of Balzac, Stendhal, Flaubert, Zola, Austen, Eliot, Dickens, and Thackeray. But perhaps it is an invisible, a tacit dependence? This is Said's argument about *Mansfield Park*, his chief exhibit.

In *Mansfield Park*, Sir Thomas Bertram travels to his estate in the West Indies for several months; while he is away, the moral order of Mansfield Park is threatened by a pair of seductive visitors from London; on his return, order is reestablished and everyone's character has been revealed. "Antigua and Sir Thomas's trip there have a definitive function in *Mansfield Park*," Said writes. Yes and no. The trip is transparently a plot contrivance. Sir Thomas might have fallen ill or gone to war; the structure and psychology of the novel would not be a whit different. The Antigua estate is alluded to only four or five times, never more than in passing, throughout this very long work. Lionel Trilling's masterly essay on *Mansfield Park* does not so much as mention it.

Said is undaunted. His interpretive strategy is bold and ingenious. "How are we to assess Austen's few references to Antigua, and what are we to make of them interpretively? . . . My contention is that by that very odd combination of casualness and stress, Austen reveals herself to be *assuming* . . . the importance of an empire to the situation at home." This is the hermeneutics of suspicion *á la folie*.

In fact, not much more can usefully be said about the relation of *Mansfield*

Park to the British Empire than that the former was written in the latter. "Extraordinary formal and ideological dependence," my foot. It is just this sort of grandiloquent assertion that excited so many people about *Orientalism* and that makes Said's celebrity so depressing. In that book, anticipating *Culture and Imperialism*, Said wrote:

> Nearly every nineteenth-century writer . . . was extraordinarily well aware of the fact of empire . . . liberal cultural heroes like John Stuart Mill, Arnold, Carlyle, Newman, Macaulay, Ruskin, George Eliot, and even Dickens had definite views on race and imperialism, which are quite easily to be found at work in their writing.

Now, like every other educated person in the nineteenth century, Arnold, Newman, Ruskin, Eliot, and Dickens had *some* views on race and imperialism, though no very definite—i.e., emphatic or precise—ones. Like most people, they were intermittently and, on the whole, vaguely aware—not "extraordinarily well aware"—of the fact of empire. One can, not easily but with determination and ingenuity, find this awareness cropping up here and there in their writing, interestingly (sometimes) illustrating the relation of political background to aesthetic or philosophical foreground. In short: conscientiously qualified, not much remains of Said's sweeping affirmation.

Myself, I find conscientious qualification much sexier than resonant exaggeration. So for me, Edmund Wilson on Kipling, V. S. Naipaul on Conrad, P. N. Furbank on Forster, and Irving Howe on anybody are all more politically stimulating than Said. Because these critics respect the boundaries—not metaphysical, to be sure, but practical—between art and ideology, because their sense of proportion is right and their discriminations are unforced, I pay attention when they do talk politics. Whereas after a few pages of Said's nagging, I'm ready to watch television or go down to the mall.

Still, no book so earnest and erudite can be quite useless. *Culture and Imperialism* compels us—if only out of exasperation—to consider some important and difficult questions, so difficult that most of us usually leave them alone. For example: Why is imperialism wrong? The principal thesis of *Culture and Imperialism* is that European culture has supported imperialism by representing subjugated non-European peoples as inferior. Said works so hard at refuting any suggestion of inferiority that he succeeds at last in provoking the question: what if they *were* inferior—would that justify their subjugation? Suppose (just for the sake of argument) we agreed that there were indeed substantial variations in average aptitude for one thing or another among racial, sexual, class, or national groups. Suppose we gave in to the continual, practically irresistible temptation to call one society or group more "advanced" or "developed" than another, even in morality or politics. Would we—should we—therefore agree that one group has a right to govern the other without the latter's consent? If so, why? And if not, then why such heroic but unnecessary efforts to demonstrate equal or equivalent group achievement?

Granted that there are evils in the world, notably imperialism. What's art got to do with it? On Said's showing, not much. Which leaves literary critics in the same boat as the rest of us: ordinary citizens without politically relevant expertise. For many people with aesthetic tastes and talents, real politics—anything likely to produce new legislation, not just new curriculum—is bound to seem like fearful drudgery. Since neither accepting irrelevance nor plunging into the pedestrian is an attractive option to most literary people, some have looked for reasons to consider the aesthetic as political. It's too difficult getting up to speed to debate economics or foreign policy with smart right-wingers. And organizing the unfortunate is appallingly dull. So, since finding evidence (however far-fetched) of the "formal and ideological dependence" of art on social structure appears to provide work both congenial and useful, it is denominated "political."

This is not such a contemptible evasion. The dilemma it is meant to resolve is a subtle one; to feel it at all is honorable. And Said has, to his credit, plunged into the pedestrian—into the details of contemporary political debate—more than most. But few of his epigoni have the energy to follow him there. Those who don't should heed Richard Rorty's astute and chastening admonition: "We humanities types are not useless, but we are not nearly as useful as [some academic leftists] think. Our skill in practicing the hermeneutics of suspicion and our flair for detecting ambiguity and latent contradiction are talents with relatively limited application."

The acknowledgment of ignorance is the beginning of wisdom. Perhaps the acknowledgment of political irrelevance will prove, for some at least, the beginning of political commitment.

Pollyanna and Cassandra

In "Literature and Science" (1883), a lecture delivered in America during the high noon of the Victorian culture wars, Matthew Arnold defended the study of Greek against utilitarian educational reformers and a newly assertive commercial class. "Literature may perhaps be needed in education," he imagines these Philistines conceding grudgingly, "but why on earth should it be Greek literature?" Because, he replies, we crave it.

> The instinct for beauty is set in human nature, as surely as the instinct for knowledge is set there, or the instinct for [right] conduct. If the instinct for beauty is served by Greek literature and art as it is served by no other literature and art, we may trust to the instinct of self-preservation in humanity for keeping Greek as part of our culture. We may trust to it for even making the study of Greek more prevalent than it is now. . . . So long as human nature is what it is, [its] attractions will remain irresistible.

Apparently human nature is no longer what it was. Around six hundred undergraduates currently major in classics each year at American colleges and universities, fewer than one in sixteen hundred new B.A.'s—a figure that probably warrants designating them an endangered species. On the other hand, though unknown in Matthew Arnold's time, business majors now account for roughly a quarter of the graduating class. Greek, it would seem, is history.

So what? Is there still any reason to read the Greeks? Martha Nussbaum[1] thinks so, and so do Victor Davis Hanson and John Heath[2]. That, however, is nearly all they agree on. Nussbaum is upbeat, engaged, optimistic about the current academic scene; Hanson and Heath are angry, marginal, apocalyptic: Cassandra to her Polyanna. Their new books make a curious pair.

Nussbaum champions cosmopolitanism: wider knowledge of the great variety of human cultures and institutions, enlivened by imaginative sympathy and brought to bear in rational and vigorous but mutually respectful deliberation about the common good, of which the Greeks were exemplary practitioners. Education for world citizenship is her theme. "A new and broader focus for knowledge is necessary to adequate citizenship in a world now characterized by complicated interdependencies. We cannot afford to be ignorant of the traditions of one half of the world, if we are to grapple well with the economic, political, and human problems that beset us." This means cultivating humanity. "Three capacities, above all," she writes, "are essential to the cultivation of humanity in today's world. First is the capacity for critical examination of oneself and one's traditions—for living what, following Socrates, we may call 'the examined life.'" The second is "an ability to see ourselves not simply as citizens of some local region or group but also, and above all, as human beings bound to all other human beings by ties of recognition and concern." The third is "an ability to think what it might be like to be in the shoes of a person different from oneself, to be an intelligent reader of that person's story, and to understand the emotions and wishes and desires that someone so placed might have."

As these examples suggest, Nussbaum is prone to platitude—she writes like a dean or a foundation officer or the chair of the National Endowment for the Humanities. No one could disagree with her bland and contentless cosmopolitanism; and indeed no one does disagree with it, just as no one professes principled opposition to peace, justice, freedom, love, rationality, or compassion. The disagreements come when one gets down to cases. Of course there's no harm

[1] *Cultivating Humanity: A Classical Defense of Reform in Liberal Education* by Martha Nussbaum. Harvard University Press, 1997.
[2] *Who Killed Homer? The Demise of Classical Education and the Recovery of Greek Wisdom* by Victor Davis Hanson and John Heath. Free Press, 1998.

in restating (in good prose, that is; bad prose always does harm) even the most respectable and uncontroversial ideal. But it doesn't help much, either.

Nussbaum does get down to cases. She has gone around the country for several years looking at curricular developments, and by and large she likes what she's seen. Ideologues may rail at political correctness on campus, and pessimists may lament pervasive dumbing down, but these complaints "bear little resemblance to the daily reality of higher education in America." On the contrary, "higher education in America is in a healthy state. Never before have there been so many talented and committed young faculty so broadly dispersed in institutions of so many different kinds, thinking about different ways of connecting education with citizenship." They are doing this good work in courses on non-European societies and cultures, the history of women, the history of sexuality, and other non-traditional subjects. Much of the book describes these courses and programs, for the most part sympathetically. And they do sound . . . nice. But they also sound a touch banal. Here is the statement of purpose for a course Nussbaum cites as a "very successful example" of an "ambitious . . . arduous, but potentially more satisfying approach" to multicultural education:

> [The] goal of the course is to develop within students a sense of informed, active citizenship as they enter an American society of increasing diversity by focusing on contemporary and historical issues of race, ethnicity, gender, social class, and religious sectarianism in American life . . . to provide students with an intellectual awareness of the causes and effects of structured inequalities and prejudicial exclusion in American society . . . to provide students with increased self-awareness of what it means in our culture to be a person of their own gender, race, class, ethnicity, and religion as well as an understanding of how these categories affect those who are different from themselves . . . to expand students' ability to think critically, and with an open mind, about controversial contemporary issues that stem from the gender, race, class, ethnic, and religious differences that pervade American society.

Thanks, but I think I'd rather study Plato with Allan Bloom, or even join the Great Books discussion group at my local public library. Yes, it is vitally important to recognize and acknowledge that one's own values and traditions are not the only ones worthy of respect—that other human beings are indeed human beings, however different. But although the acknowledgment may sometimes be morally demanding, the recognition is not, intellectually speaking, very difficult or interesting. Once you've got it, you've got it. We're not talking poetry criticism or higher mathematics.

Besides, isn't there perhaps a filament of connection between the drive for diversity and the culture of consumption? Students are increasingly seen primarily as customers by universities today; isn't the emphasis on "difference" at least partly a marketing tool? To what extent are students attracted to non-traditional subjects by an appetite for novelty or simply by mental laziness? In the hyper-stimulated world of the American campus (by the way, *Cultivating Humanity* takes very little notice of the equally vast but less stimulating world of community and junior colleges), isn't depth rather than breadth the more pressing need?

Nussbaum, however, has chosen a different text for her sermon.

> To unmask prejudice and secure justice, we need argument, an essential tool of civic freedom.

> Education must promote the ability to doubt the unqualified goodness of one's own ways, as we search for what is good in human life the world over.

> A central role of art is to challenge conventional wisdom and values.

> If literature is a representation of human possibilities, the works of literature we choose will inevitability respond to, and further develop, our sense of who we are and might be.

> However we order our varied loyalties, we should still be sure that we recognize the worth of human life wherever it occurs and see ourselves as bound by common human abilities and problems to people who lie at a great distance from us.

Amen. Yet as one endures these pious exhortations, one is reminded of Norman Mailer's exasperated comment on Paul Goodman in *The Armies of the Night*: "Mailer, of course, was not without respect for Goodman. He thought Goodman had had an enormous influence in the colleges and much of it had been, from his own point of view, very much to the good. . . . But, oh, the style! It set Mailer's teeth on edge to read it; he was inclined to think that the body of students who followed Goodman must have something de-animalized to put up with the style, or at least such was Mailer's bigoted view."

If Nussbaum is a slightly sententious Socrates, Hanson and Heath are savagely indignant Jeremiahs. "On the whole, higher education in America is in a healthy state," Nussbaum opines. Hanson and Heath take a different view. Their immediate grievance is the imminent demise of classics as a discipline. "The Greeks, unfamiliar to the general public, are now also dead in the university. Today classics embraces a body of knowledge and a way of looking at the world that are virtually unrecognized, an almost extinct species even in its own protected habitat, the academic department. We classicists are the dodo birds of academia."

True, the rate of publication in classics is at an all-time high: upwards of 16,000 articles, monographs, and books in one recent year, nearly thirty for each graduating senior in the field. This, however, is part of the problem. Most of this stuff, according to Hanson and Heath, is "silly, boring, mostly irrelevant," and above all, self-serving. "All of us who teach the Greeks anywhere, according to our station, confront daily a set of realities that say the opposite of what we learn from the Greeks: obscure and narrow publication, travel, title, pelf, and university affiliation are everything, undergraduate teaching, matching word with deed, living like Greeks relatively nothing."

"Living like Greeks"—what can that mean today? To the postmodernist left, it means the unthinkable: slavery, patriarchy, imperialism. To Nussbaum, it appears to mean an open-ended, society-wide philosophy seminar (led, presumably, by philosophy professors). To Hanson and Heath, it means something far less genteel and now scarcely recognizable. For them, the Greeks' main legacy was not Socratic dialectic or cosmopolitan humanism—valuable though these things are—but rather a "hard and peculiar way of looking at the world," austere, rooted, stoical, individualistic, plainspoken, egalitarian, mistrustful of novelty, contemptuous of luxury and vanity, jealous of economic and political independence, regardful of physical courage and mother-wit. The heroic ideal and the tragic sense are what they mean by "Homer" and what they consider just about dead.

Who's to blame? Hanson and Heath's indictment names names (including Nussbaum's) and cites documents (dozens of passages of wretched prose by academic feminists, postcolonialists, and deconstructionists). By the end there is as much blood on the floor as there was in Ithaca's Great Hall, after Odysseus killed the suitors. But of course the problems transcend classics. In every field, the star system means that senior faculty avoid teaching, junior faculty resent teaching, and both frantically publish more and more worth less and less. Financial troubles have turned university administrators into shills. French fads bemuse students; the therapeutic ethos coddles them; mass culture distracts them; and the global economy scares the bejesus out of them (hence all those business majors).

As Hanson and Heath acknowledge, all this has been said before (though rarely so well, in my opinion). What is perhaps most valuable in *Who Killed Homer?* is its continuation of the themes of Hanson's remarkable *The Other Greeks* (1995) and *Fields Without Dreams* (1996). The former is a radical reappraisal of Greek culture, which seeks to displace our interpretive focus from the polis to the countryside. "Greece alone," Hanson argues, "first created 'agrarianism,' an ideology in which the production of food and, above all, the actual people who own the land and do the farmwork, are held to be of supreme social importance. The recovery of this ancient ideology . . . explains both the beginning and the end of the Greeks' greatest achievement, the classical city-state."

Fields Without Dreams is even more original and radical: a *Works and Days* of California raisin farming (Hanson is, I have neglected to mention, a sixth-generation small farmer, and not primarily an academic), a bitter lament for American agriculture, and a fierce, despairing brief for agrarian populism. Hanson's portrait of the vanishing small farmer—"this bothersome, queer oddball"—is clear-eyed and unromantic; and his skepticism about the hollow abundance that has succeeded him is free of condenscension and nostalgia. As a diagnosis of contemporary cultural weightlessness, *Fields Without Dreams* ranks with the best of Christopher Lasch and Wendell Berry.

Hanson and Heath's Greeks are not Allan Bloom's aristocratic youths and esoteric sages nor Martha Nussbaum's proto-"world citizens"—nor, for that matter, Matthew Arnold's immortal poets and sculptors. They are *hoi mesoi*, a "society of small independent yeomen," a "republic of hoplite soldiers," each one claiming "an equal slot in the phalanx, a voice in the assembly, and a plot in the countryside." These "middling ones" created "the first freeholding citizenry in civilization" and then "crafted war and invented politics to preserve their discovery of agrarian egalitarianism." That all this sounds strikingly like late eighteenth and early nineteenth-century America—the high-water mark of democratic republicanism in modern history—is probably not a coincidence.

Is it necessary to choose between cosmopolitanism and agrarian populism? Let us hope not. The liberal virtues and the republican virtues are both indispensable. But that does not mean they are, at this moment, equally urgent or equally vulnerable. The apparently irresistible thrust of global capitalism threatens the latter virtues far more than the former, threatens rootedness and psychological integrity far more than mobility and personal growth, perhaps even—to stretch a point—threatens independence and self-reliance more than impartial benevolence. The "heroic ideal" and the "tragic sense": these phrases already sound archaic. But our civilization has not outgrown what they signify; it has merely forgotten. Cultural amnesia is not, after all, the same thing as progress. Or is it, as the critics of "progress" allege?

The Price of Selfhood

Literature has always been about love; the modern novel has been about love as a problem. More precisely, about love as one instance of the fundamental modern problem: autonomy, individuality, selfhood. Enacting one's identity, living up to one's inherited role, offered premoderns plenty of scope for literary heroism; but devising one's identity, choosing one's role, is a peculiarly modern difficulty. It has been the burden above all of modern women, the response to which has included several waves of feminism and a line of great novels: *Wuthering Heights, Daniel Deronda, The Portrait of a Lady, The House of Mirth, Tess of the d'Urbervilles, Women in Love, To the Lighthouse, The Golden Notebook, Wide Sargasso Sea*, and others by Meredith, Gissing, Forster, Cather, and more.

These novels show women—and men—struggling for self-knowledge, self-reliance, or self-definition against the weight of traditional expectations and dependencies. The terrain of this struggle is love-and-marriage, which is where—at least in the world in which those novels take place—most people have their deepest experiences and meet their most significant fates. The essays in *The End of the Novel of Love* canvass this seemingly familiar territory with urgent intelligence.

Vivian Gornick's three slender essay collections and short, lambent memoir *Fierce Attachments* (1987) contain some of the best feminist writing in recent decades. In spare, penetrating prose that leaves out little of the essential and all of the inessential, she has returned passionately, relentlessly, to a single cluster of insights: Romantic love can be—as often as not has been—a salvation myth. We are all—for historical reasons, women especially—desperately eager to be saved from the excruciating daily effort of emotional independence. What "visionary feminists have seen for two hundred years" is that power over one's own life comes not from complementary union, from two-in-oneness, but from "the steady command of one's own thought"; that "only one's own working mind breaks the solitude of the self"; that "to live consciously is the real business of our lives," and if this means living alone, hardening our hearts, refusing to melt or merge, then so be it.

The End of the Novel of Love[1] locates these insights at both the center and the periphery of modern fiction. Meredith's neglected masterpiece *Diana of the Crossways*, for example, shows one of the most appealing heroines in literature hardening her heart at "the exact moment" when heroines traditionally "melt into romantic longing and the deeper need for union." So, in similar circumstances, do Gwendolyn Harleth in *Daniel Deronda*, Lily Bart in *The House of Mirth*, and Clarissa Dalloway in *Mrs. Dalloway*. Why? Because "[each] woman has taken a long look down the road of her future. What she sees repels. She cannot 'imagine' herself in what lies ahead. Unable to imagine herself, she now thinks she cannot act the part. She will no longer be able to make the motions. The marriage will be a charade. In that moment of clear sight sentimental love, for her, becomes a thing of the past."

Each of these characters ends badly, but the spectacle of their bravery and clearsightedness arouses pity and terror. So do the real women whose lives Gornick contemplates: Clover Adams, Kate Chopin, Jean Rhys, Willa Cather, Christina Stead, Hannah Arendt. All of them tried, with varying success, to escape the undertow of convention and compromise—meaning, for most of them, a life centered on relationship and intimacy rather than on work. All of them arrived at an "awful, implicit knowledge": that the effort of soul-making "is a solitary

[1]Beacon Press, 1997.

one, more akin to the act of making art than of making family. It acknowledges, even courts, loneliness. Love, on the other hand, fears loneliness, turns sharply away from it."

This shift in our spiritual center of gravity—primarily women's, but not exclusively—leaves everything changed, including the premises of fiction. In two superb essays Gornick takes the measure of this change. "Tenderhearted Men" groups Raymond Carver, Richard Ford, and Andre Dubus as contemporary exponents of male loneliness, desolation, inarticulate suffering: a sensibility formerly (as in Hemingway) hardboiled, now tenderhearted. For all these writers' honesty and skill, Gornick finds, they have not faced up to why things are not, and cannot be, as they used to be between men and women. They do not, as Hemingway did, blame women; they like and admire women. But they yearn for what is no longer attainable and no longer even desirable: to find in romance "comfort against the overwhelming force of life."

The title essay puts the case against romantic love even more fully. Not, of course, against love as a precious experience; but against love as the meaning of life, the royal road to self-knowledge, the way down toward the deepest possibilities of thought and feeling—love, that is, as it has functioned in the modern novel: in "*Anna Karenina* and *Madame Bovary* and *The Age of Innocence* . . . as well as the ten thousand middlebrow versions of these books, and the dime-store novels too." This is no longer a plausible expectation, Gornick contends. It used to be, when marriage was sacred, sex outside marriage was sinful, pregnancy outside marriage was catastrophic, and much of the psyche was terra incognita. But love as mystery and revelation could not survive the democratization of experience and the commodification of sex. The ignorance, the suffering, the risk associated with illicit love have shrunk drastically; and so, proportionately, have the courage required and the enlightenment gained.

This is not a cause for regret. Bourgeois respectability cannot be resurrected and does not deserve to be. But it can no longer serve, either, as the main arena of self-creation for real or fictional characters. The "long line of slowly clarifying thought" that ultimately constitutes a self will have to find a new starting point; we now know too much about love. A century of feminism (with a little help from technology) has done its work; the novel of the future will have to be about something else.

The End of the Novel of Love is small in bulk but large in implication. Gornick's language and literary acumen are beyond cavil; the book is a pleasure and a stimulus: persuasive, finely wrought, quivering with intelligence. It is also disturbing, as it's meant to be. Here and in her other writing, Gornick is almost lyrical on the grim subject of loneliness. Not loneliness as deprivation but loneliness as integrity: the possible price—sometimes it sounds as though she means the necessary price—of uncompromised, fully conscious individuality. About this ideal of untrammeled selfhood there is much to be said (and much is currently being said) pro and con. Gornick's advocacy is effective, even inspiring. But modern individualism is not, it seems to me, the last word.

In recent decades we have begun to reckon the moral and psychological consequences of our almost incomprehensibly slow and complex biological evolution: how it enables and constrains us; how it reveals each of us to be a kind of organic iceberg with a tremendous hidden mass, inertial but alive and delicately engineered. The genus *Homo* is around 2.5 million years, or 125,000 generations, old. Romantic love is, for all but a minuscule elite, no more than twenty generations old; reliable contraceptive technology, perhaps three. We do not yet know how much of our sexuality and psychology is hard-wired, but probably a lot. In which case, we will need a better wiring diagram before we can wisely adopt any ideal of selfhood.

Notoriously, the theory of evolution cut no ice with D.H. Lawrence; he didn't, he scoffed, "feel it in my solar plexus." Nevertheless, his misgivings about modern individualism—the weightiest that have yet been expressed, in my opinion—rested on kindred intimations of animality. "To live consciously is the real business of our lives," Gornick writes, out of a feminist and rationalist tradition that Lawrence encountered in the shapes of Bloomsbury and Bertrand Russell, two of its finer manifestations. Lawrence would have demurred; he thought that instinct, impulse, and reflex, physical grace, emotional vividness, and ritual unison were no less important than critical judgment and self-conscious individuality. Consciousness, he believed, is accessory, epiphenomenal, "the glitter of the sun on the surface of the waters," as he wrote on one occasion; and on another: "I conceive that a man's body is like a flame, and the intellect is just the light that is shed on the things around."

Lawrence, too, wrote in a tradition: the Romantic critique of the Enlightenment. It has had its incautious, even unsavory exponents; and Lawrence too, as everyone knows, lurched down many a rhetorical blind alley. It's hard, after all, to be explicit about primal realities. But it's essential to try. Somewhere between, or beyond, these two great traditions, with their complementary imperatives—intellect and imagination, analysis and instinct, freedom and rootedness, individuality and communion—is the best way we can live now.

Yes to Sex

For thirty years, in a wide arc from the *Village Voice* and *Social Text* to the *New Yorker* and *Mirabella*, Ellen Willis has been the Sixties' best exponent and a savvy interpreter of American politics and culture. Her output thus far is small—two sterling collections, *Beginning to See the Light* (1981) and *No More Nice Girls* (1992)—so one eagerly welcomes her new book[1] (notwithstanding the false note struck by its title, which insinuates cluelessness on the other side—always a polemical dud move).

What do the Sixties have to say to the Nineties? In essays on crime, race, censorship, globalization, Bosnia, the Republican ascendancy, the culture of austerity, Zippergate, and right-wing libertarianism, Willis advocates left-wing libertarianism. The left should contend for the maximum of individual development and expression; and what it has to contend against are external constraints imposed by gross economic inequality and internal ones arising from the inculcation early in life of a rigid, self-denying morality. Among the tenets of left libertarianism:

[1] *Don't Think, Smile: Notes on a Decade of Denial* by Ellen Willis. Beacon Press, 1999.

that the point of life is to live and enjoy it fully; that genuine virtue is the overflow of happiness, not the bitter fruit of self-denial; that sexual freedom and pleasure are basic human rights; that endless work and subordination to bosses are offenses to the human spirit; that contempt for the black poor is the middle class's effort to deny that *we are next*; that Mom is not going back home again and so we need to rethink domestic life, child rearing, and the structures of work; that democracy is not about voting for nearly indistinguishable politicians but about having a voice in collective decision-making, not only in government but at home, school, and work. Naturally this vision should be accompanied by tough-minded analysis, in the first instance a thoroughgoing critique of the new economic order and its accelerating class war.

Attention to the internal as well as the external yields much astute commentary. Willis's discussion of crime, "Beyond Good and Evil," takes note of its obvious roots in material deprivation but also subtly and rigorously links the "psychopolitics of crime" to the "dynamics of domination." "The Ordeal of Liberal Optimism" addresses the liberal critique of affirmative action, suggesting persuasively that it takes too little account of racial psychodynamics. Both essays are notable for lucidity, fairmindedness, and sureness in getting at the marrow of bitterly contested questions.

An essay on censorship and free speech starts out, like most feminist approaches to the anti-pornography debate, considering the "politics of sexual representation." But Willis moves quickly to "the politics of speech as such," where "the case against the censors is not so obvious after all." There turns out to be more substance to the critique of First Amendment absolutism than one might have supposed. Catherine MacKinnon and others argue with some plausibility that the boundaries of speech protected by the First Amendment can only be specified by taking no less seriously the constitutional mandate of equality set out in the Fourteenth Amendment. Speech undeniably has consequences, sometimes entirely predictable ones. "Distinguishing talk about inferiority from verbal imposition of inferiority may be complicated at the edges," MacKinnon writes, "but it is clear enough at the center with sexual and racial harassment, pornography, and hate propaganda."

Willis avoids the untenable absolutist rejoinders: that the First Amendment is unambiguous and that speech can infallibly be distinguished from action. She acknowledges, as one must, that speech is a particular kind of action; and of course she does not deny that legally actionable harassment can sometimes be purely verbal. But while MacKinnon's argument stops there, content merely to demote speech from categorical uniqueness, Willis goes on to root a defense of controversial speech in a theory of freedom, which is in turn derived from a theory of moral psychology. It's not that speech is never wounding, she argues, but that freedom is healing.

> Symbolic expression, however forceful, leaves a space between communicator and recipient, a space for contesting, fighting back with one's own words and images, organizing to oppose whatever action the abhorred speech may incite. Though speech may, and often does, *support* the structure of domination, whether by lending aid and comfort to the powerful or frightening and discouraging their targets, in leaving room for opposition it falls short of *enforcing* submission. For this reason the unrestrained clash of ideas, emotions, visions provides a relatively safe model—one workable even in a society marked by serious imbalances of power—of how to handle social conflict, with its attendant fear, anger, and urges to repress, through argument, persuasion, and negotiation (or at worst grim forbearance) rather than coercion. In the annals of human history, even this modest exercise in freedom is a revolutionary development; for the radical democrat it prefigures the extension of freedom to other areas of social life.

I think this takes the debate a step beyond Stanley Fish's *There's No Such Thing as Free Speech*—no small achievement.

Throughout these essays it's a pleasure to watch the deployment of Willis's extraordinary dialectical skills. But not all her targets are equally deserving. A good deal of the book is devoted to rebuking the "economic" or "populist" or "majoritarian" left for insufficient attention to the psychocultural roots of inequality and domination. To those who suggest that perhaps a thoroughgoing demystification of truth, beauty, objectivity, morality, authority, law, and love can wait until the minimum wage goes up a dollar or two and not quite so many American households (currently one in three) are only a major illness away from bankruptcy, Willis replies that freedom and equality are indivisible. If Americans "do not feel entitled to demand freedom and equality in their personal and social relations," she insists, "they will not fight for freedom and equality in their economic relations." Furthermore, "people are not 'distracted' by the moral and cultural issues that affect their daily existence as much as the size of their paychecks; they care passionately about those issues."

Isn't there a non sequitur here? A popular majority might, after all, agree broadly with the left about freedom and equality in economic relations but disagree broadly about freedom and equality in personal relations. People no doubt care passionately about both economic issues and moral/cultural ones, but their views about the former may be much closer to those of economic leftists than their views about the latter are to those of cultural leftists. Actually, these are not merely logical possibilities. According to Alan Wolfe in *One Nation After All*, that's the way things are. Needless to say, Wolfe's book is not the last word, but he offers plenty of evidence.

And if this *is* the way things are, what follows? Would economic populists then be entitled, and inclined, to show cultural libertarians the door? I'm not nearly so sure as Willis. Which door, anyway? A little comradely recrimination may be good for the ideological blood pressure; but beyond that, I don't see what's at stake in this strategic debate. There is no left-wing party or other organization awaiting its outcome, ready to carry the approved word far and wide. It won't and shouldn't lead anyone to drop one kind of political activity and take up another. Economic radicals and cultural radicals can pretty much count on each other's handful of votes, and neither has any resources or patrons to be raided by the other. The masses rarely peruse the *Nation* or *Dissent*; they're busy or tired or glued to the screen, and we're not on the local newsstand anyway. So by all means let's fire away at one another, but with popguns rather than heavy artillery.

In any case, economic democracy is surely the best thing that could happen to cultural radicalism. During his quixotic 1968 mayoral campaign, Norman Mailer won over an emphatically skeptical Bella Abzug by roaring back at her: "I can tell you that regardless of my views on women as *you* think you know them, women in any administration I could run would have more voice, more respect, more real opportunity for argument than any of the other candidates would offer you." Exactly. A little (or better, a whopping) redistribution of wealth would put cultural radicals—most of whom, I suspect, inhabit the lower four-fifths of the income scale—in a much stronger position to ignore the rest of society, press their claims on it, or construct alternatives to it.

Willis's quarrel with the "culturally conservative" or "pro-family" left is more substantial. In recent years public discussion of abortion, divorce, welfare, and crime has been marked by near-universal deference for words like "virtue," "responsibility," "self-control," "discipline," "stability," "community," "family," and the like. Willis is deeply suspicious of this rhetorical tendency. It serves, she argues, to shore up a familiar system of domination and hierarchy based on self-denial and the subordination of women. The premise of traditional morality is some version of original sin; it "assumes the need to combat the human incli-nation toward evil by imposing coercive social controls as well as the internal controls of conscience and guilt." The agency of this repression is the family: "it is the parents' job to suppress their children's evil impulses and assure that they develop the requisite inner controls." These "evil impulses" are erotic: desires for bodily satisfaction and pleasure, which are imagined as potentially limitless and progressively consuming in later life if not firmly curbed in infancy and then, in childhood, channeled into forms of expression (i.e., maleness and femaleness) that allow for social order and continuity. The cost of these "inner controls" is a pervasive, largely unconscious unease: fear and submissiveness alternating with rage and resentment. "In demonizing children's desire, the family provokes the very destructive impulses it must then imperfectly repress."

The child's thwarted impulses persist in adulthood, this argument contin-ues, where they are countered by an array of external controls—religious, legal, medical, economic, etc.—that teach and enforce one or another version of hier-archy. They are also countered by the need to repress the acutely painful memo-ries of rage and humiliation that an open acknowledgment of long-unsatisfied desires would provoke. In addition, social, sexual, familial, economic, and other hierarchies are less oppressive for some (males, whites, parents, employers) than for others—an incentive for the more fortunate to make the best of a bad but ap-parently natural and inevitable situation.

Hence, according to Willis, our society's precarious equilibrium. "A mor-al system based on repression and coercion, on the stifling of desire, generates enormous stores of anger and frustration that can never be totally controlled. When those emotions find expression in destructive behavior, it is seized on as proof of intractable human evil and the need to maintain or increase repression. The result is a closed circle, a self-perpetuating, self-reinforcing system of tragic dimensions."

The way out of this circle is the conquest of scarcity. As long as societal survival was not assured, hierarchical subordination and the disciplining of individual desire were self-evidently necessary. Over the last two centuries, however, it has become possible to see traditional morality as a strategy of social self-preservation, a strategy bound to be superseded and indeed already in retreat. When pleasure—or at least its material prerequisites—is more abundant, self-denial can cease to be the foundation of all collective life, and morality as a structure of internalized coercion, along with the patriarchical family that reproduces it, will wither away.

And what might come after? The only place Willis hints at an answer is a passage in her well-known 1979 essay "The Family: Love It or Leave It."

> The logical postpatriarchial unit is some version of the commune. Groups of people who agreed to take responsibility for each other, pool their economic resources, and share housework and child care would have a basis for stability independent of any one couple's sexual bond; children would have the added security of close ties to adults other than their biological parents (and if the commune were large and flexible enough, parents who had stopped being lovers might choose to remain in it); communal child-rearing, shared by both sexes, would remove the element of martyrdom from parenthood.

A little sketchy, this. But even those who are dubious about Willis's postpatriarchical alternative must acknowledge that her libertarian-socialist utopianism is based on something more than a sentimental attachment to Sixties slogans. It is, on the contrary, a highly plausible deduction from the prevailing conception of modernity, which defines the good life in terms of leisure and abundance and envisions history as continuous moral and material progress, made possible by the spread of scientific and social rationality. Nearly all secular thinkers of both left and right subscribe to this conception, and in their case Willis's exasperated exhortations to "think radically" are very much to the point.

At least one secular leftist, however, thought quite as radically about modernity as Willis and came to different conclusions. Christopher Lasch was not a believer in original sin but in what might be called original limits. These are limits imposed not by material scarcity or political inequality but by the process of individuation itself. Lasch's account of psychic development, like Willis's, focuses on the infant's response to frustration, but more convincingly. (Willis's fullest account is in "Toward a Feminist Sexual Revolution" in *No More Nice Girls*; I have outlined Lasch's ideas at considerable length in an earlier essay.) Willis's "demonizing of desire" implies parental intent, a contingent matter. But as Lasch points out, some—in fact a great deal—of infantile frustration is inevitable, as are the outsized fantasies with which the infant typically responds. These fantasies, of omnipotence or terrified helplessness, of annihilating rage or undifferentiated union, of perfectly benevolent or implacably threatening parents, must gradually be mastered, reduced in scale, if the child is to assume the contours of a self.

Living down these otherwise disabling fantasies is the essence of psychological maturation. It requires the continual experience of love and discipline, gratification and frustration, from the same source. This can best—arguably can only—be done in the constant presence of the fantasied objects, i.e., the child's parents. Until the last two centuries, it usually was. But the displacement of household production by mass production drastically altered the child's relation to its father; and the centralized, interventionist state, overshadowing and sometimes replacing parental authority, complicated maturation still further. The result was frequently a weak self—which is the clinical meaning of "narcissism." (It has nothing to do with an excess of self-love, the popular meaning of the word.)

The essence of modernity is mobility and choice; the essence of premodernity was immobility and ascription. It *looks*, vexingly, as though successful individuation requires an irreducible minimum of the latter. The bearer of this bad news was understandably greeted with something less than grateful enthusiasm by many of his political comrades. But when Lasch criticized modernity, he had in mind mass production and the centralized state, not sexual equality. He believed that the family needed to be defended, not against feminism but against the effects of the separation of home and work. He was skeptical of "progress," not from a dislike of equality or pleasure but from a preference for the genuine rather than the ersatz articles. He maintained that freedom meant overcoming emotionally-charged dependence on individual or local authorities, not taking for granted an abstract, universal dependence on distant, bureaucratic authorities.

Culture and psychology are central to politics; Willis is right about that. But cultural politics must reckon with our psychic ecology: the sum of our adaptations, over the course of two million years, to infantile dependence, territoriality, scarcity, mortality, and the other hitherto inescapable limits of human existence. We are organisms; we cannot flourish at just any tempo, pressure, or scale. Imagination itself is, as I have suggested, an evolutionary adaptation, whereby we master a threatening environment when young by binding or investing fantasy within nearby entities—parents, neighborhood, church, ethnic group. These intense primary identifications can and should be gradually left behind, but they cannot be skipped, on pain of shallowness, instability, and—paradoxically—an inability in later life to stand firm against authority.

Cultural politics should aim to reform rather than abolish marriage, the family, hierarchy, authority, morality, and law. These institutions and practices evolved to serve essential purposes. They are not purely, or even primarily, strategies of exploitation. To consider them prisons rather than temporary outposts is not radical but superficial, like considering religion and myth mere lies rather than inadequate attempts at explanation. Cultural radicals will sometimes, in fact, need to defend these institutions; i.e., insist that some way be found to achieve their formative or protective purposes. As the global economy and mass culture lay siege to inwardness, plow up our psychic root system, and alter the very grain and contour of our being, conservation increasingly becomes a radical imperative.

Foucault remarked sourly: "We must not think that by saying yes to sex, one says no to power." There are, of course, plenty of other good reasons for saying yes to sex and to pleasures of (nearly) every other kind, as well as for demanding a fairer distribution of pleasure's prerequisites—money and leisure. But the strength to persevere in such demands and also to pursue the sublimer, more strenuous pleasures—of craft, of thought, of devotion, of emulation—is not only, as Willis contends, "the overflow of happiness"; it is also the "bitter fruit" (tart, anyway) of self-discipline. Premodern cruelties and superstitions still bulk large; left-wing libertarianism is still the best answer to them. To recognize the subtler entrapments of modernity requires, however, another variety of radical imagination.

South of Eden

In Lampedusa's novel *The Leopard*, the philosophical Prince Fabrizio explains sadly to a visitor, a liberal reformer urging Italian national unity, why nineteenth-century Sicily will not join the modern world: "The Sicilians never want to improve, for the simple reason that they think themselves perfect; their vanity is stronger than their misery." A curious and pathetic illusion, this. Mortification would seem a more appropriate response to Sicilian history and culture than vanity. The guiding principles of Sicilian society, at least as it is portrayed in nineteenth- and early twentieth-century Italian literature, are envy, jealousy, superstition, avarice, low cunning, unremitting suspiciousness, and everlasting vindictiveness. The stubbornly adhered-to—and frequently romanticized—Sicilian ideals of *onore*, *vendetta*, and *omertà* mean, in practice, that all women are property, that all grievances are mortal, and that all outsiders are untrustworthy. D.H. Lawrence, who probably knew and loved Sicily better than any other non-Italian, was aghast at the mores of the Sicilian village: "so squalid, so pottering, so despicable; like a crawling of beetles." At their worst, Sicilians of the traditional stripe can make the wiliest and most grasping of Balzacian villains seem like the most ethereally pure of Dickensian heroines. The Mafia and the Inquisition, the two most successful institutions in the island's history, are about what they (being only a couple of generations removed, perhaps I should say "we") deserve.

229

Nevertheless, from this unpromising human material some enduring literature has been fashioned. Giovanni Verga, one of the founders of European naturalism, produced several renowned novels and stories set in Sicily, as did the young Luigi Pirandello, for all his later cosmopolitanism. Southern Italy, with its similar social and cultural conditions, was the setting of Ignazio Silone's widely admired fiction, including his masterpiece, *Bread and Wine*. And one of the most popular Italian books of this century, Carlo Levi's *Christ Stopped at Eboli*, chronicles the encounter of an urban intellectual from the North, exiled by Mussolini to a remote village in the rural South, with his premodern countrymen.

To this slender but distinguished line one may add the contemporary Sicilian writer Leonardo Sciascia. Born in 1921, he has spent most of his life as a schoolteacher. In the 1950s he began to write historical/political sketches of his native region, which were collected in his first book, *Salt in the Wound*. Around the same time, he began writing fiction; *Sicilian Uncles* is his first collection. His subsequent fiction became progressively more playful, allusive, and oblique. *Candido* is an updated version, with modern Italian characters, of Voltaire's fable. *The Council of Egypt* is a historical tale about a forged manuscript; though not quite as baroque as *The Name of the Rose*, it is nearly as erudite and as epistemologically suggestive. *Mafia Vendetta*, *A Man's Blessing*, *Equal Danger*, and *One Way or Another* are detective novels, all of them featuring murder, political conspiracy, and an ambiguous outcome in which, true to Sicilian reality, something less than justice is done. *The Wine-Dark Sea* is a collection of short stories, Pirandellian in their combination of whimsy and melancholy. Although Sciascia is one of Europe's most eminent living writers, English translations of all his works have been in and out of print; so every new translation or reissue, like this one from Carcanet, is an event.

Sicilian Uncles[1] is the most political in content and the most conventionally realistic in form of Sciascia's fiction, and it is arguably his best. It consists of four novellas. In "The American Aunt," a boy observes the arrival of the occupying American army and the subsequent metamorphosis of his town—a ritual of Sicilian history—from hostility to hospitality. He cadges cigarettes from the

[1]Translated by N.S. Thompson. Carcanet, 1986.

soldiers and sells them to his layabout uncle, who mourns for the "respect" and "glory" that Mussolini's conquests had brought Italy. Along with the soldiers, there begin to arrive a stream of parcels from the townspeople's American relatives. It is like a first installment of the Marshall Plan, and like the later installments, it is accompanied by frequent exhortations to vote against the Communists in the postwar elections.

Eventually the boy's aunt arrives from Brooklyn with her family and a trunkful of gifts, whose distribution is supervised by the Sicilian uncle, formerly pro-Fascist but now staunchly pro-American. The aunt's triumph is a little muted: she finds the island not quite so poor and primitive as in her girlhood memories and her fantasies of benevolence. But she finds something else, too: a husband for her daughter in the canny, courtierlike uncle. This encounter between New World and Old World subtlety is, in its way, reminiscent of Henry James—though nothing could be less Jamesian than Sciascia's laconic style.

The Italian post-World War II elections, in which the Communists lost to the Christian Democrats, took place in 1948. Exactly a century earlier, the specter of revolution had likewise haunted Sicily, and was likewise beaten back. The narrator of "Forty Eight" is also a boy. His father is the gardener of Baron Garziano of Castro, who, along with the Bishop and the Prefect, incarnates the traditional triple nemesis of the Sicilian peasantry: Church, state, and landed aristocracy. When the European revolution of 1848 sets off tremors even in Castro, the terrified Baron and the wily Bishop manage to ride out the storm and return to their customary pursuits: the Baron to adultery and the Bishop to embezzlement. But a dozen years later the specter returns in the form of Garibaldi, whose troops (including the narrator, now a young man) are in the process of unifying Italy. Ever a survivor, the Baron welcomes and abjectly flatters Garibaldi—though enough of the Red Shirts see through his cajolery to suggest that the old order is no longer invulnerable.

In both these stories, the ingenuousness of the child-narrator highlights the ubiquitous, ineffable rascality of Sicilian adults. This contrast is the source of much of Sciascia's humor. For example, the pro-Fascist uncle in "The American Aunt," who grumbles that Mussolini is too soft on political opponents, is full of terrors when the tide turns:

"The Communists!" he said. "Neither you nor your father understand anything of what's going on. They're coming now. You'll see those murderers arrive right here, burning the churches, destroying families, pulling people from their beds and shooting them." My uncle was thinking of himself. He was in bed at least sixteen hours a day. I pictured him being dragged from his bed by the feet—which pleased me—though I wasn't so pleased at the thought he might be shot.

The note of compassion in that last sentence is characteristic of Sciascia. Notoriously, Sicilian speech is sly and melodramatic by turns; the effect is ridiculous but endearing. Sciascia renders it sardonically, unsentimentally, with affection but without condescension.

"The American Aunt" and "Forty Eight" are exquisitely wrought stories, in part because their author maintains his aesthetic distance: the comic invention is so exuberant that moral and political meaning remain latent. The other two tales in *Sicilian Uncles*, "Antimony" and "The Death of Stalin," are more directly political; Sciascia's wry humanism is closer to the surface. But if they are not quite so coolly elegant, they are even more affecting.

In "The Death of Stalin," the shoemaker Calogero Schirò is a loyal Communist and a fervent admirer of Stalin, whom he defends against the continual imprecations of the parish priest. The Nazi-Soviet Pact of 1939 tests his faith and gives the priest something to gloat over. But, helped by the appearance of Stalin in a dream, he reasons it out: the Non-Aggression Pact is a trap for Hitler; Stalin is biding his time. The priest is skeptical, but Calogero is gleeful at his discovery: "'Stalin's the greatest man in the world,' he said. 'To think of traps like that you need a brain as big as a fifty-pound sack of flour.'"

There are other troubling developments—the annexation of Poland, the invasion of Finland, the liquidation of Stalin's generals, the loss of the postwar elections—but Calogero keeps the faith. Then the hardest blow falls: Stalin dies and his "mistakes" come to light. Even the party admits them. Calogero is shaken; the priest exults. Again he tries to reason it out: Stalin's "brain was beginning to crumble with always having to think about the benefit of mankind: at a certain point he became eccentric." But he's too honest not to end up dissatisfied and confused.

"The Death of Stalin" is extremely funny. But even more important, Sciascia shows that although Calogero was deceived, he was something more dignified than a dupe. To acknowledge the horrible crimes of Stalinism, and at the same time do justice to the honorable aspirations it exploited, is difficult; it has rarely been done better than here. As the Germans retreat before the victorious Russian armies, Calogero has a reverie:

> Stalin was coming down into the very heart of Europe, bringing Communism and Justice. Thieves and usurers were trembling, and all those spiders who wove the world's riches and its injustices. In every city that the Red Army reached, Calogero imagined dark swarms in flight: the men of oppression and injustice convulsed with animal terror; while in the light-filled piazzas the workers mobbed Stalin's troops. Comrade Stalin, Marshal Stalin, Uncle Joe, everybody's uncle, protector of the poor and weak, the man with justice in his heart. Calogero closed every reasoning out of the things wrong with Regalpetra and the world by pointing to the portrait, "Uncle Joe'll take care of it," and he thought it had been he who had invented the familiar nickname, which by that time all the comrades in Regalpetra were using. On the contrary, all the farm labourers and sulphur miners in Sicily, all the poor who believed in hope, used to call him "Uncle Joe," as they once had done to Garibaldi. They used the name "Uncle" for all the men who brought justice or vengeance, the hero or the *capomafia*: the idea of justice always shines when vindictive thoughts are decanted. Calogero had been interned, his comrades there had instructed him in doctrine, but he couldn't think of Stalin as anything other than an "Uncle" who could arm for a vendetta and strike decisively *a baccagliu*, that is, in the slang of all Sicilian "Uncles," against the enemies of Calogero Schirò: Cavaliere Pecorilla, who had sent him into internment; Gangemi, the sulphur miner, who had refused to pay him for resoling a shoe; and Dr. La Ferla, who had distrained him of over two hundredweight of wheat to pay for an operation on his groin, which a butcher could have done better.

There is no need to detail the ironies in this passage, or the fate of Calogero's hopes. I could hardly bear to, in any case. Still, this homely vision—this jumble of ancient grievances, local prejudice, and personal pain—seems to me as worthy of respect as the loftiest flights of Gramsci.

Stalinism and Fascism had another fateful encounter: the Spanish Civil War. George Orwell's *Homage to Catalonia* begins with a now famous anecdote: his brief meeting with an illiterate Italian militiaman, who symbolized for him everything brave and decent about the Republican cause—everything that, like Calogero Schirò's vision, was frustrated and betrayed by Stalinism. The protagonist of "Antimony" is also a young militiaman, this time on the Fascist side, one of the many unemployed Italians shipped to Spain by Mussolini to fight for Franco. But the Fascist firing squads nauseate him, and he comes to realize that the people he is fighting in Spain and the people he lives among in Sicily—the peasants and the sulfur miners—have a common enemy. "I would say that the least peasant in my home district, the most 'benighted,' as we say, that is, the most ignorant, the one most cut off from a knowledge of the world, if he had been brought to the Aragon front and had been told to find out which side people like himself were on and go to them, he would have made for the Republican trenches without hesitation." It is a memorable political education. Despite its brevity, "Antimony" ranks with *Homage to Catalonia* and André Malraux's *Man's Hope* as one of the finest imaginative products of the Spanish Civil War.

By the end of that war W.H. Auden was to write, in deepest disillusionment, that "intellectual disgrace/Stares from every human face." Very few politically engaged writers have emerged from this century's ideological wars with their intellectual honor intact. Sciascia may be numbered among them. The humanism that shines through the fiction of Silone, the films of de Sica, the essays of Chiaromonte, Camus, Orwell, and Dwight Macdonald—this, leavened with the bittersweet humor of the immemorially defeated Sicilian, is Sciascia's sensibility as well. The miracle, even more in his case than in theirs, is that so much disillusionment and defeat could yield so much generosity and hope.

"All my books taken together form one," Sciascia has written: "a Sicilian book which probes the wounds of past and present and develops as the history of the continuous defeat of reason and of those who have been personally overcome and annihilated in that defeat." Defeat, yes; but there is hope in Sciascia's "Sicilian book" too. In *Politics and the Novel* Irving Howe paid tribute to Silone in terms that will do equally well to sum up Sciascia's achievement: "He remains hopeful, with a hopefulness that has nothing to do with optimism, that from the hidden inarticulate resources of the poor, which consist neither of intelligence nor nobility, but rather of a training in endurance and an education in ruse— that from all this something worthy of the human may yet emerge."

Fearlessness

The afterlife of Italian poet, novelist, critic, and filmmaker Pier Paolo Pasolini brings to mind some familiar lines from Auden's "In Memory of WB Yeats":

> Time that is intolerant
> Of the brave and innocent . . .
> Worships language and forgives
> Everyone by whom it lives . . .

Time has doted on Pasolini's friends, countrymen, and sometime antagonists Eugenio Montale and Italo Calvino, but has neglected the once equally celebrated Pier Paolo. His films have never gone into full eclipse, but his poems, fiction, screenplays, literary criticism, and political commentary, which engaged all literate Europe during his lifetime, have seldom traveled across the Atlantic. "Mad Ireland hurt you into poetry," Auden continued, addressing Yeats. Though the young Pasolini worshipped language, mad and ineffably wicked Italy eventually hurt him into idiosyncratic politics and extravagant rhetoric. He adopted one medium after another, fascinated at first by new formal possibilities but soon distracted into perfervid polemic. His preaching was sometimes inspired; it was also, inevitably, time-bound. He was braver and more innocent than Montale, Calvino, or virtually anyone else among his contemporaries. But political passion overwhelmed aesthetic concentration, and so, outside Italy at any rate, he has forfeited literary immortality.

Pier Paolo Pasolini was born in 1922 in Bologna. The family spent summers with relatives at Casarsa, in Italy's northeastern corner. The local peasantry spoke an ancient dialect, Friulian, in which Pasolini wrote his first poems and plays. Interest in dialects was reviving in mid-twentieth-century Italy, and Pasolini became one of the foremost practitioners and critics of Italian dialect poetry.

After the Second World War, with a degree from the University of Bologna, the beginnings of a literary reputation, and a secure job teaching secondary school, Pasolini was happy with provincial life. But for the first of many times, his uncontainable sexuality landed him *al brodo*—in the soup. Accused of paying for sex with teenage boys—his lifelong, unashamed practice—he was expelled from the Communist Party and forced to resign from public school teaching.

Self-exiled to the anonymity of Rome, he spent the first months of the 1950s as a walker in the city, discovering the slum districts and absorbing *romanesco*, the Roman dialect. Though his work—teaching private school and freelance writing—was poorly paid and exhausting, his passion for the life and above all for the *ragazzi* of the Roman streets was inexhaustible. By the end of the decade, his novels (*The Ragazzi* and *A Violent Life*) and his first film (*Accatone*), full of vivid sex, colorful and often incomprehensible slang, and a murderous poverty that belied postwar Italy's "economic miracle," exploded him into national prominence, while *Gramsci's Ashes* (1957), an anguished meditation in verse on the condition of Italy, was hailed by Calvino as "one of the most important facts of Italian postwar literature and certainly the most important in the field of poetry."

His career thereafter was a dazzle of publicity and controversy. Anna Magnani and Maria Callas both emerged from legendary seclusion to make films with him. (Callas was also to fall in love with him, only to suffer bitterly when he could not reciprocate.) *The Gospel According to Matthew*, the first (perhaps the only) great religious film by a homosexual Marxist atheist, nonplussed both the Church and the Left. Alternating with the harsh realism and surrealistic symbolism of his contemporary subjects, he made film versions of the Oedipus story, *Medea*, an African *Oresteia*, the *Decameron*, the *Canterbury Tales*, and the *Arabian Nights*. He was arraigned for immorality thirty-three times, usually in connection with the banning of one or another of his films, an ordeal that pro-voked parliamentary protest and contributed to the liberalization of Italy's postwar constitution. He was regularly invited to speak or write in various Com-munist forums and regularly denounced in others. The *Corriere della Sera*, Italy's *New York Times*, offered him an unprecedented front-page column. In 1975, at the zenith of his fame and talent—his last year's columns set all of newspaper-reading Italy on its ear and drew responses from Calvino, Alberto Moravia, the Italian prime minister, and thousands of others—he was murdered by a teenage boy he had picked up.

His life was a maelstrom of contradictions: the anarchical Communist; the anticlerical Christian; the sexual revolutionary with grave reservations about le-galizing divorce and abortion; the scholar of antique poetic forms who became an avant-garde cineaste; the cordial hater of the bourgeoisie and its minions, who nevertheless scoffed at the student revolt of 1968 and instead defended the police; the notorious transgressor, almost the living negation, of traditional values, who nevertheless inveighed incessantly against "false modernity," called for the aboli-tion of television, compulsory education, and long hair, and told an interviewer that "the people I respect most are those who haven't gone beyond the fourth grade."

What explains Pasolini's chaotic sensibility, if anything does, is (in his own words) "a violent load of vitality." His molten temperament made aesthetic re-serve, rhetorical restraint, or analytical detachment impossible. And besides, so much seemed to him at stake: not merely institutional change but the extinction of a form of life, the paganism of rural Southern Italy and of the "paleoindustrial" Roman *borgate*, where adolescents had "barely even heard of the Madonna" but at least lived and judged from firsthand rather than predigested experience.

"I have become convinced," he wrote near the end of his life, "that poverty and backwardness are not by any means the worst of ills." Has the (partial) conquest of premodern poverty and servitude been worth the price in psychic stability and in physical rootedness, spontaneity, and grace? In one form or another, this question has troubled a great many modern intellectuals. Along with its blessings, moder-nity has entailed, or at least been accompanied by, a vast blight of uniformity and superficiality. The disappearance of the dialects, with their unique rhythms and nuances, destroyed by "the horrendous language of television news, advertising, official statements," was Pasolini's first clue, which he followed up brilliantly, even if sometimes eccentrically (as in his pronouncement that the sex organs of the Roman underclass had decayed from one generation to the next). Consumerism, he warned, is "a genuine anthropological cataclysm," threatening to eclipse "the grace of obscure centuries, the scandalous revolutionary force of the past."

He raged against television, not only for homogenizing language and deadening imagination but also for fostering a meaningless, weightless sexual permissiveness. "It is television," he charged, "which has brought to a close the age of *pietà* and begun the age of *hedone*." Many people were astonished by this, coming from the avatar of cinematic sensuality. What he meant, as biographer Barth David Schwartz put it (in his magnificent *Pasolini Requiem*), is that "the demystification of sex has passed directly into its predictable and obligatory merchandising," leaving most people—or so he judged—neither freer nor wiser nor happier.

It was not always clear—in fact, it was scarcely ever clear—exactly what Pasolini opposed to the depredations of "progress." (Calvino once wrote that debating him was "like hailing a racing car driver circling the track, to ask for a ride.") He admitted freely that he was often too impatient and too exasperated to make sense, that he only had time and strength to articulate "the full force of cold rejection, of desperate useless denunciation." Here is a typically maddening and illuminating specimen of Pasolini's sublime, crackpot antimodernism:

> Young males are traumatized nowadays by the duty permissiveness imposes on them—the duty always uninhibitedly to have sex. At the same time, they are traumatized by the disappointment which their "scepter" has produced in women, who formerly either were ignorant of it or made it the subject of myths while accepting it supinely. Besides, the education for and initiation into society which formerly took place in a platonically homosexual ambiance is now, because of premature couplings, heterosexual from the onset of puberty. Yet the woman is still not in a position—given the legacy of thousands of years—to make a free pedagogic contribution: she still tends to favor definite rules, a code. And this today can only be a codification more conformist than ever, as is desired by bourgeois power; whereas the old self-education, between men and men or between women and women, obeyed popular rules (whose noble archetype remains Athenian democracy). Consumerism

has therefore ended by humiliating the woman, creating for her another intimidating myth. The young males who walk along the street, their hand on the woman's shoulder with a protective air, or romantically clasping her hand, either make one laugh or cause a pang. Nothing is more insincere than the relationship to which that consumerist couple gives concrete, unwitting expression.

Daft, of course. Still, I'm not sure that Michel Foucault, who spent the last decade of his life assembling immense, arid tomes about sexuality, produced in them a more suggestive paragraph.

Pasolini called himself "the most ancient of the ancients and the most modern of the moderns." What he meant by that, and what he hoped to accomplish, is hinted at in another remarkable passage, a comment on the *Oresteia*:

> After Athena's intervention, the Furies—unbridled, archaic, instinctive, out of nature—also survive; and they too are gods, they are immortal. They cannot be transformed while leaving their irrationality just as it is; transformed, that is from Curse-makers into Blessing-givers. Italian Marxists have not, I repeat, posed themselves this problem ... the transformation of Curses into Blessings, of the desperate, anarchical irrationalism of the bourgeoisie into an irrationalism ... that is new.

Notice: not the old, premodern irrationalism, but one that is "new," i.e., free, egalitarian, fully modern.

In his last column, published two days before his murder, Pasolini complained poignantly: "I am, finally, angry at the silence that has always surrounded me. . . . No one has intervened to help me forward, to develop more thoroughly my attempts at an explanation." Nor has anyone since. Instead, what Norman Mailer had written a few years earlier about D. H. Lawrence in *The Prisoner of Sex* now seems true of Pasolini, too: "The world has been technologized and technologized twice again in the forty years since his death, the citizens are technologized as well. . . . What he was asking for had been too hard for him, it is more than hard for us; his life was, yes, a torture, and we draw back in fear, for we would not know how to try to burn by such a light."

Stories from the City of God[1] is a small garland of narratives and essays that chronicles Pasolini's ambivalent relationship with Rome. In the stories, most of the protagonists are young boys from the slums. The youngest of them, an urchin whom Pasolini befriends at a public beach, is innocent, generous, trusting. All the rest are hustlers. ("Hustlers" is actually the meaning of *ragazzi di vita*, which is the Italian title of Pasolini's first novel, *The Ragazzi*.) Some are amusing, like Romoletto, who steals a big fish at the fish market, finds that it's rotten, and figures out how to sell it anyway. For the most part, though, they're not particularly clever or vital. What interests Pasolini, more than their beauty or wit, is their pathos. Their bodies have not yet thickened, their intelligence narrowed, or their sympathies withered, but they are afflicted nonetheless by a dim sense that all this is inevitable. The book opens with a lovely sketch of a nameless Trastevere boy, a chestnut vendor. ("Trastevere" means "across the Tiber," where the slums are.) "I would like to understand," Pasolini writes, "the mechanics by which the Trastevere—pounding, shapeless, idle—lives inside of him." "Trastevere Boy" was written in 1950; by the end of the decade Pasolini had fulfilled his ambition.

The best of the stories here is the longest, "Terracina." Luciano and Marcello steal a couple of bicycles and ride out to the fishing village of the title, where Marcello has relatives. Uncle Zocculitte takes them on as assistants. The age-old routines of Mediterranean fishermen are briefly but vividly described against the charmed background of sea and bay, which are separated by the stony promontory of Circeo, where Circe bewitched Ulysses. Luciano is also bewitched, but unlike Ulysses he doesn't escape. He takes the boat out alone one Sunday and foolishly, longing for a first taste of freedom, passes beyond the promontory into the open sea, where a gale blows the boat over. Terracina is an idyll, but Trastevere is a fate.

"Women of Rome," seven short vignettes written in 1960 to accompany a book of photographs, is more trenchant and melancholy, less tentative and wistful, than the sketches of ten years before. There is a brief portrait of Anna

<hr>

[1]*Stories from the City of God: Sketches and Chronicles of Rome, 1950-1966* by Pier Paolo Pasolini. Handsel Books, 2003.

Magnani at a party, as elemental and magnetic as onscreen. There is another couple walking down the street, this one pre-consumerist, their handclasp signifying a "right of ownership," in which she is "silently, sadly complicitous." There are open-air fruit sellers, "strong as mules, hard as stone, ill-humored." And with good reason: "Their lives are limited to two or three things: a small, dark house, old as the Colosseum, in a dark alley behind the Campo dei Fiori . . . two, three or four children, half boys and half girls, half toddlers and half adolescents, perhaps one of them in the army; and a husband with a beat-up car, who speaks as if he had a boiling hot battery in his throat, red in the face and pasty-skinned, with a face so wide you can fit a whole village in it." It was by no means only Rome's *ragazzi* that Pasolini knew, cared about, and despaired over.

The essays or "chronicles" in this collection are slight but marvelous. They are mostly short reports for newspapers or magazines: some humorous, like "The Disappearing Wild Game of the Roman Countryside," about the travails of hunters at the hands of the Italian bureaucracy, and "The Corpse'll Stink All Week Long!", about styles of soccer fandom; others on slang, the postwar *literati*, urban renewal, and (naturally) the psychology of the *ragazzi di vita*. There is a powerful trio of pieces on new and old Roman shantytowns (written for the Communist journal *Vie nuove*, where PCI leader Togliatti had once tried unsuccessfully to bar him from appearing because "such a man is unfit for family readers"); an uncharacteristically solemn but moving report on the funeral of a well-known labor leader, tens of thousands of workers silently raising and lowering their fists as the coffin plods down the Corso d'Italia behind a band; and a witty throwaway "day in the life" piece about being cheated by film producers and party-hopping with his friend Moravia. In Marina Harss's lively translation, these "chronicles" are more concrete and colorful than the furious polemics of Pasolini's last years (only a few of which are available in English, as *Lutheran Letters*, (translated by Stuart Hood), to which they make an excellent prelude.

The Sicilian writer Leonardo Sciascia—wry, skeptical, reserved—could not have been more different from Pasolini. One might have expected antipathy. And in fact, they often disagreed. But they understood each other. After one or another of Pasolini's provocations, an editor asked Sciascia for a response. Pasolini "may be wrong," Sciascia replied, he "may contradict himself," but he knows "how to think with a freedom which very few people today even aspire to."

Exactly. Like Lawrence, Pasolini had no truck with common sense or conventional wisdom, and he paid the price. The deepest fear of any intellectual is making a fool of him- or herself. Pasolini was fearless.

III. Fantasia

Extrasensory

Progress and decline are spatial metaphors. They suggest a curve headed upward or downward over time. The more points through which a curve is plotted, the better defined it is; so the farther backward and forward we can plausibly—without floating away in fantasy—extend the temporal axis, the better we'll understand cultural tendencies like the decline of verbal literacy, about which Sven Birkerts wrote so perceptively in his now-classic essay "Into the Electronic Millennium."[1]

Backward, then, into the prehistoric mists. What was it like before there was writing? Whatever other categories may be useful for imagining the differences between then and now, surely immediacy is. Between perception and reaction, between stimulus and response, there lay no shadow, no complex processing, no translation of cipher into referent into meaning (to adapt Birkerts' handy terms). The large parts of our neurophysiology needed to decode, store, and retrieve written information went instead to speed and intensify the reflexes of pre-literate man. No writing meant fewer options to search out and compare

---

[1] *Boston Review*, October 1991; reprinted in *The Gutenberg Elegies*, 1994.

before any decision (and fewer decisions, naturally); fewer competing perspectives or frameworks to choose among. Instinctual conflict, sometimes; but no pale cast of thought. I would guess that Homeric, or at any rate Neanderthal, heroes really did "leap" into battle, really did "embrace" death. Imagine their orgasms.

But this was not an entirely benign, nobly primitive condition. Humankind has not evolved biologically very much since the invention of writing, so pre-literate people had roughly the same neurophysiological capacity, the same quantity of imagination, as us. But since they were forced to deploy it within very much narrower dimensions, the results were exotic, even bizarre. They didn't just charmingly endow snakes, trees, and waterfalls with personality, and sometimes divinity. They often heard them speak, and sometimes died of fright. Nearly every oral culture seems to have been a theocracy, and an amazing number of them (on the evidence of Julian Jaynes' *Origins of Consciousness in the Breakdown of the Bicameral Mind*) were based on hearing the voices of gods, i.e., on mass delusion. Imagine their nightmares.

Loss and gain, then. The things that matter most to us, the terms in which we tell our life stories—loves, beliefs, tastes, ambitions—presuppose a degree of vicarious experience, an extent of information, inconceivable 50,000 years ago; while our ancestors' significant life-experiences—to have lived among intimately familiar and subtly discriminated flora and fauna; to have enjoyed or endured sensations and enacted impulses with a vividness, spontaneity, and intensity unattainable now—involved a radically different balance of direct and vicarious experience, of intensive and extensive information. Our existence is immeasurably more mediated, less immediate, than theirs.

Birkerts' essay plausibly describes a transition from our era to one in which most people's experience will be still more vicarious and less direct, their information more extensive and less intensive. This may seem an oddly neutral way to characterize the chilling prospects his essay holds out. I do indeed share Birkerts' unease about the near-to-medium term and will wail and gnash my teeth presently. But something at the margins of his vision, and in particular his allusion to the eclipse of individuality, calls for a few less despairing remarks.

Let me try for a moment to disconnect the what from the how; the evolutionary process from its political context; what Birkerts calls "electronic collectivization" from the fact of its design and exploitation by business, the media, the entertainment industry, and the state. Let's disregard, in imagination, these extrinsic, distorting influences on cultural development and suppose that we the people freely, democratically, and wisely controlled our cultural evolution. What difference would this make to the fate of writing?

Every text, we know, has a context; and the more artful the text—whether poem, tale, picture, argument, or equation—the larger the relevant context. Texts of sufficient richness we call ineffable: the body of direct and vicarious experience, of extensive and intensive information, needed to register their whole force and depth is unattainable for beings with our capacities.

Depth is not the only dimension in which our aesthetic/intellectual reach exceeds our grasp. An aspiration to breadth or universality—to "all-sidedness," to assimilate the best that has been thought and said and be one of those on whom nothing is lost—only became a cultural ideal in modern times, just as its realization began to be impossible. The impulse to master the still (barely) masterable corpus of mid-eighteenth-century knowledge produced the *Encyclopédie*, which is, in respect of this ideal, the high tide of modernity. After the confidence of the *philosophes* comes the titanism (and ultimate resignation) of Goethe, the exquisite melancholy of Matthew Arnold and Henry James, the delirium of Pound and the High Modernists, and the white noise of postmodernism.

Along with the marketing requirements of late twentieth-century capitalism and the (related) spread of a narcissistic or pre-Oedipal character structure, one contributing cause of postmodernism may be despair over the impossibility of assimilating more than a fraction of the best that has been thought and said "on all the matters which most concern us" (Arnold, *Culture and Anarchy*); of achieving "a harmonious perfection, developing all sides of our humanity." To know even a single branch of culture both intimately and exhaustively will soon exceed the capacity of just about anyone. In the arts as in science and politics, the division of labor has made available an abundance and variety of experience and information that are no longer merely stimulating but arguably overstimulating, even overwhelming. We can try, as Richard Rorty urges, "to admire both Blake and Arnold, both Marx and Baudelaire, both Nietzsche and Mill, both Trotsky and Eliot, both Nabokov and Orwell"; we can hope to understand "how these men's books can be put together to form a beautiful mosaic." But it's a stretch. Add to this list Wittgenstein, Bartok, Rilke, Balanchine, and Levi-Strauss, and we begin to stagger. Add further—and who could bear to omit?—Duke Ellington, Robert Bresson, Jasper Johns, Frank Lloyd Wright, Martha Graham, Michel Tournier, and we have long since passed a limit. Though we may know enough to admire, we cannot really comprehend, cannot possibly devote to all these masters and masterpieces the patient, deeply informed attention they require.

And if *per impossibile* we could, we would scarcely have begun to do justice to "all the matters which most concern us." I'm helpless to evoke, can't even properly name, the beauties of science and mathematics. But no one, I suppose, believes they're inferior to those mentioned in the preceding paragraph? Look steadily and whole at the misery for which, as an American citizen, one bears one's mite of moral responsibility, and an interior voice sounds: you must change your life. But where to find the time, the energy, the spare imagination?

It's too much. "Harmonious perfection" is out of the question. We must either accept cultural overload, partial vision, mutual incomprehension, or else find some way to extend our range, augment our capacities, enhance our neurophysiology. Actually, there's a good deal to be said for the first alternative. Why does there need to be anybody who can "put together" all of culture? If print remains our principal medium of expression and communication, we can hold on, at least for a while, to the present rhythms and grain of our mental life, the architecture of our selves. "Privacy" and "autonomy" may be only names for our current balance of direct and vicarious experience, of intensive and extensive information. But it is *our* balance; it is us. No doubt our way of life will continue to change. I can no more imagine the cultural primacy of books lasting another 50,000 years than, say, theism or meat-eating or the nuclear family or private ownership of the means of production. But (for reasons I'll explain in a moment) I'm more than ambivalent, I'm positively alarmed, about beginning the transition now.

Still, the transition will begin someday, and should. Though I don't fully understand why—here I can only appeal to intuition, shared or unshared—there does need to be someone (or something) that can put together all of culture. Birkerts's figure/ground analogy for human identity is apt. But in the limit case, when the ground—the sheer scope of cultural possibilities, even considering only those available in traditional forms—alters drastically, qualitatively, then the implications of the analogy cease to be conservative. The figure must change dimension, perhaps radically, in order to maintain differentiation.

If this requires a new neural network, perhaps one extending outside our skin, then sooner or later, evolved or constructed, we will have one. *Pace* Birkerts, networks need not be exclusively "constitutive of the immediate present." Networks can embed hierarchies, temporal as well as logical: memory, tradition, culture itself are such networks. Organic rather than electronic ones, to be sure; but then, it's synergy rather than substitution that I look forward to.

Of course memory can be constricted and history flattened by commissars, spin-doctors, or profit-maximizing advertising executives and media managers. The design of a culture, the shape of a species' "collective sensibility" is a political question. Right now that question is being begged, whence my (and Birkerts') alarm. Ideally, verbal literacy would be subsumed or transcended in the course of cultural evolution, not simply eroded. The attrition of civic memory and craft knowledge, a reduced attention span and loss of discrimination, the attenuation of nuance and the homogenization of vocabulary—in all these ways the decay of literacy serves both the manufacture of consent and the accumulation of capital. A populace that cannot recognize rhetorical devices, make moderately subtle verbal distinctions, or remember back beyond the last election or ad campaign is defenseless against official propaganda and commercial hype. Only rootedness makes sustained resistance to the modern Leviathan—state, corporations, and media—possible. And an important form of rootedness is our internalization of the Word in one form or another: sacred scripture or poetic tradition or civic mythology or family lore. Benign cultural evolution, genuine emancipation, would lead us to work through such traditions, preserving even while going beyond them. As it is, we are merely being distracted from them.

The deepest and bitterest of all current disagreements is about whether modernity itself is an example of benign cultural evolution. In the creation of modern cultural and economic individualism, premodern communal traditions were similarly undermined without being worked through. For the most part, the people of Europe did not make their own painful way beyond village, kin network, handicraft, and local religion into a brave new world of mobility and rationality, city and factory. By and large, they were bulldozed. In that case as in this, the transition was shaped and paced, though not entirely motivated, by the needs of elites. True, a democratic transition to modernity in Europe would have taken centuries longer, and might not even now be consummated. But it would not have given rise to the twin spectres of antimodernist fundamentalism and post-modernist nihilism.

Marx and Freud made parallel and profoundly true observations, one about social practices and the other about individual beliefs. If a practice or belief is over-thrown prematurely, is repressed rather than outgrown, the result is pathology. To suggest that humankind is now ready to leave behind verbal literacy, when only a tiny, fortunate fraction have savored its pleasurable possibilities to the full, is not hubris. It is fatuity; worse, cruelty. At this stage of our political and cultural development, electronic collectivization would produce not new, marvelously complex and efficient forms of cognition and communication but historical amnesia and mass manipulation.

Language, Birkerts' essay memorably concludes, is our culture's "ozone layer." Someday, perhaps, we will no longer need an atmospheric ozone layer. Of course we must immediately stop depleting atmospheric (and linguistic) ozone or else face catastrophe. But eventually we will decipher the genetic code and redesign our skin, our immunological system, and probably much more. I hope, though, that it takes a few millennia. To think what the "free" market or the authoritarian state would do with genetic engineering is awful, just as it's awful to see the transformative possibilities of electronics squandered on weapons production, law enforcement, advertising, the credit industry, and the entertainment industry.

That our organic senses, including memory, will someday be joined, in a way we cannot now conceive, to electronic ones is something I certainly can't prove yet don't really doubt. Our perennial desire to integrate and master all knowledge can no longer be accomplished with our present sensorium. But we will not get there by continuing to dissipate our linguistic heritage. We are not transcending verbal literacy; we are merely forgetting it. Contemporary post-modernism is a false dawn because the finest possibilities of modernity have not begun to be realized. For the same reasons, the electronic millennium is now a threat rather than—what it may yet prove to be, in the farther reaches of cultural evolution—a promise.

Publication History

The foregoing pieces were published in the following places (sometimes under different titles):

Agni:
"Demos and Sophia: Not a Love Story" (Fall 1988)
"Inside the Cave" (Winter 1989)
"No, in Thunder!" (Fall 1991)
"Cultural Imperialism" (Fall 1993)
"The Sealed Envelope" (Spring 1994)
"A Ravaged History" (Winter 2001)

Boston Phoenix:
"An Exemplary Amateur" (5/8/84)
"South of Eden" (1/13/87)

Boston Review:
"Extrasensory" (February 1992)
"Our Ancestors . . ." (December 1994-January 1995)
"The Price of Selfhood" (December 1997)
"The Liberal Intelligence" (December 2002)

Dissent:
"Agonizing" (Fall 1991)
"The Lady and the Luftmensch" (Spring 1994)
"A Whole World of Heroes" (Summer 1995)
"Living by Ideas" (Fall 1995)
"Requiem for the Enlightenment" (Fall 1996)
"Pollyanna and Cassandra" (Fall 1998)
"Puny Expectations" (Summer 1999)
"Yes to Sex" (Fall 1999)

Grand Street:
"What Are Intellectuals Good For?" (Spring 1988)
"Privilege and Its Discontents" (Winter 1989)

Harvard Review:
"The Worst Policy" (Fall 1994)

LA Weekly:
"A Critical Life" (2/18/91)

n+1:
"Farewell, Hitch" (#2, 2005)

Nation:
"Disenchantment and Democracy" (12/4/89)
"Citizen Karp" (8/23/93)
"Only Words" (1/31/94)
"Fearlessness" (2/9/04)

Village Voice:
"Dying of the Truth" (4/19/83)
"The Promise of an American Life" (*VLS*, February 1985)
"Grand Disillusions" (*VLS*, December 1985)